W9-CXZ-999

VIRTUAL THEATER
FROM DIDEROT TO MALLARMÉ

Kazem Ghassemieh Saturday, February 21, 1998
1:15 PM.
Towson, Maryland

VIRTUAL THEATER

THEATER

FROM DIDEROT TO MALLARMÉ

———

EVLYN GOULD

———

THE JOHNS HOPKINS UNIVERSITY PRESS
BALTIMORE AND LONDON

© 1989 The Johns Hopkins University Press
All rights reserved
Printed in the United States of America

The Johns Hopkins University Press
701 West 40th Street
Baltimore, Maryland 21211
The Johns Hopkins Press Ltd., London

The paper used in this publication meets the minimum requirements of
American National Standard for Informational Sciences—Permanence of
Paper for Printed Library Materials, ANSI Z39.48-1984

Library of Congress Cataloging-in-Publication Data

Gould, Evlyn.
Virtual theater from Diderot to Mallarmé / Evlyn Gould.
        p.   cm.
Bibliography: p.
Includes index..
        ISBN 0-8018-3822-3 (alk. paper)
1. French drama—19th century—History and criticism.   2. Verse drama,
French—History and criticism.   3. Psychoanalysis and literature.
4. Romanticism—France.   5. Diderot, Denis, 1713–1784—Dramatic
works.   6. Mallarmé, Stéphane, 1842–1898—Dramatic works.   I. Title.
        PQ543.G6   1989
        842'.009—dc19   89-1794
                        CIP

To my parents

Contents

CONTENTS

Acknowledgments

I am particularly indebted to Leo Bersani, Bertrand Augst, and the late George House for their inspiration and insightful comments throughout the duration of my work on Virtual Theater. I would like to express my appreciation to them all for providing me with a theoretical framework for my fascination with theater, a fascination they all share. I would also like to thank Ann Smock, Denis Hollier, Linda Orr, and Steven F. Rendall for their enthusiasm about and help with my project, especially in its early stages; Scott S. Bryson and Elisabeth Lyon for their emotional and intellectual support throughout; Suzana Michel for her research into sources for existing translations; Larry Busenbark for his further work on translations, his tireless editorial remarks on my revisions, and his proofreading; Wayne A. Gottshall for his help with the electronic production of the manuscript; the students in my courses on Virtual Theater both at the University of Oregon and at the University of California, Berkeley; and my husband, Henry M. Ponedel, for providing the ideal work-space necessary to the completion of my project as well as for his patience and encouragement. Finally, I am eternally grateful to Andréa Karlsen and the late Sidney Johnson for my training in dance and music, discipline and beauty.

My work on Diderot and the German Romantics was made possible in part by a University of Oregon Faculty Summer Research Grant.

VIRTUAL THEATER
FROM DIDEROT TO MALLARMÉ

What Is Virtual Theater?

Virtual Theater illuminates a history of ambivalence about the theater from Denis Diderot to Stéphane Mallarmé. "Virtual" is a term borrowed from optics which refers to the potential or energetic existence of optical counterparts for objects that only occur within a psychical or mental space but give the impression of existing in a physical reality. Freud intimates its association with psychoanalytic theory in the *Interpretation of Dreams*: "Everything that can be an object of our internal perception is *virtual*, like the image produced in a telescope through the passage of light-rays."[1] The optical system of the telescope offers a scientific or technological metaphor for the psychical apparatus so that the term "virtual" identifies the elusive figurations emanating from unconscious thought processes that bend or refract conscious foci as the telescope does the light rays. "Theater" supposes the externalization of these optical phenomena in a physical space designed for representation. "Virtual Theater" is thus a paradox that proposes the externalization of internal and energetic optical phenomena in the physical space of textual representation. Mallarmé evokes this act of theatricalizing the virtual when he writes: " . . . libérer . . . même comme texte, la dispersion volatile soit l'esprit" (". . . to liberate, even as text . . . the volatile dispersion be it the mind").[2] I have coined the expression "Virtual Theater" to describe an odd collection of unrepresentable or "ideal" theater pieces that use the textual configurations of a theatrical format to represent the nature of subjectivity.

Virtual Theater from Diderot to Mallarmé is therefore a purely theoretical history constituted through the specific examples of "writerly" or "ideal" plays that I propose to study in the pages that follow: Diderot's *Le Neveu de Rameau*, Vigny's *Daphné*, Stendhal's *Racine et Shakespeare*, Hugo's *Le Théâtre en liberté*, Flaubert's *La Tentation de Saint Antoine*, and Mallarmé's *Hérodïade* and *L'Après-midi d'un faune*. What links these heterogeneous theaters and makes them "virtual" is that they each propose a theory of the theater caught in an indistinction between, on one hand, the metapsychology of an actual spectator whose identifications offer insight into the nature of representation and, on the other hand, a Platonic Idealism that scorns the theater while at the same time moving toward Freudian psychoanalysis by exploiting a theatrical format in order to insert into a textual surface the dynamic movements of speculative thinking. In other words, the authors of these plays investigate the theoretical questions posed by actual spectatorship and those posed, as well, by the literary representation of philosophy. They thereby discover the principles of representability outlined only later by Freud in his psychoanalytic inquiry into the nature of dreams.

Though this history is clearly not exhaustive[3]—ambivalence about the theater does not finish with Mallarmé nor does it necessarily first appear in the work of Diderot—its specific dimensions are designed to carve out a space of tension that links late-eighteenth-century Romantic re-readings of Plato to the nineteenth century's anticipation of Freud's use of a theatrical metaphor to describe the potential interaction of conscious and unconscious thought. For it is with the advent of Romantic thought—beginning roughly with Diderot—that literature begins to theorize this ambivalence in such a way as to cause a reassessment of both Plato and Freud. This particular period, then, is of interest not because it consciously exploits psychoanalytic theory but because it manifests the tensions produced by Romantic, philosophical ideals as they are slowly eroded by those modernist tendencies most appropriately understood by way of Freudian psychoanalysis. The history circumscribed by Virtual Theater is thus something akin to what Mallarmé called an "interregnum" and Flaubert an "uneasy transition" between Platonic philosophy and Freudian psychoanalysis.[4]

The significance of Virtual Theater's association of Plato and Freud is that although much modern theory (in large part championed by Jacques Derrida) espouses the notion that a newly revised Freud represents a reversal of Platonic Idealism,[5] the authors of virtual plays write a history that resituates this binary thinking by identifying a spatial (and Freudian) theatricality already inherent in the philosophical process as it is presented in Plato's dialogues. That is, in its odd mixture of theatrical and philosophical concerns, Virtual Theater steps outside of the history of philosophical discourse insofar as that discourse is understood—as it is by Michel Foucault—as an attempt to overturn Platonism.[6] The strength of Virtual Theater lies in its return to Plato. Though Diderot and Mallarmé appear to be more obviously indebted to Plato than, say, Hugo and Flaubert—Diderot by virtue of his reconception of the philosophical dialogue, Mallarmé by virtue of his own peculiar Idealism—each of these authors begins with a philosophical inquiry into the nature of representation that finds a model for its discourse in the polyphony of dialogue. Like Plato, the authors of Virtual Theater criticize theater but use theatrical models to correct its deficiencies. Unlike Plato but like Freud, these authors also envision their models in terms of the structural dimensions of theatrical space. In other words, they repeat the work of Plato in Freudian terms.[7]

Curiously, in the same way that Virtual Theater finds in Plato's dialogues a model that disrupts (by repeating) Platonic Idealism, it also uncovers, in its anticipation of Freudian psychoanalysis, models that Freud both revealed and overlooked.

The same ambivalence that marks the Platonic dialogue in relation to its own theatricality also characterizes the fate of Freud's use of a theatrical metaphor to characterize the interaction of consciousness and the unconscious. Plato attacks the theater but theatricalizes the philosophical process in the polyphony of dialogue; Freud finds a metaphor for his psychical apparatus in the family dramas of *Oedipus Rex* and *Hamlet*[8] but overlooks the formal or structural dimensions of those dramas in favor of the sexual anecdotes that their stories relate.[9] In each case, the shape of theater so central to both discourses is lost in an effort to secure authority.[10] In Virtual Theater, however, the shape of the theater is restored so that both Freud and Plato work together, despite themselves, to explain the theatricality at stake in a textual representation of the configurations of subjectivity.

In this context, the history of Virtual Theater is designed in part to elucidate the tendency in modern or "postmodern" critical theory to exploit figures of theatricality as an image of itself.[11] This tendency is itself caught in an ambivalent interaction with Freudian psychoanalysis, and in particular, with Freud's theatrical metaphor. Indeed, Freud's metaphor assumes an espousal of the esthetics of classical representation on which it is based while at the same time providing a model for theories of subjectivity and textuality that are at odds with those esthetics. As a result, "postmodern" philosophers often criticize the traditional esthetics inherent in the stage/audience division supposed by Freud's metaphor while, at the same time, nuancing it into a theory of textual performance. This line of thinking leads to the notion that Freud reverses Plato. Modern psychoanalytic theorists, on the other hand, work to redefine the dynamics of that very same division in an attempt to find in the spectator of actual representations the mechanisms of unconscious identification that regulate and disrupt his or her conscious attention to the stage. This line of thinking leads to the notion that Freud revises himself.

Given these seemingly opposed but, in fact, parallel positions, a brief look at the peculiar fate of the history of Freud's metaphor is in order. It begins in 1897, in a letter to Wilhelm

Fleiss on the subject of hysterical identification in which Freud compares the content of his own incestuous fantasies to the tragedies *Oedipus Rex* and *Hamlet*.[12] In this letter, Freud not only identifies an incestuous compulsion supposedly common to all of us, he also implies that the relationship of a subject to the fantasm is like that of a spectator to the stage.[13] However, as the work of Jean Laplanche and J.-B. Pontalis in particular has shown, Freud comes upon this theatrical analogy at the same time he is elaborating an Oedipal complex, a theory of the fantasy in infantile sexuality, and the seduction theory with its notion of hysterical identification. Unfortunately, during this period, the interrelation of these theories is not yet articulated so that the fantasy loses its structural, theatrical dimensions, its true nature obscured by theories of sexuality (Laplanche and Pontalis, "Fantasy," 6–7, 9), while the Oedipal complex comes to overshadow the other issues, becoming a highly charged focal point for modern critical theory.

Insofar as the Oedipal triangle has been redefined in post-Lacanian psychoanalysis as a structure inherent in the unconscious which defines a series of positions available by way of identification to a thinking subject rather than as an image of parental figures, the theatrical metaphor remains crucial to the work of modern psychoanalytic theorists.[14] For Laplanche and Pontalis, the multiple positions of the theatrical metaphor provide the framework for an important redefinition of the fantasm as a subject's own particular staging of desire ("Fantasy," 17). For Mikkel Borch-Jacobsen, the metaphor becomes a way of talking about unconscious identification in Freud's own autoanalytic project (*Le Sujet freudien*). In its particular relationship to the theatrical experience, the same metaphor has been repeatedly exploited by André Green and Octave Mannoni as well as by various film theorists—Jean-Louis Baudry, Christian Metz, Thierry Kuntzel, and Raymond Bellour—in whose work it has become a way of specifically addressing the question of a spectator's identifications at the theater or cinema.[15] This last group of psychoanalytic theorists is, as a rule, less interested in apprehending the elusive "subject" of Freudian psychoanalysis than in understanding the metapsychology of an actual spectator at the theater and its relation to the multiple points of view offered by the fantasm. Nonetheless, what they all have in common is a tendency to emphasize the theatrical structure of the fantasm in such a way as to move Freudian psychoanalysis away from the obsessive scenes of a particular infantile sexual organization toward a theory of the fantasm as a means of apprehending the ways in which structures in a "text"—written or performed—may give rise to both psychic and semantic indeterminacy. In so doing, they also move away from an "Oedipal rock" toward a more fluid conception of both libidinal economy and the thinking subject, away from family anecdotes on stage toward an inquiry into the structural dimensions of theatrical space as a description of subjectivity. The significance of these shifts is that they isolate the fantasm as the real subject of psychoanalytic inquiry.

Those who remain leery of Freud's metaphor, while at the same time acknowledging their indebtedness to it, are the "postmodern" philosophers. Though their attitudes toward the theatrical metaphor vary, they include Gilles Deleuze and Félix Guattari who flatly reject it; Jean-François Lyotard who deconstructs but reconsiders it; and Philippe Lacoue-Labarthe who, by way of Jacques Derrida, readopts it as a model for philosophical discourse itself.[16] On the whole, these philosophers take issue with Freud's recourse to classical representation—primarily his use of *Oedipus Rex*—to illustrate a theater of "psychic reality." This use assumes some unified subject of consciousness whose unconscious "reality" would be hidden but just as unified or logical. The theatrical metaphor thus provides the illusion of a unified subject of thought that these writers of philosophy consistently undermine. Yet in their efforts to map the disruptions of these unities, these philosophers are themselves attracted to modern representations: the choreography of Merce Cunningham, the music of John Cage, or quite simply, "modern art."[17] In this way, philosophy's self-portrait remains essentially theatrical insofar as it finds, in modern performance, a figure for itself that is mul-

tiplied and polyscenic, musical and mobile; we might even refer to it as an antirepresentational mode of representation.[18]
The irony of this position is that it replaces Freud's use of the
model provided by classical representation with the more
modern model provided by contemporary performing arts. A
new theatrical space thus takes the place of Freud's.

In light of these two versions of theatricality—the first a
description of the essentially structured mobility of a thinking
subject, the second a description of the disruptive dynamics of
a theatricalized textual performance—I shall argue that Virtual Theater revises their interrelations by providing a literary
history for them. This revision supposes that Freudian psychoanalysis will help to uncover structures common to each
of the virtual plays which identify a growing concern with the
theatrical role of the unconscious in writing philosophy, but
it also supposes that these plays will in turn elucidate what
Freud proposed, then overlooked: the structural relations that
regulate and deregulate a subject's interaction with textual representations. For just as the virtual plays may be said to
"correct" Platonic Idealism by finding in the textual configurations of dialogue an ideal model for the theatricality of
thought itself, they may also be said to "correct" Freud's theatrical metaphor in that they shape themselves according to
the structure and logic of the fantasm: a double scene in
which a divided subject is infinitely re-figured in imaginary
self-representations. In other words, like the philosophers, but
unlike Freud, Virtual Theater rejects the esthetics of classical
representation. Nonetheless, like the psychoanalytic theorists
and therefore also like Freud, Virtual Theater theorizes the
metapsychology of the spectator of those representations. The
result, for the authors of Virtual Theater, is the writing of a
play that cannot be staged. An accommodation by modern
theory of the very same assumptions, however, results in a
theoretical discourse that becomes a dance or play of speculative fictions since it can no longer admit any one single voice
of authority. These philosophers and theorists repeat, thereby,
the work of the authors of Virtual Theater who themselves
repeat the work of Plato's dialogues. That is, the modern ten-

dency to conceive of theory as theatrical and choreographic, because it is speculative, or as mobile and musical, because it is no longer monologic, is already at work in the virtual plays.

Ultimately, it is precisely this shifting of the theatrical metaphor away from a classical, philosophical model for representation toward a modern psychoanalytic theater of disruptive psychic intensities that is recorded by the authors of Virtual Theater. These authors seem to have come to terms with their ambivalence about theater through the writing of a philosophy that uses theatrical space to represent the drama that subjectivity is. Our history begins, therefore, with Diderot's creative adaptation of the theatricality of Plato's philosophical dialogues and finishes with Mallarmé's theoretical theaters that equate the energy of performance with textual virtuality.

ONE

From Plato to Diderot

In their *L'Absolu littéraire*, Philippe Lacoue-Labarthe and Jean-Luc Nancy reconsider the question of Romanticism in light of the theoretical speculations on literature and philosophy that preoccupied the German philosophers at Jena.[1] The importance of their study is that it re-situates Romanticism within a philosophical context and associates the emergence of the modern concept of "literature" with this context.[2] The German philosophers struggled with philosophy as a writing problem, that is to say, with the essentially literary nature of philosophical discourse (*L'Absolu*, 264). Ironically, this reassessment of the place of literature in philosophy found its originary model in Plato's Socratic dialogues. The German Romantics saw in Plato's dialogues an ideal "mixture of genres" capable of gathering within itself all modes of discourse and of producing its own self-conscious theory (*L'Absolu*, 268).[3] In this Romanticism, then, dialogue—or more precisely, something akin to Bakhtin's "dialogism"[4]—became a privileged place in which to mark philosophy's indistinction with literature while at the same time taking "literature" as the object of its own theoretical speculations (*L'Absolu*, 264–70).

The philosophers themselves used this re-reading of Plato to engage a collective philosophical discourse in the hopeful elaboration of their "Ideal Book," a "speculative epic" or literary *opus philosophicum*, designed to reflect the nature of human beings and of the universe (*L'Absolu*, 248–50).[5] However, their work also highlights a more generalized desire in the late eighteenth century to see the Platonic dialogue as the most appropriate mode of exposition for the representation of speculative thinking. Whereas the Renaissance, tainted by Augustine's Christian Neo-Platonism, read in Plato the meta-language of a philosopher who speaks of *Laws*, the late eighteenth century's "Romantic" re-reading of Plato was more attentive to the pluralized discourse of a philosopher who writes dialogues.[6] The former gives birth to the monologic tradition of the philosophical treatise, to the concept of an authoritative subject of philosophy and, eventually, to Freud's "science" of psychoanalysis with which postmodern philosophers take issue. The latter, on the other hand, nourishes a polyphonic tradition in philosophy, a literary genre that Nietzsche referred to as "philosophical drama" and that Lacoue-Labarthe and Nancy call a "drama of subjectivity," intimating its kinship with a newly revised Freud (*L'Absolu*, 183–84).[7] Indeed, these theatrical rubrics for the polyphony of Plato's dialogues underscore the essentially theatrical nature of philosophical textuality in terms that explain why postmodern philosophy must itself come to terms with Freudian psychoanalysis in its desire to describe itself as a musical or theatrical performance.

In the context of this "second" history of philosophy concerned, like the German Romantics, with the literary or theatrical dynamics of its own presentation, Virtual Theater is a concept designed to evoke an opposite, if parallel, trajectory by studying the theoretical questions posed by literature's presentation of philosophy. This trajectory accentuates an indistinction of philosophy and literature and it also invokes the late eighteenth century's modern reading of Plato's polyphony.

Unlike the history initiated by German Romanticism, however, Virtual Theater associates the dialogue with the history of theater. In its attempt to underscore the limitations of a "philosophical" subject, Virtual Theater borrows theater as a written form to represent the logic (and lack of logic) of modern subjectivity. Indeed, theater as a written form accommodates a mixture of discourses while securing a distinction between two separate kinds of textual space: the space reserved for an actor who engages in dramatic dialogue and the space of dramatic *didascalia* reserved for a playwright who can narrate, describe, or simply think. As a result, theater as a written form allows a philosophy that is polyscenic and a philosophical subject who is multiple or polyvalent. Like the Platonic dialogue but belonging to an essentially literary tradition, Virtual Theater produces an ambivalent mixture of literary and theoretical discourse that cannot have any certain or authoritative message because it offers a process for readers and writers rather than a product to be understood at a distance. Therefore, in the pages that follow, I shall propose that Platonic philosophy is intimately tied to the theater both formally and contextually—that the dialogues themselves are a theatricalized philosophy—and that the late eighteenth century's use of this polyphonic model engenders a modern literary history for philosophy's indistinction with theater which begins with the writing of Denis Diderot.[8]

Diderot initiates the "history" of Virtual Theater by openly exploiting Plato's ambivalence about the theater while at the same time accommodating the disruptive designs of unconscious thinking provided for by Freud's use of a theatrical metaphor. With his *Le Neveu de Rameau*, in particular, Diderot proposes a polyphonic philosophy or better, a kind of philosophical fugue that is theatrical yet antirepresentational because it borrows the Platonic dialogue to illustrate the theatrical nature of subjectivity. In this way, as I have already obliquely suggested in my introduction, Diderot deemphasizes the indebtedness of his "philosophical drama" to what Jonas Barish has identified as a Platonic tradition of "antitheatrical prejudice" while highlighting its reliance upon an Aristotelian—and what can be called, prematurely, a Freudian—tradition of theorizing about the theater. On one hand, in his transformation of philosophy into a theatrical or psychoanalytic problem, Diderot assumes, in contradiction to Platonism, a likeness between the philosopher and the actor. Like the Freud who transforms Aristotle's catharsis into a question of the spectator's libidinal economy, Diderot transforms a philosopher's encounter with an actor into a question of unconscious identification.[9] On the other hand, however, Diderot also exploits the theatricality of the Platonic dialogue itself by enclosing it within the framework of an imaginary theater. In much the same way that Freud's dreamer realizes an intimate drama that can only be played out within the confines of his or her own mind, the world of Diderot's dialogue is contained within the speculations of one single philosopher whose text becomes the stage of the philosopher's own unique drama of subjectivity. As a result, the world of Diderot's dialogue only exists as a virtual world—one that replaces or even "forecloses" the real world in the very act of thinking that world.[10]

In relation to the Platonic dialogue, we could say that the philosopher/subject of Diderot's Virtual Theater occupies the positions of Socrates, of the Sophists, and of Plato himself, emphasizing, unlike Plato but like the German Romantics, the *writing* of philosophy and the shifting registers of subjectivity.[11] Moreover, by displacing attention away from the philosopher/ruler and onto the philosopher/writer, Diderot's Virtual Theater becomes conscious of its own internal theatricality, making the thinking subject of philosophy into the very subject of the play. Therefore, although Plato himself was not openly interested in admitting the theatrical nature of a philosophical subject, I shall argue, after Lacoue-Labarthe and Nancy, that he initiated, perhaps despite himself, a speculative inquiry into the nature of subjectivity that finds in his dialogues the ideal model for a polyphonic or musical and theatricalized philosophy.

THE POLYPHONIC PLATO:
TOWARD A *THEATRUM PHILOSOPHICUM*

The question of drama or theater in philosophy might be seen as both central to and disruptive of the internal workings of Platonism itself. The question of theater emphasizes, like the work of Diderot, what might be called a moment of Platonic oversight. This oversight has to do with recognizing (or not) the theatrical nature both of philosophy and of the philosophical subject. As Lacoue-Labarthe and Nancy demonstrate, Plato condemns, in his *Republic*, what Genette calls a genre of "mixed diegesis"—a mixture of epic narrative and "mimetic" or dramatic form—but Plato exploits this mixed form in most of his major dialogues (*L'Absolu*, 271). In this way, there is a disjunction, in Plato, between a philosophical system and a philosophical writing practice, between a philosophy of essences and the material problems posed by its own representation. The former bans from the ideal republic any actor or dramaturge, any false dissimulator who hides his discourse behind the voices of others and thus disperses the authorial subject, whereas the latter allows Plato to disperse himself as he hides behind the voices of Socrates and the Sophists. There is, in other words, another way of conceptualizing Plato's relation to theatricality or *mimesis* which makes of him the silent "other" in a history of the theater.[12]

The dialogues represent this "other" of the theater because they stand at the threshold of two theatrical metaphors. They mark the initiation of a theatrical or polyphonic "genre" in philosophy—I shall call it, after Michel Foucault, the "*theatrum philosophicum*"—but in so doing, they may be said to interiorize a metaphor that the drama would exteriorize, the metaphor of the *Theatrum Mundi* or theater of the world.[13] Presenting a brief history of this second metaphor, Curtius notes that it originates in Plato's *Laws*. In Book I, we read: "May we not regard every living being as a puppet of the gods, which may be their plaything only, or may be created with a purpose?" (I.644d–e Jowett) and in Book VII: "Man is made to be the plaything of God, and this, truly considered, is the best of him" (VII.803c).[14] The first quotation, like a dialogue, asks a question about man's role in the universe, whereas the second, six books later, appears to answer that question. Here the monologic seems to replace the dialogic. Nonetheless, it is the coexistence of the speculative and the dogmatic in Plato that gives rise to historically conflictive readings of Platonic philosophy.

The irony of Plato's substitution of fact for speculation is that the conflict inscribed in the speculative citation not only marks the entire history of Western drama from antiquity through the nineteenth century (Curtius, *European Literature*, 138–44) but it also lies at the heart of Plato's lifelong desire to envision a utopian republic. The first passage, from Book I, points to a conflict between a theocracy (a vertical structure of power in which an individual would be the mere plaything of the gods, a servant to their absolute authority), and a theatrocracy (a horizontal or circular structure of power in which each citizen stands equidistant from the political center, having the right and obligation to determine his own fate or purpose). In other words, this passage emphasizes the conflictive nature of the Athenian's place in the universe, conflictive because it is accounted for by two different theories: one, a religious and hierarchical model in which truth is defined by classical ontology, the other, a geometrical or mathematical model borrowed from Anaximander's cosmology in which truth is determined as a common enterprise through the confrontation and reconciliation of several points of view.[15] Is one a plaything—as the theory of Ideas would suggest—or must one design one's own fate—as the model of the dialogic education supposes?

In a general way, one could argue that the tragedies of antiquity address human despair before this very dilemma. Jean-Pierre Vernant, in his revaluation of Freud's reading of *Oedipus Rex*, has noted that it was precisely the difficulty of situating oneself in the religious order of the world that explains the birth of tragedy at the turn of the sixth and fifth centuries B. C.[16] Greek tragedy from Aeschylus through Sophocles to Euripides responded to a complex network of political, social, and religious conflicts by representing a tension between two orders or planes: the human and the divine.[17] The tragic hero appears therefore to be both projected into a mythic past of legendary kings and religious forces and living in the modern age of the city-state as an Athenian bourgeois who relies upon his own initiatives and is solely responsible for their outcome (Vernant, *Mythe et tragédie en Grèce ancienne*, 82). In other words, he is caught between taking his purpose too seriously and at the same time, being inevitably controlled as a plaything of the gods. In this sense, the politicoreligious conflict pinpointed by the question in the first of Plato's quotations is materialized in the action and physical dimensions of an actual stage setting. The theater has become the ideal setting for the *Theatrum Mundi* in its representation of our conflictive relationship to our world.

It is significant to note in this context that Derrick de Kerckhove, in his brilliantly imaginative "Theory of Greek Tragedy," agrees that tragedy has conflict as its basic structure but disagrees that the conflict is political, religious, or moral in nature.[18] Derrick de Kerckhove argues, after F. M. Cornford, that the tragedy reflects and reconciles a crisis of perception having to do with two notions of space that ultimately coincided in the theater of Athens, physical space and a purely theoretical geometrical space (27). He then goes on to liken this reconciliation to Lacan's mirror stage, arguing that the theater presented, through its actors, an image of the single body as autonomous from its environment. According to Kerckhove, in the spectator's introjecting of the situation of the actor on stage, the spectator then began to conceive of a "self" as an entity contained in the unlimited space of the world (30).

Kerckhove's discussion is primarily concerned with the use of Greek theater as one of the developments of the phonetic alphabet (23) and is therefore not specifically related to Plato's "theater," but he does make three points worth discussing here. First, for Kerckhove, the Greek stage enacted a "process of exteriorization for a new way of being-in-the-world"

(29). That is, as the comparison to the mirror stage supposes, the Greek stage literally programmed modes of consciousness in a world-space conceived as a theater or *Theatrum Mundi*. Second, the exterior or material experience of theater would eventually lead, in the nonliterate members of Athenian culture, to an internalization or acquisition of private consciousness that was already available, through the use of the phonetic alphabet, to those who could read and write (23). Finally, Kerckhove sees the birth, development, and extinction of Greek tragedy as several stages in a "specific pattern of identity buildup" that can be traced from before Aeschylus through Sophocles to Euripides (and then again, from before Corneille, through Racine and Shakespeare to Voltaire). Simply stated, these stages are described as (1) the "formation of private identity" due to a compromised confrontation with the establishment; (2) a period of crisis in which conflict is situated within the hero himself; and finally, (3) a stage of resolution characterized by rational argumentation and democracy during which the old order is flatly denied (Kerckhove, 35).

Whether or not one agrees with this compelling if schematic overview of Greek tragedy, one could argue in an equally schematic manner that in the realm of philosophy Socrates, Plato, and Aristotle seem to define a similar development. For Socrates' conception of the *psyche* did identify a newly conceived "formation of private identity" (Jaeger, 2:38–44); Plato's dialectical method does situate Socrates' conversational analysis within the mind of the thinker himself; and Aristotle does emphasize what Jaeger calls the "empirical element in Platonism," a reading that democratically denies Plato's arbitrary division of the world into universal ideas and things of sense (Jaeger, 2:164–65, 323). Though it is clearly outside of the scope of this essay to defend this speculative trilogy, it seems useful insofar as it highlights Plato's position in the stage called "crisis," thus suggesting that whereas the theater enacted a "process of exteriorization" for new modes of consciousness, Plato's dialogues, aimed at the literate, enacted a process of internalization for new modes of consciousness—modes that were also visual and theatrical.

Indeed, the Platonic dialogue appears to re-create, in a metaphysical, philosophical sphere, the dilemma laid out by the tragedy except that the mind has become the theater of this same conflictive universe. That is, tragedy represents humanity's conflictive relation to the universe whereas the dialogue proposes a process by which to individually confront and assess that conflict. As a result, whereas the tragedy may be said to resolve itself in an ultimately didactic end (whether negatively as for Plato or positively as for Aristotle), the dialogue remains unresolvable, providing only the path by which to analyze.[19] The metaphor of the *Theatrum Mundi* thus escapes the confines of Platonic philosophy to be taken up by the dramas of antiquity but the metaphor of the *theatrum philosophicum* is taken up by the dialogues themselves as a way of spatializing the work of the thinking mind and of pluralizing its different points of view.

The *theatrum philosophicum* as a form initiated by these dialogues itself initiates a mode of discourse particularly well suited to the representation of an individual's internal questioning especially at moments of crisis. Mikhail Bakhtin identifies dialogue as a subversive form in literature and situates the source of this subversion in the Socratic dialogue.[20] Similarly, Lacoue-Labarthe and Nancy study the subversive nature of the dialogue in philosophy and point out that it appears to occur most frequently in response to moments of political, social, and cultural crisis.[21] Indeed, according to the French authors, it is in response to crisis that the dialogue comes to be seen as what I am calling the *theatrum philosophicum*—a literary form for philosophy that may be said to theatricalize subjectivity. The use of dialogue assumes the undermining of philosophy as a discourse of truth because the ground on which the transcendental ego of the philosopher would stand is itself constantly shifting. Instead of a logic of exclusion, a movement of "either this or that" toward an ultimate absolute truth or resolution, philosophy as it is represented by the dialogue admits a polyvalent logic of indeterminacy,[22] a logic contaminated by the "musicalized" thought processes of something akin to a psychoanalytic or divided subject.

RE-READING PLATO

The late eighteenth century's renewed interest in Platonism as a polyphonic or theatricalized philosophy is not surprising when we consider that Europe would undergo a politico-religious and sociocosmological crisis strikingly similar to the one undergone by Athenian society.[23] The return to Plato in this context was undoubtedly partly due to Friedrich Schleiermacher's rediscovery of the "original" Plato at that time. That re-reading initiated both the vision of Plato as the philosopher par excellence and the notion that his philosophy was first and foremost a method, a dynamic imitation of thinking (Jaeger, *Paideia*, 2:79). However, it is clear that the German Romantic reappraisal of Platonico-Aristotelian poetics resulted, more specifically, from an effort to theorize the cultural crises of their age.

In *L'Absolu littéraire*, Lacoue-Labarthe and Nancy outline three modes of crisis essential to this reappraisal: the social and economic crisis caused by the growing bourgeoisie during the late eighteenth century; the political crisis exemplified by the French Revolution; and the philosophical crisis inaugurated by Kant and his discussions of the subject of philosophy (13–14).[24] Lacoue-Labarthe and Nancy are primarily interested in the third of these crises since it makes of philosophy an esthetic problem by concentrating on the individual's capacity to reason and to speculate but also to imagine and to fantasize (46). In other words, Romanticism is inescapably associated with philosophy's contestation or acceptation of Reason; it stands in opposition to the ideals of the *Aufklärung* while at the same time representing their logical conclusion. This relation to Reason explains why German Romanticism took one step back from Aristotle's universals and found itself attracted to Plato's polyphonic form of philosophy.

In the anonymous text that opens *L'Absolu littéraire* called "Das älteste Systemprogramm des deutschen Idealismus" ("The Earliest System-Program of German Idealism"), the end of philosophy as a system of registers or tables and exclusive categories—the end of a monologic metalanguage—is also the repositioning of philosophy as a mere play of ideas, a purely esthetic category. Though this text appears to generally reflect the style of Schelling's *System of Transcendental Idealism*, it has also been attributed to Hegel and was supposedly influenced by Hölderlin (*L'Absolu*, 39–40).[25] Despite the singular voice of its author, therefore, it can be read as a kind of collective "manifesto" of German Romantic thought. In this manifesto, as the French authors translate it, we read:

> Je suis convaincu que l'acte suprême de la raison, celui par lequel elle embrasse toutes les idées, est un acte *esthétique* et que *vérité et bonté ne sont soeurs qu'unies dans la beauté*—le philosophe doit avoir autant de force esthétique que le poète. Les hommes dépourvus de sens esthétique donnent nos philosophes de la Lettre seule [*unsere Buchstaben philosophen*]. La philosophie de l'Esprit est une philosophie esthétique.[26]

In this text, a philosophy of the mind is called an esthetic philosophy because "the supreme act of reason is an esthetic act" but also because, as Schelling writes in his *System*, art alone can objectify the "subjective illusions" of philosophy (Simpson, 127–30). In German Romantic thought, then, the democratic esthetics of the Platonic dialogue are espoused while the vertical model of Platonic Idealism is dismantled. An idea is no longer conceived as the feeble, material representative of an ideal realm but as the product or re-presentation of a purely intellectual and individual world created by a free, because self-conscious subject.[27]

This horizontalizing of Platonic Idealism reconceives of the nature of subjectivity itself by incorporating three assumptions that rely upon but also displace the theories of Kant: (1) A thinking subject always contains within himself all truths (moral or other) and all authority. Truth is not to be found in

Plato's ideal realm but is "united with goodness in beauty" by ideas themselves. (2) The world is a corollary to or creation of this subject. It therefore only exists insofar as this subject can conceive of or recreate it in a world of art. (3) Any "moral" subject, the conception of whom assumes interaction with a vertical or theocratic model, is transformed into a "free" subject, one who is thoroughly self-conscious and thus constantly re-creating new self-representations (*L'Absolu*, 48). Therefore, to paraphrase Lacoue-Labarthe and Nancy, the "I" has become an empty subject, a construct that permits us to interact through language or to designate ourselves in logic but which no longer confers any unity (*L'Absolu*, 43). Once again, then, this "I" quite clearly anticipates that of the subject of psychoanalysis who comes to replace "unsere Buchstabenphilosophen" in Diderot's Virtual Theater.

Toward a "Virtual Theater"

Though this reconception of subjectivity is probably best articulated, theoretically, by the German Romantics at Jena, its literary representation as a Virtual Theater is probably best exemplified by what might be called the fantasmatic source of German Romantic theory, the work of Denis Diderot and primarily his *Le Neveu de Rameau*.[28] All of Diderot's philosophical endeavors were, like those of the German Romantics, contaminated by creative literary forms: fragmentary thoughts, letters, dialogues, and theatrical novels. Moreover, *Le Neveu* is known to have circulated at Jena in the form of Goethe's translation. More important, however, with this piece Diderot crosses the threshold of modernism by offering a literary representation of the German Romantic re-reading of Platonism.[29] *Le Neveu* can be seen as a modern instance of Plato's *theatrum philosophicum* but one that also highlights the predicaments with which the German Romantics would want to come to terms. Like Plato's dialogues, *Le Neveu* stages a tension between the values of a theocratic hierarchy and the democratic autonomy of an individual's ethics and it does so in the conflictive and ultimately ambiguous terms typically as-

sociated with the Platonic dialogue.[30] *Le Neveu* repeatedly
defers any ultimate resolution of conflict by rejecting a meta-
language of philosophical truths in favor of an open-ended
dialogical fiction of opposing viewpoints. In fact, in his study
of *Le Neveu*, H. R. Jauss points out that critics have wrongly
associated the dialogue's subtitle, "satire second," with the
model of Horace rather than recognizing its indebtedness to
the open Socratic dialogue and to its seriocomical relative, the
Menippean satire.[31] On the other hand, Diderot's *Neveu* anticipates the ideals of the Romantics. It presents Friedrich
Schlegel's desired mixture of philosophy and poetry (*L'Absolu*, 272) as well as Schelling's notion of art as the setting for
an objectified philosophy (Simpson, 123), and it exploits the
satire as a mixed genre to illustrate the instability of the speaking subject.[32] In this way, whereas the German philosophers
merely theorized an ideal philosophy of the mind, writing
fragments for a project that never came to fruition, Diderot's
Neveu materializes their ideal. For *Le Neveu* is a mental theater in which the subject has become a multiplied collection
of unstable self-representations whose world unfolds according to the logic of a musical fugue.

Indeed, as *Le Neveu* opens, we are privy to the subtle
thoughts of the philosopher/writer whose world has become
a "corollary to its subject," an unstable presentation of the
theater of thought itself:

> Qu'il fasse beau, qu'il fasse laid, c'est mon habitude d'aller sur les
> cinq heures du soir me promener au Palais Royal. C'est moi qu'on
> voit, toujours seul, rêvant sur le banc d'Argenson. Je m'entretiens
> avec moi meme de politique, d'amour, de gout ou de philosophie.
> J'abandonne mon esprit a tout son libertinage. Je le laisse maître
> de suivre la premiere idée sage ou folle qui se presente comme on
> voit dans l'allée de Foy nos jeunes dissolus marcher sur les pas
> d'une courtisane a l'air eventé, au visage riant, a l'oeil vif, au nez
> retroussé, quitter celle cy pour une autre, les attaquant toutes et
> ne s'attachant a aucune. Mes pensées, ce sont mes catins.[33]

With the striking metaphor of wenches or prostitutes for
thought, Diderot summons up a startling image of the un-

wieldy, illogical, and desire-driven nature of thinking. A mind abandoned to its own "libertinage" is like the young debauched man who chases any and all ladies and the movement of the thoughts themselves is as varied and mad as this array of ladies. From the outset then, the mental gyrations of this soon-to-be-identified philosopher step outside the logic of cause and effect, the logic of exclusion: this or that, "beau" or "laid," "sage ou folle" ("beautiful" or "ugly," "wise or foolish") to become a logic of desire, a logic of inclusion or of multiplication: this and this and this.

This mobilizing of the systematic categories of logical philosophical thinking anticipates the undermining of "unsere Buchstabenphilosophen," but it also represents, in microcosm, the primary issue at stake in the dialogue to come. The Nephew, once he appears, will have as his goal to render relative each of the philosopher's assumed categorical truths. More important, the dialogue itself between the philosopher's monologic certainty and Rameau's polyphonic speculations only exists within the confines of the philosopher's own impulsive mind. As Julia Kristeva notes in her study of *Le Neveu*, the Nephew's constant contradicting takes place, in a dialectic sense, as the representative of the other in the philosopher's "I," thus highlighting the productive division of the writing subject.[34] In this opening interior monologue already theatricalized or "objectified" by the supposition of an implied observer ("C'est moi qu'*on* voit," literally, "It is I that *one* sees" [my emphasis]), this mind is clearly divided; it is both the subject and the object of its own speculations. And with the further statement "Je m'entretiens avec moi meme" (literally, "I discuss me with myself"), it is as if this "I" finds itself in three positions at once, the observer of an interior dialogue between himself and him (or his) self.

As the dialogue begins, the three positions delineated by this "*Je m'*entretiens avec *moi* meme" come alive in a literal and material way as the Nephew, now introduced, finally happens along. At this point, the present tense of the philosopher's silent thoughts has given way to the past tense of a narrator which in turn gives way to the immediate presence of dramatic dialogue:

> Vous etiez curieux de scavoir le nom de l'homme, et vous le sca- vez. C'est le neveu de ce musicien celebre qui nous a delivrés du plain-chant de Lulli. . . .
> Il m'aborde. . . . Ah, ah, vous voilà, Mr le philosophe; et que faites-vous ici parmi ce tas de faineants(?) Est-ce que vous perdez aussi votre temps a pousser le bois? C'est ainsi qu'on appelle par mépris jouer aux échecs ou aux dames.
> M O I. —Non; mais quand je n'ai rien de mieux a faire, je m'amuse a regarder un instant, ceux qui le poussent bien. (*Le Neveu*, 6–7)[35]

In this opening reference to an already discussed game of chess and, thus, once again to the mutation of a hierarchical order into a play of strategic moves (it is not who wins but how you play the game), we can see a slightly altered version of Kristeva's analysis of pronominal instances in the dialogue. The "I" of the philosopher/writer who, in the opening mono- logue, addressed an indeterminate "one" (including both him- self and any others) now becomes both the "I" of the philoso- pher/narrator who addresses the "you" of an implied reader and the "I" of the philosopher/character "Moi," who ad- dresses the character "Lui." As a result, the subject of this text—the philosophical subject of literature—is, as the chess game and Kristeva would suggest, mobile and indeterminate ("La Musique parlée," 163), an "empty form" that accom- panies the philosopher's self-representations. To put these roles in theatrical terms, one could say that the philosopher is at once a writer or dramaturge, a spectator—"Il m'aborde" ("He accosts me")—and an actor in the dialogue who plays the role of the philosopher "Moi."

This subtle distinction between his various positions or roles in and around the dialogue does not in itself prove that the entire dialogue is nothing more than the projected image of the philosopher's own capricious thoughts. Yet the capacity to play both spectator and actor simultaneously recalls other of Diderot's dialogues, notably "Paradoxe sur le comédien," in which it is this very duplicity that defines the nature of the man of genius, whether a great actor, a great painter, a musician, or a writer.[36] The association of the two texts seems inevitable when we consider in this context, first, that Moi's opening remarks give way to a discussion of precisely this genius—a discussion that forms an obsessive leitmotif throughout the dialogue—and second, that the two characters Moi and Lui come to mimic the duality of this one exceptional mind. For Moi and Lui come to represent, in an extreme way, the two types of thought processes characteristic of an actor.

Rameau is characterized by a lack of conventional values and a constantly shifting and uncertain identity ready at any moment to inhabit multiple, musical roles. He is the best example of the worst of Plato's fears concerning false dissimulators, for in inhabiting other roles, he lives without a livelihood and even without a self. Nonetheless, in Diderot's acting system, Rameau has the makings of a great actor since it is only by having no character that an actor can play them all ("Paradoxe," 1035). Unfortunately, the energy and verve of Rameau's multiple identities constitutes what Diderot calls a "comédien ébauché" ("the outline of an actor") because, without inner judgment, "l'ouvrage d'une tête froide" (1051; "the work of a cool [ergo unemotional] head"), his performance can only be an ephemeral moment of genius lacking gradation, preparation, and unity (1050). In other words, the role of the philosopher is to complement Rameau's talents because he is the impartial spectator who coldly observes and judges the world (1006). Here again, however, such talents are limited, for, curiously, whereas the "Paradoxe" is one-sided insofar as it is particularly interested in demonstrating that judgment is necessary to the portrayal of sentiments on stage, we could say that the role of the philosopher in Le Neveu fills in the gaps of Diderot's theatrical theory. Indeed this role suggests that judgment alone is not enough. The genius, whether actor or writer, also needs the input and energy of creative, even illogical, ideas. Therefore, without Lui, the philosopher is nothing more than the mask of a man overly concerned with maintaining his intellectual integrity. He lives by a code of fixed conventions based on an arbitrary system of blacks and whites to which he submits all of his observations. As a result, any details that might de-center the system or the self are flatly dismissed. This is why, when Rameau seems to be more logical than he, the philosopher inevitably changes the subject.[37] However, at the end of *Le Neveu*, the mutual dependency of the two extreme characters becomes more and more apparent: Moi can write though he only writes "truths" (*Le Neveu*, 94), that is, only dry philosophy (he is one of Romanticism's "bookish philosophers"); Lui is more creative and spontaneous but does not have the discipline to write (96–98). The supposition is that, where writing is concerned and as the "Paradoxe" will suggest, the genius needs a combination of each of these characters' skills. In other words, as the German Romantics suggest, philosophy without poetry or Reason without fantasy cannot adequately apprehend the nature of the mind.

In the "Paradoxe," Diderot illustrates the interaction of these two extreme halves of one mind by explaining that great actors or writers must temper the flow of their own passionate emotions by separating themselves from them in a kind of self-conscious distancing. To do so, they must call upon both their great imagination and their finely tuned skills of observation and judgment in the creation of an ideal imaginary model (1008–9). This model is then held in the mind's eye where it can be heard, seen, repeated, and judged at will. In fact, in a commentary that anticipates Freud's description of a patient preparing for a psychoanalytic session as well as Stanislavski's description of his famous acting method,[38] Diderot says of the actress La Clairon: "Nonchalamment étendue sur une chaise 'longue, les bras croisés, les yeux fermés, immobile, elle peut, en suivant son rêve de mémoire, s'entendre, se voir, se juger et juger les impressions qu'elle excitera. Dans ce moment elle est double: la petite Clairon et la grande Agrippine." (1007–8).[39] Here the actress has a mental picture of an imagined role that she scrutinizes with her inner eye. That is, in a subtle identification that splits the mind into two instances at once, the actress/genius both inhabits this model and watches herself as she does. As in a daytime fantasy, she is both an actor and a vigilant spectator.[40]

In the *Interpretation of Dreams*, Freud makes a similar comparison between the work of the genius and that of the daydreamer as he identifies two instances necessary to poetic creation (135). Quoting Schiller, Freud explains that in the creative mind, the "Gates of Reason" must be opened in order to allow a free flow of visual representations emanating from the pre- (and theoretically, because of its contiguity, the un-) conscious. Consciousness must then screen these "subjective illusions" to produce art. Without this "subjective" input, the writer remains "uninspired." Indeed, if we blithely apply Freud's distinctions to the two characters in *Le Neveu*, we can say that Diderot anticipates an interaction between the selective choosing of conscious thought and the energetic displacements of the unconscious, except that in Diderot's text, both characters seem to be able to call upon both of these instances. That is, in *Le Neveu*, it is easy to suggest that Rameau and the philosopher represent the two sides of a dichotomous mind: an eccentric and mad flow of visually and aurally represented passions and energies repeatedly tempered by the philosopher's "gates of reason." But the text of *Le Neveu* is much more subtle and complicated as both Moi and Lui can be said to independently possess this doubled mind. Both can coldly observe the input of their "subjective illusions" because both can play the roles of the spectator and of the actor.

We have already seen that the philosopher/writer who introduces the play takes up both of these positions, if somewhat surreptitiously, in his roles as narrating spectator, on one hand, and as the actor/character Moi, on the other. But Rameau can also perform the model quite admirably and does so, repeatedly. In one instance, to demonstrate to Moi his illustrious, if contemptible, skills as a "mediator of love intrigues," Rameau takes on the same roles as the philosopher/writer. First Rameau addresses himself:

LUI. —... combien de fois je me suis dit: Comment, Rameau, il
y a dix mille bonnes tables à Paris, à quinze ou vingt couverts
chacune; et de ces couverts-là, il n'y en a pas un pour toi!... est-
ce que tu ne scaurois pas mentir, jurer, parjurer, promettre, tenir
ou manquer comme un autre?... est-ce que tu ne scaurois pas
encourager ce jeune homme à parler à Mademoiselle, et persuader
à Mademoiselle de l'écouter, comme un autre? (*Le Neveu*, 22)[41]

We can see Rameau's tendency to become impassioned and
emotional but also self-deprecating as he distinguishes between the esthetics and the morality of his talents. Like the
philosopher/writer, "il s'entretient avec lui meme" ("he discusses him with himself"). Then, he summons this passionate
energy in the creation of an imaginary theater playing both
himself and the role of this imaginary Mademoiselle:

—Mais mon papa. —Bon, bon; votre papa! il s'en fachera d'a-
bord un peu. —Et maman qui me recommande tant d'etre hon-
nete fille?... —Vieux propos qui ne signifient rien. (23)

In this dialogue which undermines each of the girl's bourgeois
social conventions, Rameau finally convinces her to meet the
supposed intended by pretending that this man has written
her a note. To explain this to Moi, his implied "reader," he
takes on a third role, that of a narrating spectator before this
now "objectified" scene: "Deja le coeur lui tressaillit de joye.
Tu joues avec un papier entre tes doigts ... Qu'est cela? —Ce
n'est rien" (23). In this performance, Rameau plays both characters in the dialogue while at the same time addressing Moi
in his role as a narrator. In other words, Rameau can at least
mimic the talents of the man of genius even if he refuses to do
so on moral grounds. His impassioned excesses are tempered
into an imaginary scene, which he both watches at a distance,
in his role as a narrator/spectator, and plays as a doubled
actor. The result is, as Diderot suggests in the "Paradoxe," a
believable, because objectified, character.

By comparing the structure of Rameau's imaginary theater
to that of the philosopher/writer, we can see that both can
simulate the activities of the genius. Both Rameau and the

philosopher are doubly doubled as they create dialogues with
themselves on two sides of an imaginary proscenium arch. For
example, in this scene, for the benefit of Moi:

Rameau, the	Rameau, the
character	"mediator"
addresses	addresses
Rameau, the	Rameau, playing the
spectator/narrator	role
"tu"	of Mademoiselle

Likewise, in the larger structure of the text itself and thus, for
the benefit of the actual reader, we can see that the philoso-
pher/writer mirrors Rameau's roles.

In the opening	While throughout the
monologue:	play:
The philosopher's	The philosopher as
capricious	the
thoughts	character Moi
converse with	converses with
The philosopher as silent	Lui, a character this
spectator	philosopher plays.

In both cases, the energy of impassioned thinking is controlled
by a "tête froide" in the creation of an imaginary scene or
model. Then, inhabiting the model, each character is both inside and outside the theater of his own fantasies. In other
words, despite the obvious differences between the philosopher and Rameau as characters, structurally speaking, they
appear to be mirror images: identical and, at the same time,
binomially opposed.

The importance of this similarity is to show first that neither of the characters can be called a unified subject since each
is an actor/spectator, and second, that Diderot has taken great
pains to delineate two separate characters in two separate
ethical worlds only to illustrate that their distinction is negli-
gible. Both characters are masters of the art of manipulation
but whereas Moi manipulates surreptitiously, supposedly unaware of his own dishonesty, Rameau performs for Moi only

to prove his unwillingness to exploit these dishonest talents (*Le Neveu*, 24). Such talents are not art but manipulation. In this way, Rameau, insofar as he represents society as a whole, comments on the philosopher's fixed values and sense of uniqueness by showing us that the world is a theater with society as its players. The philosopher, on the other hand, shows us that thought is also a theater but one that constantly projects new roles to play, unconsciously. That is, to know thyself or to remain conscious of oneself is to see oneself outside of oneself in the theater that is the world. However—and this may be the real lesson of *Le Neveu*'s elaborate structure—to create art is to "un-know" oneself and in a Platonic sense, to become a-moral, since it involves losing one's sense of self as a unique identity in the creation of multiplied self-representations. For as the philosopher/writer looks out onto the world, he finds there an image of himself, repeated.[42]

In the context of German Romanticism, we might evoke here Schelling's distinction between art (*Kunst*) and poetry (*Poesie*). The former defines a learned and practiced, deliberate activity of consciousness; the latter combines this talent with the free, involuntary activity of the unconscious (Simpson, 122–23). Thus far, Rameau has clearly shown us his conscious and deliberate efforts to create convincing characters. The strange thing about Rameau is the fact that although he can simulate the activities of the man of genius in the service of artful manipulation, he cannot seem to summon the same power when it is truly a question of producing poetry (*Le Neveu*, 165–66). For this, he will need the cold eye of his interlocutor in a momentary fusion with him which stages the creative act itself. As Schelling suggests, it is only the resolution of a contradiction between conscious and unconscious activity that will finally engender poetic production.

This fusion of the two characters in a representation of the creative act occurs in the section of the dialogue referred to as Rameau's "chant en fugue" (*Le Neveu*, 76). In it, the two characters discuss a theory of imitative arts initiated by Rameau's response to Moi's question "What is a song?" Rameau explains:

> Le chant est une imitation, par les sons d'une echelle inventée par l'art ou inspirée par la nature, comme il vous plaira, ou par la voix ou par l'instrument, des bruits physiques ou des accents de la passion; et vous voyez qu'en changeant la-dedans, les choses a changer, la definition conviendroit exactement a la peinture, a l'eloquence, a la sculpture, et a la poesie. (*Le Neveu*, 78)[43]

This theory, like that of the genius, assumes that the energy of passions or natural sounds must be tempered or molded, "imitated" or translated by a scale or system of values inspired by nature or purely invented. The likeness of this theory to that of the genius is of particular importance here since the two characters follow their discussion with a performance of the theory. That is, the look of the cold philosopher with his systematic vision of the world combines with Rameau's sounds and passions to create what can only be called poetry itself. As a result, both characters seem to disappear in the representation of the writer's art.

This disappearance is signaled first by the slippage of the narrator's typical discourse of opposites—either this or that, black or white, wise or foolish—as it becomes contaminated by a poetic effort to describe Rameau as he sings, acts, dances, and plays. Ultimately, the performance is transformed into an idealized model with which the philosopher then identifies:

> Que ne lui vis-je pas faire? Il pleuroit, il rioit, il soupiroit; il regardoit, ou attendri, ou tranquille, ou furieux; c'etoit une femme qui se pame de douleur; c'etoit un malheureux livré a tout son desespoir; un temple qui s'eleve; des oiseaux qui se taisent au soleil couchant; des eaux qui murmurent [*sic*] dans un lieu solitaire et frais, ou qui descendent en torrents du haut des montagnes; un orage; une tempete, la plainte de ceux qui vont perir, melée au sifflement des vents, au fracas du tonnerre; c'etoit la nuit, avec ses tenebres; c'etoit l'ombre et le silence; car le silence meme se peint par des sons. (*Le Neveu*, 84–85)[44]

The syntax of the opening sentence expresses the philosopher's growing confusion as the distance between himself and the object of his narration begins to shrink. That is, his seemingly objective observation of what are here the most out-landish of Rameau's histrionics is troubled. The discourse of opposites becomes more subtle—the crying and the laughing are tempered by the sighing; between tranquil and furious, there is now a place for tenderness—and the past tense of the narration gives way to the present of an immediate experience that transforms Rameau's performance of character-types into an imitation of nature: a temple, silent birds, murmuring or torrential waters, the lamentation of the doomed mixed with the blowing of the winds.

In this passage, we can see that the conscious activity of a deliberate description is transformed into poetic creation through the subtle interaction with something akin to what Schelling calls the involuntary or unconscious aspect of genius. In his *System*, Schelling explains that esthetic production takes place in the synthesizing of talent and a more spontaneous "gift" of inspiration and that this synthesis or closure results in a "feeling of an infinite harmony." He then adds, "This feeling, which accompanies the closure, is at the same time an *emotion*, a being *moved* [*Ruhrung*]" (Simpson, 123). Despite Schelling's overly euphoric account of "esthetic production," his description "reads" Diderot's text as an instance of this production, for all of the discursive instances of the dialogue have been "moved." Not only has the overly cold Moi been moved by this interaction—indeed, his textual designation has been missing for some time since it has been moved or given over to the narrator's point of view—but Rameau, too, finds himself moved: "Sa tete etoit tout a fait perdue. Epuisé de fatigue, tel qu'un homme qui sort d'un profond sommeil ou d'une longue distraction; il resta immobile, stupide, etonné. Il tournoit ses regards autour de lui, comme un homme egaré qui cherche a reconnaitre le lieu ou il se trouve" (*Le Neveu*, 85).[45] In other words, in his performance of a musical fugue, he has exhibited the characteristics of that psychopathological amnesia referred to as a "fugue state." As a result, both characters are absent in this moment of poetic production, thus suggesting that the two distinct figures have merged or fused in the service of art or *Poesie*. Finally, however, the narrator/spectator has also been moved, for he evokes, in his description of Rameau, not what he sees before his eyes but what he sees inside his mind. In so doing, he gives up his control as a narrator and eliminates the object of his narration.[46] In short, the objectified look upon Rameau's energetic but illogical music has drawn the narrator into the performance so that his point of view is given over to that of the writer.[47]

The interest of these losses of conscious identity lies in their relation to Schelling's undefined but obsessive reference to an unconscious. For whereas Schelling's unconscious "gift" echoes what we commonly think of pejoratively as a "romantic" notion of the inspirational aspect of esthetic production, Diderot provides it with a structure—indeed, a theatrical model theorized only later by psychoanalysis as a dream or fantasy scene created by a subject who both watches and acts, who is both subject and object.[48] Clearly, the indeterminate nature of subjects and objects in Diderot's text is already underscored by the use of the disjunctive pronouns *moi* and *lui*, which, unlike any other pronouns in French, can function interchangeably as either subjects or objects: I or me, he or him. This ambivalence of subjects and objects is further highlighted by Diderot's textual designation of two separate spaces, the inside and the outside of an imaginary stage that come to be mirror opposites. Though for the most part the philosopher as narrator remains a passive spectator before the scene of the dialogue, thus insuring a distinction between himself as a conscious subject and the object of his gaze, he is drawn, in this last scene, into an unconscious identification in which both his conscious identity and his capacity for analytical logic are undermined. It is not enough to say that he identifies with Rameau, for he does not become a histrionic musician; rather, in appropriating the musical movement and energy of Rameau's performance, his own personal fantasy materializes before his eyes. He ceases to record what Rameau is doing for he is lost in a scene created out of his own unconscious associations. For this one fleeting moment, he is both the subject and the object of his own internal fantasy. In other words, philosophy as a set of exclusive values is indeed undermined but not in the philosopher as a character; rather it is undermined in the subtle, formal play of the text itself as it elucidates the work of the writer.

In terms of the larger structure of the text, an essential question is therefore posed about the place of music in the relationship of philosophy and literature. It seems that the logic of a traditional philosophical discourse, represented by Moi, has been "musicalized" by the illogical energy of Lui. Formally speaking, both philosophical discourse and the subject of philosophy have been undone by a fugue. It can be argued, I believe, that the *Neveu* is itself structured along the outlines of a fugue, the least structured of polyphonic musical forms characterized by the interweaving of at least two independent but simultaneous melodies.[49] In the fugue, an exposition, in which all the themes are given, is often followed by a "counterexposition," "countersubject," or "answer," in which each theme is repeated in counterpoint, one voice following the other. The narrative opening of *Le Neveu* does indeed expose all of the themes of the dialogue, suggesting, as I have argued, that the whole is contained within the writer's own private textual theater but also that the dialogue itself is nothing but the repetition of an already stated chain of events; Rameau's paradoxical habits, his lung capacity, his frustrations, his famous dinner party chez Bertin, and his awful, inhuman uncle are each events prescheduled in the opening exposition which in turn form the basic skeleton of the dialogue to come. There is no new material discussed in the dialogue proper, only an objectified or theatricalized replication of those original silent thoughts, a repeat performance. The subsequent interaction of Moi and Lui as a series of contrapuntal contradictions and "harmonic digressions" seems to then mimic the counterexposition in what are often called "episodes," subsidiary subjects or themes based on material from the exposition. Near the fugue's *dénouement* or conclusion, which is not necessarily a resolution, there can be a "stretto," a moment of crisis or intensity in which the two voices become indistinguishable, as we saw in Rameau's "chant en fugue." Since, in addition, at the end of the dialogue neither character has been persuaded by the other, the assumption is that their discussion may well take place again and again, indeed, ad infinitum as in the case of an obsessional fantasy scenario or even as in a musical score. As opposed to Plato's movement of logic across several voices, we have here the logic of desire, a series of "repetitions in difference" on the theme of the man of genius. A dialectics of truth thus becomes a musical performance.

Ultimately, then, whether or not *Le Neveu de Rameau* is actually composed as a fugue, its likeness to the musical form emphasizes its displacement of an act of communication in favor of a language performance by drawing a relationship between the movement of thought and the movement of music. Julia Kristeva refers to this displacement, in semiotic terms, as a "signifying economic" which replaces the linearity of philosophical metalanguage with the spatiality of the theater in its material production of the signifying process itself ("La Musique parléé," 169). She adds, in modern Lacanian terms (which nonetheless echo those of Schelling and of Freud), that this process relies upon "other," that is, musical, signifying systems in order to represent the veering of the unconscious into the field of the signifier (169). In other words, in order to stage the work of an active conscious mind constantly undermined by the digressive additions of unconscious activity, Diderot's text borrows the logic of music. Moreover, although Kristeva does not see the whole of *Le Neveu* as reflecting the structure of a fugue, she does refer to Rameau's "chant en fugue" and to Diderot's ideas about music as the sign of a synthesis of rationalist univocity and musical pluralization, of the exigencies of the reality principle and the pulsions of the primary processes (190). If this is true, then Diderot's text offers itself as a remarkable anticipation of Freud's theatrical metaphor, for it appears that the theatrical structure of *Le Neveu de Rameau* is designed to show that the mind is indeed a divided scene—a fixed structure that insures the endless polyphonic movement of thoughts as well as the pleasurable productivity of losing one's rational or conscious identity.

According to Kristeva, it is this synthesis of conscious rational logic and the musical, energetic impulses of unconscious thinking that, beginning with Diderot, inaugurates the modern novel (201). However, this "modern novel," which, for Kristeva, is best represented by Joyce's "rhythmic pluralization of meanings" (202), might be better understood, in the context of Diderot, as nothing more or less than the Ideal Book of the Romantics. As a repositioning of Plato's *theatrum philosophicum, Le Neveu* corresponds to each of the Romantics' definitions of this illusive, supposedly unrealizable "genre." It is at once an "interior or ideal" fusion of art and philosophy (*L'Absolu*, 280), a drama of subjectivity that mixes and yet dissolves genres, a theater destined to be read and not to be seen (*L'Absolu*, 283–84). In sum, it is what we have here described as a "Virtual Theater." Ultimately, following Diderot's literary exploitation of the *theatrum philosophicum*, we can identify subsequent manifestations of this genre-that-is-not-one which continue to walk a fine line between theater and philosophy from Hugo, Vigny, and Stendhal to Flaubert and Mallarmé.

T W O

Mixed Literature and Philosophy

If Diderot's *Le Neveu de Rameau* plays out what Georges Poulet refers to as a Romantic or pre-Romantic examination of consciousness, it also proposes a unique theatrical shape for this philosophical endeavor that I have called Virtual Theater.[1] It is this same theatrical shaping of self-conscious examination that preoccupies the early-nineteenth-century French Romantics whether or not they owe a direct debt to Diderot, for Romanticism in France is characterized by an exceptional interest in theater. Although the generalized goal of this obsession with theater is usually understood as the expression of a desire to create a Romantic tragedy powerful enough both to oppose Racine's classicism and to rival the dramaturgy of Shakespeare, Calderon, and Schiller, this goal is indeterminately confused with the type of theatrical shaping evident in *Le Neveu*.[2] Indeed, in an effort to conceptualize a French-style Romantic drama, French thinkers would produce manifestos questioning notions of classical representation, translations, adaptations, and imitations of the great foreign masterpieces as well as a prodigious number of unrepresentable plays, "closet dramas" or "ideal theaters."

There are several explanations for this great number of bookish theaters. Claude Duchet considers it to be a manifestation of the desire to create a "drame historique" within (or outside of) the confines of the severe demands of censorship.[3] This reading supposes that authors wrote bookish theaters because of either material or political excesses, that is, the borders of the stage were simply too narrow to accommodate the *mise en scène* of history. Musset's *Lorenzaccio* or Hugo's *Cromwell* might indeed fall into this category though Hassan El Nouty argues, ironically, that *Lorenzaccio* was composed during a brief moment when censorship was lifted.[4] Moody Prior sees the writing of ideal theaters as an expression of open contempt for the stage, that is, as an intentionally provocative attack on theatrical conventions.[5] Pierre Salomon concurs, citing Mérimée's *Théâtre de Clara Gazul* as an instance of this kind of provocation,[6] and Musset reiterates a similar stance in the preface to his own *Spectacle dans un fauteuil*.[7]

From a slightly different perspective, as suggested by the title of his *Théâtre et pré-cinéma*, Hassan El Nouty does not believe that ideal bookish theaters were a reaction to censorship or that they were really proposing provocative and new kinds of dramaturgy (117–48, 273). Though he does partially agree with Duchet's explanation, he also renders it more subtle by insisting on the confluence of three factors. He includes the desire to dramatize history but adds the tendency to subordinate representations of human beings to that of the world and the growing importance of Gautier's "spectacle oculaire" which, for El Nouty, represents a fusion of ideal theater and cinematic esthetics (117, 271–74). The last of these factors is questionable since it leads El Nouty to suppose that most ideal theaters are simply awaiting more advanced modes of representation such as the cinema or video (274).[8] The second of the factors—subordinating the representation of human beings to that of the world—is also problematic, either too simple or too politically motivated, because it counters the view held by many that Romanticism and its ideal theaters were an expression of what Barish calls "inwardness" (*Anti-Theatrical Prejudice*, 326), and Poulet, an examination of consciousness. If we consider, for example, the cases of Edgar Quinet's *Ahasvérus*, Pierre-Simon Ballanche's *Orphée*, or even Diderot's *Neveu*, it seems evident that certain bookish theaters may be seen as the *mise en scène* of a single mind which has become one with the universe as Poulet suggests (*Entre Moi et Moi*, 27). In other words, instead of awaiting more adequate modes of representation or being stifled by efforts to represent the world, certain ideal theaters were merely opting for a theatrical format in an attempt to represent subjectivity itself.

In emphasizing the Romantic goal of revitalizing the theater in the creation of a new kind of drama, these critics have overlooked the "writerly" significance of choosing a dramatic format in the creation of a theater designed solely to be read. Another way of getting at these dramatic writing strategies, therefore, is to examine the aspect of Romantic criticism that concentrates on what Meyer Abrams has referred to as the slipping of the preeminence of tragedy in favor of lyric poetry. Charles Affron, for example, underscores the fact that Romantic drama offered a new setting for lyric poetry by creating a new context for poetic consciousness. Of Hugo and Musset, he writes: "In their avidity to explore the various dimensions of art they project their imagination into formal combinations that wrench poetry from its immediately recognizable contexts." Though Affron's analysis of new "formal combinations" does not include Virtual Theater—indeed, he is primarily concerned with truly stageable drama—he does begin to note some of the writing problems that preoccupy the early Romantic authors and that explain why they may have chosen to write plays not intended for the stage. For, according to Affron, the use of dramatic form allows poets to scatter their voices among the various roles of a play, to abolish theatrical time in favor of timelessness and to transcend rhetoric through the use of metaphor.[9]

In a similar vein, Jonas Barish notes that for Romanticism the theater was a place designed for social interaction, whereas the poem was a space in which to enjoy the solitude of self-conscious examination. Citing authors as varied as Auguste Compte, John Stuart Mill, and Byron, among others, he notes a tendency to distinguish between theater and drama: the first is a superficial and generally corrupt social interaction and the second connotes a "pure expressiveness that knows nothing of the presence of others" (*Anti-Theatrical Prejudice*, 326). In other words, for the Romantics in Barish's study, Platonic antitheatricalism is transformed into an antisocialism such as we might associate with Vigny, Flaubert, or Mallarmé. Though this reasoning is compelling, it still does not explain why certain authors did not simply write poems instead of plays, that is, why so many of them persisted in writing plays that were designed to remain on paper. Barish does note instances of ambiguity or ambivalence about the theater in such authors as Mallarmé and Maeterlinck who hoped to envision a new kind of truly poetic but nonetheless stageworthy theater (337–40). Unfortunately, he does not offer further insight into this ambiguity because it might threaten, one suspects, that lumping together of all bookish theaters under the rubric of antitheatricalism.

It is this ambivalence about the theater in Romantic thought that interests me. Although it may not explain the general phenomenon of "closet" dramas or "library" plays, it does point to the fact that theater has become a focal point for the philosophy of literature in general as well as a format for the exposition of philosophy in literature, an ideal model for the representation of a theatricalized self-consciousness. For this reason, I shall examine three very different examples of the way in which literary philosophy or the philosophy of literary esthetics in early-nineteenth-century France would find itself caught between analyzing and being theater. Hugo's *Littérature et philosophie mêlées*, Vigny's *Journal d'un poète*, and Stendhal's *Racine et Shakespeare* each offer unique examples of the ways in which theater would come to lodge itself somewhere between literature and philosophy.

Across the work of these three authors who are indeed representative of Romanticism in France, we shall see that the question of theatricality is cautiously relocated. Out of Hugo's concerns about actual representation, the question of theater moves away from the real stage to become a paradigm for the philosophy of esthetics. Although Hugo promulgates the use of theater as a didactic act of communication and believes language to have the transparency capable of rendering this type of communication, the theatricality of his own journal suggests that theater might also describe the nature of subjectivity. Vigny, relying upon the assumption Hugo overlooks, comes to see theater as a model for subjectivity, now understood as a drama of consciousness. In his efforts to conceive of a format adequate to the representation of that drama in writing, he experiments, in his journal, with mobilized points of view and creates a *mise en abîme* of dialogues. This in turn takes the emphasis away from the person of the author and displaces an act of communication in favor of a language performance whose purpose is no longer to teach but to afford pleasure. Stendhal, because of the extraordinary pervasiveness of theater in his work and because of his literary use of the philosophical dialogue, demonstrates the way in which writing always theatricalizes subjectivity and he comes to imply that theater is the place in which philosophy meets and is undone by literature. In short, Hugo poses the question of literature and philosophy in terms of theater; Vigny introduces philosophy into literature by exploring modes of theatrical exposition; Stendhal uses similar modes of theatrical exposition to show the inevitable entrance of fiction into any discourse, and, by exploiting the theatrical nature of the philosophical dialogue, the inevitable entrance of literature into philosophy. Each proposes a theatricalized version of philosophy that sets the stage for the nineteenth century's production of Virtual Theater.

"HUGO'S EGO"

> Pourquoi, en effet, ne pas confronter plus souvent qu'on ne le fait les révolutions de l'individu avec les révolutions de la société? [10]

As Philippe Lacoue-Labarthe has suggested, Hugo's *Littérature et philosophie mêlées* is symptomatic of an era.[11] First, as a personal journal, it is a good example of the growing popularity of journals as a genre, a popularity that Thibaudet relates to a new fascination with the persons of authors but which also is clearly related to the general tendency to exploit the act of self-examination.[12] Hugo himself offers his journal in part as the natural complement to the reading of his novels *Han d'Islande* and *Notre-Dame de Paris* because it offers an "unpremeditated" account of the evolution of his thinking between 1813 and 1843.[13] Second, Hugo's journal is a mixture of genres, as its title suggests, made up of projects for the theater and for government, poems, satires, epigrams, critical and historical essays, and personal observations. Third, the journal demonstrates its author's theory that social and political revolutions will be followed by literary revolutions.

In the "But de cette publication" that opens his journal, Hugo introduces the work as a chaotic mixture whose only logic is to represent the confluence of these three forces: self-examination, mixed genres, and literary revolution:

> Tout cela va, vient, avance, recule, se mêle, se coudoie, se heurte, se contredit, se querelle, croit, doute, tâtonne, nie, affirme, sans but visible, sans ordre extérieur, sans loi apparente; et cependent . . . au milieu de toutes ces idées contradictoires qui bruissent à la fois dans ce chaos d'illusions généreuses et de préjugés loyaux . . . on sent poindre et se mouvoir un élément qui s'assimilera un jour tous les autres, l'esprit de liberté, que les instincts de l'auteur appliqueront d'abord à l'art, puis, par un irrésistible entraînement de logique, à la société; de façon que chez lui . . . les idées littéraires corrigeront les idées politiques. (*Littérature*, 1:11)[14]

The haphazard nature of the journal works in its favor to stand for liberty of thought but also to represent, quite literally, its own tumultuous times filled with debates, quarrels, affirmations, and contradictions. The passage itself performs these opposing tensions. In fact, if the highly personal and chaotic contents of the journal have a purpose, it is that their chaotic nature insures a "disinterested" or impartial mirror of the development of one man's mind which thereby reflects the "physionomie d'une époque" (*Littérature*, 1:9; "physiognomy of a century"). That is, the publication of this journal is justified, in Hugo's mind, because of its unwavering honesty and lack of ulterior motive. These qualities lend it a certain objectivity and thus, a certain historical value. In this sense, Hugo's journal provides a perfect example of what Poulet calls "le romantisme socialiste" (Poulet, *Entre Moi et Moi*, 35–36) for it is at the same time individual and universal.

In presenting the unarranged and unpremeditated thoughts of one mind, Hugo argues that the journal realizes a kind of social mission that transforms an individual act of self-conscious examination into a philosophy of social responsibility:

> Dans des temps comme les nôtres, où les événements font si rapidement changer d'aspect aux doctrines et aux hommes, il [l'auteur] a pensé que ce ne serait peut-être pas un spectacle sans enseignement que le développement d'un esprit sérieux et droit qui n'a encore été directement mêlé à aucune chose politique et qui a silencieusement accompli toutes ses révolutions sur lui-même, sans autre but que la satisfaction de sa conscience. (*Littérature*, 1:6–7)[15]

Revolutions, in this passage, describe the spectacle of self-examination which, once recorded, becomes a didactic spectacle. The choice of silent revolutions is striking since Hugo notes that the journal has no political motives and that it is a purely disinterested record of his own thoughts. In other words, revolutions, here, stand for an act of self-manipulation and self-discovery during which one would theoretically turn the mind over and over in order to scrutinize its contents without at the same time influencing those contents. One wonders how this utterly self-indulgent exercise in self-awareness can be a didactic spectacle.

The answer to this perfectly logical query lies in Hugo's notion of social purpose and in his sense of himself as a "spectacle." For the spectacle becomes didactic only if it is imitated, that is, only if Hugo's readers are willing to follow his own autoanalytic model:

> L'auteur pense que tous ceux de nos contemporains qui feront de bonne foi le même repli sur eux-mêmes, ne trouveront pas des modifications moins profondes dans leur pensée, s'ils ont eu la sagesse et le désintéressement de lui laisser son libre développement en présence des faits et des résultats. (1 : 13)[16]

In this passage, Hugo is exhorting the reader to examine his or her own consciousness in much the same way he did by looking back upon his own journalistic commentaries. It gives us therefore, a better sense of what kind of autoanalysis this journal really provides. Indeed, there is a double movement involved in this process which may explain why Hugo sees his journal as a spectacle. To achieve an "objective" self-scrutiny, one must engage in the activities associated with Diderot's actor and Freud's creative artist: a random flow of "disinterested" ideas—in Hugo's case, the chaos of thought directed uniquely by the spirit of liberty—is to be analyzed through a folding back onto oneself, a "repli," which requires the distance of a kind of speculating eye. Thus, for Hugo, the philosophical act constituted by writing a journal has to do with recording oneself in writing, that is, as literature, and then, examining this supposedly impartial record in order to glean a better and more objective sense of oneself. The process is philosophical insofar as it assumes as its outcome the discovery of ontological truths but it is literary and, indeed, theatrical in that it involves becoming an imaginary actor and spectator.

This same process of folding back onto oneself describes the relationship of the journal to its preface. The journal itself is made up of three parts: first, the *Journal des idées d'un royaliste de 1819;* then, the *Journal des idées d'un révolutionnaire de 1830;* finally, a selection of fragments presented in chronological order from 1823 to 1834, bringing it up to the date of the preface. Because the greater part of the preface itself is devoted to a discussion of the current status of the author's opinions about art and society, one could say that it continues the progress inscribed in the journal, adding yet another stage in the development of the author's mind and another "repli" onto himself. However, it also adds an artificial arrangement to the volume, despite its author's insistence to the contrary, because it finishes by describing its own revolution. It is as if having finished the journal, the reader could theoretically begin again, gleaning less a sense of the progress of Hugo's ideas than a sense of the revolutions of thought itself. One begins to have the sense that the journal is performing its point, performing rather than explaining that which it is talking about.

The same might be said for the preface itself. It is striking that this preface also contains its own "repli" insofar as it is made up of two distinct parts that seem irrelevant to each other. On one hand, there is a justification for the publication of a personal journal which, as we have seen, presents the "spectacle" of self-conscious examination. On the other, however, Hugo offers a philosophy of representation that discusses the history of the French language from the Renaissance through the nineteenth century, the question of poetic style or prosody, and, finally, the seminal importance of theater in modern society. Though these two halves of one preface seem to be entirely unrelated, the concept of the "repli" elucidates their interaction. For whatever is true of Hugo's "spectacle" of subjectivity is also true of representation in general.

Hugo begins his discussion of theater by defining it as the centerpiece of his philosophy of representation. He writes that

> s'il nous était permis de hasarder une conjecture sur ce qui doit advenir de l'art, nous dirions qu'à notre avis, d'ici à peu d'années, l'art, sans renoncer à toutes ses autres formes, se résumera plus spécialement sous la forme essentielle et culminante du drame. . . .
>
> Aussi les quelques mots que nous allons dire du drame s'appliquent dans notre pensée . . . à la poésie toute entière, et ce qui s'applique à la poésie, s'applique à l'art tout entier. (*Littérature*, I : 23)[17]

As Hugo's piece is already highly symptomatic of his century's concerns, it is not surprising to find that the theatrical model stands here as a paradigm for representation in general. This undoubtedly offers some insight into the early nineteenth century's fervent interest in theater and suggests why its theoretical successes far surpassed its accomplishments on stage.

For Hugo specifically, focus on the theater has to do with his belief that if art is to touch society, it can best do so on a public stage where great numbers of people can be taught and civilized (1:43–45). For Hugo, the dramatic poet has a social and philosophical mission that resembles the one Hugo has already defined for himself by publishing the journal. In relation to the Romantic polemic concerning whether theater should be designed to satisfy the needs of the public by favoring spectacle or, rather, the needs of artists by presenting intellectual and philosophical ideas,[18] Hugo recasts the issue by emphasizing the philosophical nature of the theatrical experience itself:

> Le drame sans sortir des limites impartiales de l'art, a une mission nationale, une mission sociale, une mission humaine. Quand il [the author] voit chaque soir le peuple si intelligent et si avancé, qui a fait de Paris la cité centrale du progrès, s'entasser en foule devant un rideau . . . il s'interroge avec sévérité et recueillement sur la portée philosophique de son oeuvre. . . . Le poète aussi a charge d'âmes. . . .
> Le théâtre, nous le répétons, est une chose qui enseigne et qui civilise. (*Littérature*, 1:43–45)[19]

For Hugo, the theater, and therefore literature in general, has become the ideal setting for philosophy. Its national, social, and human mission is to educate and civilize the people, while at the same time remaining impartial. By this, Hugo means that theater, like his journal, should not be concerned with contemporary politics or transitory "parti pris." On the contrary, theater should use its objective means of representation to teach "les sept ou huit grandes vérités sociales, morales ou philosophiques" (1:55; "the seven or eight great social, moral, or philosophical truths"). Essentially then, Hugo espouses Aristotelian notions of theater: art should represent the universal essence of human nature in order to teach or correct that nature.[20]

According to Hugo, a crowd of people should be attracted to drama as a bird to a mirror (*Littérature*, 1:53), finding there a reflection of itself:

> C'est par des peintures vraies de la nature éternelle que chacun porte en soi; c'est en nous prenant, vous, moi, nous, eux, tous, par nos irrésistibles sentiments de père, de fils, de mère, de frère et de soeur, d'ami et d'ennemi, d'amant et de maîtresse, d'homme et de femme; . . . c'est en sondant avec le *speculum* du génie notre conscience, nos opinions, nos illusions, nos préjugés; c'est en remuant tout ce qui est dans l'ombre au fond de nos entrailles; en un mot, c'est en jetant . . . de larges jours sur le coeur humain, ce chaos d'où le *fiat lux* du poète tire un monde! —C'est ainsi et pas autrement. —Et, nous le répétons, plus le créateur dramatique sera profond, désintéressé, général et universel dans son oeuvre, mieux il accomplira sa mission et près des contemporains et près de la postérité. (1:51)[21]

The poet's philosophical mission consists of pulling ontological truths out of the chaos of opinions, illusions, and prejudices that is consciousness and illuminating, with his speculum, the murky depths of subjectivity. The assumption is that there exists a concrete entity of being, even a collective consciousness, at the innermost center of each of us which will be touched or moved by representations of familial dramas. This is why art is didactic. By being impersonal and impartial, the poet's works will represent true paintings of our universal and eternal natures.

Ironically, however, the most striking thing about this passage is the fact that this essentially Aristotelian notion of theater's mission is not unlike Hugo's own mission writing and publishing his journal. The journal itself is described as a chaos of opinions, illusions, and prejudices. And within this chaos a reader can sense the essential nature of one man whose mind is also a mirror of society. Like the theater, Hugo's journal presents universal, philosophical truths only because it is impartially composed or "désintéressé." Moreover,

the image of the dramatic poet's speculum with which he examines the nature of consciousness, echoes both the reader's
and Hugo's own philosophical act in approaching the journal.
It is by means of a speculating eye that Hugo performs revolutions upon himself and that readers might accomplish an
autocritical "repli" onto themselves. Finally, like the theater,
Hugo's journal is conceived as a didactic spectacle. In other
words, the question of theater has become much more all-
consuming than even Hugo seems to suspect. A connection
has been made between the two types of representation, making the journal itself into its own kind of theater. Therefore,
whereas Hugo attempts to proceed by examining his previously written presentation of subjectivity along philosophical
lines, making it a didactic spectacle, his text provides another
kind of spectacle, a kind of unconscious theater of thought
itself. As a result, universal truths and impartial representation turn into just the opposite because the philosophical act
constituted by writing, then reading oneself, is also inevitably
a theatrical one.

In fact, this process of writing and reading involves becoming both an actor and spectator. Like an actor, Hugo performs roles in his journal: he is a royalist in 1819, then a
revolutionary in 1830. Like a spectator, he examines himself
acting, "objectively," with the supposed intent of gleaning
truths about his subjective nature. Yet this self-examination
does not lead to any intrinsic, unchanging self. On the contrary, it produces those "contradictory ideas" that come and
go, believe and doubt, negate and affirm in a dynamic display
of chaotic self-representations. The theater, then, is not only a
model for representation in general, a focal point for the philosophy of literature, but also a model for the representation
of subjectivity. The implication is that philosophical mastery
of oneself, that self-examination by which one attempts to discover ontological truths, is undone by the very theatricality
inherent in the act of self-examination. We could say that in
writing about the subject of theater, the writing subject himself becomes theatricalized. Or more specifically, a theatricalized textuality frames the voice of authority and thereby dis-

pels the very possibility of finding truths about one's own subjectivity. As Roland Barthes expressed it, "C'est la 'fonction' du texte que de 'théâtraliser' . . . ce travail par quoi se produit la rencontre du sujet et de la langue."[22] Hugo, writing, never quite coincides with Hugo the philosopher; the subject is never quite himself. So while Hugo speaks on, unaware that the possibility of recording subjectivity is always fated to confront this inescapable gap, his philosophy is undone by its own internal literature as his text theatricalizes its author's encounter with language. Clearly, it is this question of subjectivity and the difficulties of its representation as or in philosophy that is to a large extent hidden by the century's overwhelmingly theoretical interest in theater. This makes Hugo's *Littérature et philosophie mêlées* a symptom of its times, not because in it the individual becomes universal, but because it signals a crisis in subjectivity and representation with which subsequent authors will want to come to terms.

BETWEEN VIGNY AND VIGNY

> Je dois donc dire que j'ai cru démêler en moi deux êtres bien distincts l'un de l'autre, le *moi dramatique*, qui vit avec activité et violence, éprouve avec douleur ou enivrement, agit avec énergie ou persévérance, et le *moi philosophique*, qui se sépare journellement de l'autre moi, le dédaigne, le juge, le critique, l'analyse, le regarde passer et rit ou pleure de ses faux pas comme ferait un ange gardien. Les deux personnes parleront tour à tour dans ce livre et je me persuade qu'on reconnaîtra facilement le son de leur voix.[23]

Alfred de Vigny is another Romantic poet concerned with the interaction of literature and philosophy in his writing. Like Hugo, Vigny exploits the metaphor or figure of the theater in order to dramatize that interaction in his own mind, and like Hugo's journal, *Littérature et philosophie mêlées*, Vigny's *Journal d'un poète* serves as the space in which to envision and analyze that theater. Unlike Hugo, however, who publishes his journal in order to propose a model for self-examination as a socially corrective measure, Vigny is re-

---

leased from a sense of social responsibility. The journal itself alternates between states of literary inspiration and philosophical argumentation but the recording of these states is uniquely designed to help Vigny understand himself. As he puts it, "Je présente ces considérations, non pour poser des principes, mais pour expliquer les miens et faire comprendre quelles idées me décidèrent à imprimer à mes ouvrages la forme que je leur ai donnée."[24] In other words, Vigny engages in self-analysis only to understand the meandering of his own creative imagination. In opposition to Hugo's notion of self-control or philosophical mastery, Vigny's efforts suggest an awareness of the unconscious element in writing and creativity that an analytical distancing may help to expose.

Indeed, what Vigny realizes and what Hugo seems to only passively perform is that literature and philosophy are not two separate disciplines that should be combined in art in order to give it social purpose but, rather, two separate faculties contained in one mind which express themselves in a work of art as two separate points of view. In 1837, Vigny writes:

> (*A mettre dans la préface de mon prochain drame*).
> Il y a dans les oeuvres d'art deux points de vue. L'un philosophique, l'autre poétique. —Le point de vue philosophique doit soutenir l'oeuvre, drame ou livre, d'un pôle à l'autre précisément comme l'axe d'un globe, mais le globe dans sa forme arrondi et complète avec ces couleurs variées et brillantes est une image de l'axe de l'art qui doit être toujours en vue, en tournant autour de la pensée philosophique et l'emportant dans son atmosphère. . . . Rechauffer plutôt qu'enseigner. (*Oeuvres*, 2:1082)[25]

According to this passage, philosophy's didactic nature could be enveloped by the rounded axis of art, thereby allowing it to be a structural ordering principle without being seen. Interestingly enough, philosophy's entrance into art displaces its goals in favor of those of fiction; the purpose of representation is to warm, that is, to give pleasure, and not to teach. Hugo's desire to mix the endeavors of the poet and the philosopher is thus also evident in Vigny, but not because the poet has a philosophical and social mission, rather because Vigny has found both points of view in his own mind: a dramatic self whose energetic changeability is subject to the guidance of an other, philosophical self.

When it comes to the theater, Vigny's attitude is ambivalent precisely because of his desire to represent or coalesce these two selves in a work of art: "Jeu de marrionnettes que le théâtre! pas assez de place pour le développement des caractères et la philosophie!" (2:937; "What a puppet show the theater is! not enough room for the development of characters and philosophy!"). In this passage, it is evident that both axes of good drama, philosophy and art (the creation of characters belonging to the latter domain—2:904), seem to be too time-consuming for the confines of the theater. In another passage, Vigny notes that even when these elements are present, vulgar audiences miss the point. After a production of his *Quitte pour la peur*, for example, Vigny is deeply disappointed by "la multitude": "Elle a réussi à comprendre l'événement mais n'a pas compris la satire philosophique et la question sociale lui a échappé" (2:988; "It [the multitude] has succeeded in understanding the happening, but has not understood the philosophical satire, and the social question escaped it"). This in turn leads him to his oft-repeated renunciation of the theater: "C'est par la partie commune de son talent que l'on réussit au théâtre, comme dans la vie publique on est populaire par les qualités vulgaires" (2:989; "It is by the common part of one's talent that one succeeds in theater, as in public life one is popular for vulgar qualities"). Unlike Hugo who promulgates theater for social good, then, Vigny rejects it precisely because it is social.

Insofar as Vigny is a social aristocrat who scorns the "spectacle" of theater, he is like many of his contemporaries who, as El Nouty puts it, exhibit the elitist sense that the people have no taste (*Théâtre et pré-cinéma*, 66–67). Yet Vigny's disdain is not a product of a Platonic antitheatrical prejudice. On the contrary, Vigny criticizes Plato in his *Stello* for valuing the intellectual domination of judgment over the work of the imagination (*Oeuvres*, 1:739). Unlike Plato, Vigny recognizes his essentially double or theatrical nature and its relevance to theatrical composition. The problem for Vigny is that the theater exchanges the force of the poet's words for the force of playacting:

> J'ai longtemps cherché quelle secrète antipathie m'éloignait d'écrire pour le théâtre, antipathie étrange en moi dont le principal instinct ou talent est la composition dramatique. En analysant l'art théâtral je l'ai trouvé. C'est qu'il y a dans cet art une partie qui reste toujours flottante, celle du *jeu* qui appartient à l'acteur, et ce qu'on appelle le *jeu* n'est rien moins que l'expression des sentiments, le dessin des tableaux et celui des scènes, c'est-à-dire trois des sources d'émotion. (2:931)[26]

It is precisely the lack of control over the total dramatic effect, over the part of drama, that best touches society, over the material realities of representation contained in the actor's act but lost to the writer's, which keep Vigny from doing what he does best.

The conflict between Vigny's disdain for the theater and his natural talent for dramatic composition does not, however, keep him from writing theater. For although Vigny's plans are thwarted by censorship, still his interest in drama persists:

> Arrêté le plan de *Daphné* qui n'était pas assez simple. Ceci est trop tragique pour un poème. C'est un Drame que je ne puis garder pour la scène parce que nul gouvernement ne le laisserait représenter. (2:1058)[27]

As we witness in this passage, *Daphné* is at once too complicated and too shocking for the stage and yet, necessarily drama.[28] In the case of *Daphné*, politics are part of the problem as the play would theoretically associate the fall of the Roman Empire with the fall of the ancien régime to democracy (*Oeuvres*, 2:1295). However, when we consider the form of this unrepresentable play we shall see that Vigny's project for the theater is not only thwarted because of censorship but also because it is a philosophical drama, the staging of Vigny's own drama of subjectivity.

Indeed, throughout much of his journal, between the years 1831 and 1863, Vigny is obsessed, much like the German Romantics, with the dramatic composition of an Ideal Book to

be entitled *Daphné*. Though some of the composition has sur-
vived showing *Daphné* to be a second volume in the philosophical drama of Stello and Docteur Noir (2:771–857),
Vigny's persistent and indecisive references to it suggest that
the form of the drama was of constant concern, variously
confused with Vigny's thoughts on epic and on theater. As
F. Baldensperger has evasively suggested in the *Oeuvres complètes*, the initial conception of *Daphné* appears to have been
born out of one of the first tragedies Vigny ever wrote, *Julien
l'Apostat* (2:769). In 1832, Vigny refers to the manuscript of
"Julien" written in 1816, announcing that he has just burned
it (2:950) but in 1833, he notes his continued interest in the
figure of Julien:

> Je ne puis vaincre la sympathie que j'ai toujours eue pour Julien
> l'Apostat.
> Si la métempsycose existe, j'ai été cet homme.
> C'est l'homme dont le rôle, la vie, le caractère m'eussent le
> mieux convenu dans l'histoire. (2:988)[29]

Julien is thus Vigny's ideal alter ego, a focal point for the
drama of subjectivity that Vigny would like to write as a
sequel to *Stello*. Paradoxically, this close relationship between Vigny and Julien might explain why *Daphné* was never
completed.

As of 1837, Vigny began to think about *Daphné* as an epic
drama (2:1062). That is, *Daphné*, like *Stello* or *Servitude et
grandeur militaires*, would be constructed as "une idée en
trois actes" (2:1065; "one idea in three acts") thus making
Julien's drama into one of the three acts, not unlike Thomas
Chatterton's in *Stello*. Alongside the story of Julien would be
those of Philip Melanchton and of Rousseau, "all three Pla-
tonists" (2:1073) and "counterrevolutionarie[s]" (2:1070),
making the "philosophical negation of Christianism" (2:
1087–88) into the "philosophical axis" of the epic. In this
case, *Daphné*, like *Stello*, would be constructed as three stories read or recounted by Docteur Noir to the sensitive Stello,
resulting, at the close of all three stories, in a lesson or "or-
donnance" for the poet. The second title associated with

Daphné, "La Deuxième Consultation du Dr. Noir," tends to support this conception of the work. Moreover, we know that Vigny envisioned four consultations between Stello and the doctor. The first, *Stello*, represents three examples of poets misunderstood by society: Joseph Gilbert, Chatterton, and André Chénier. The second, *Daphné*, would represent three examples of religious fervor in Julien, Melanchton, and Rousseau. The third, never written, would theoretically concern political men—and in one instance we read: "Faire défiler Monk, Marat, Julien l'Apostat" (2:1013; "Make Monk, Marat, Julien the Apostate parade"), and the fourth would interrogate the idea of love (2:1013). From these outlines for the consultation projects, it is clear that the figure of Julien is caught, in Vigny's thinking, between politics and religion, exactly like Vigny himself.

Julien is also caught, however, between theater and epic. For surrounding the confused conception of *Daphné* as one part of a four-part epic, the concept of a theater piece on Julien also persists. As late as 1857, we see two journal entries that confirm Vigny's continued interest in using the figure of Julien in a drama for the stage. On February 5, Vigny notes:

> *Julien l'Apostat*. Comme il parlait toujours grec, j'écrirai le drame des Stoïciens en prose. . . .
>
> Le drame sera intitulé "les Stoïciens." . . . Cet ouvrage que je rêve depuis tant d'années n'a pas encore sa forme définitive dans mon esprit.
>
> Elle approche. Lorsque je la verrai assez belle, je l'écrirai. (2:1329)

Then on May 11 of the same year,

> *Julien l'Apostat*.
>
> Je suis sans cesse poursuivi par cette pensée. Peindre la lutte intérieure de l'âme de ce grand homme, conservateur de l'*Empire Romain* et prévoyant l'invasion de la Barbarie. Craignant le christianisme parce qu'il affaiblit la *défense* de l'Empire en décourageant les *guerriers* de la *guerre*.
>
> Discute cette question avec saint Martin.
>
> Intituler la pièce: *les Stoïciens*. (2:1330)[30]

Clearly, *Les Stoïciens* would have as its subject matter the questions posed and confronted in *Daphné* so that one is lead to believe that *Les Stoïciens* or *Julien l'Apostat* might work, like the story of Chatterton, as both a play and a novelistic drama or epic.

The confusions concerning the form of *Daphné*, drama or epic, are further complicated by the inclusion of yet another character, Lamuel or Emmanuel, whose story or destiny would surround the telling of the three stories of *Daphné*. As Vigny put it, an imaginary story, that of Lamuel, would envelope three historical representations of religious fervor all passing before the eyes of Stello and the Docteur Noir (2: 1080–81). That is, in this conception of *Daphné*, *Daphné* itself would be part of a much larger composition in which Docteur Noir would read it to Lamuel (2:1056), a sensitive soul who, like Julien and Stello, also ends by committing suicide (2:1004, 1017, 1057). The book, *Daphné*, would then be found by both Melanchton and Rousseau who, like Lamuel and Stello, identify with Julien (2:1076). In this case, *Daphné* is at once the name of the epic, the location of Julien's story, and a book which functions, like a theatrical prop, to link the three different time periods of the three different stories.

The result of this elaborate if inconclusive composition is, like the prop *Daphné* would suggest, a nested specular structure or *mise en abîme* in which the figures of Stello and Docteur Noir are reproduced threefold, both vertically and horizontally, so to speak. While from story to story each historical hero repeats Julien's conflict and identifies with him, Stello remains outside of the stories as a spectator who watches a parade of figures who function as parables for his own situation. That is, he identifies with each of the heroes and with Lamuel. Moreover, as spectators outside of the drama of Lamuel, Stello and Docteur Noir reproduce or mirror the conflict of Lamuel (2:1058, 1063) which in turn mirrors the conflict of Julien taking place within the drama being read and called *Daphné* (2:1076). Witness this journal entry of February 2, 1837:

Ecrit le chapitre: Christ et Antéchrist. —Qu'il y ait à la fin du
volume un *Dialogue imaginaire entre Julien et Jésus.* —Stello
l'entend distinctement.
—L'*Amour*, le Poète, Stello, cherche le beau et le bien; l'*In-*
telligence, le Philosophe, le Docteur-Noir, cherche le vrai. . . .
Vous voyez, dit le Docteur-Noir, que Lamuel aurait mieux fait
de jeter ses idées comme vous ferez des vôtres, dans une forme
toute philosophique ou poétique, que de se jeter, à corps perdu,
dans le flot grossier pour lui faire rebrousser chemin. Mais il ne
pouvait que ce qu'il a fait parce qu'il n'était ni tout à fait Poète ni
tout à fait Philosophe. (2:1057)[31]

In this journal entry it seems that Stello and Docteur Noir
are situated, like spectators, outside of the drama of Lamuel
which serves as an example for Stello. For this reason, they
are able to objectively discuss the tragedy of Lamuel which is
also a representation of Stello's own subjective drama. For Lamuel, like Stello (and of course, like Vigny himself), is caught
between his poetic and his philosophical natures. Since we
know that Lamuel's drama envelopes the other three, it would
appear that this lesson occurs at the end of all three stories
and that Stello, at this point, is able to recall, on his own mental stage, an imaginary dialogue between Julien, the hero of
the first story, and Jesus. In other words, an attempt is being
made to make it appear that the entire epic takes place in the
thoughts of Stello.

A later journal entry of 1839 conceives of a potential prelude to *Daphné* which would link the composition back to
the original *Stello*, by showing us a similar capacity to visu-
alize past memories. Under the title "Qu'est-ce que Daphné?"
("What is Daphné?"), we see an anxious Stello, "agité par l'activité de ses pensées, activité violente que les songes avaient
multipliée" ("agitated by the activity of his thoughts, a violent
activity that dreams had multiplied"). The passage continues:
"Il croyait voir devant lui les visages mélancoliques de Gilbert,
de Chatterton et d'André Chénier et la voix ferme et inflexible
du Docteur-Noir résonnait encore suave dans ses oreilles. . . .
il se prit à songer au peuple de l'Univers qui avait le mieux
compris la tristesse de la vie: les Juifs" (2:1122–23).[32] The

end of this passage thus places Stello in the world of the fourth century, the world of *Daphné*, of Lamuel, and of Julien the Apostate.

This potential prelude connecting *Daphné* to *Stello* illustrates the fact that the epic *Daphné* with all of its stories was undoubtedly supposed to take place on the stage of Stello's imagination. It may also explain why Vigny was never quite able to finish the project. For it is almost as if we need to await Flaubert's *Tentation de Saint Antoine* in order to understand Vigny's conception. Indeed, as in Flaubert's drama, it appears that Vigny is trying to write a series of self-representations in which Stello would look into a mirror where he finds Lamuel who in turn looks into a mirror where he finds Julien, Melanchton, and Rousseau, only to finish in a circular structure that allows Stello to think back in his imagination to the first of the stories, perhaps underscoring their similarities. When we consider in this light that Vigny gave his unfinished manuscript to Flaubert's confidante, Louise Colet (2 : 12), the association with Flaubert seems entirely possible.

In any case, while Stello remains outside of the dramas as a spectator who finds himself repeated in each of the heroes passing before his eyes, Docteur Noir moves from his role as spectator, alongside Stello, to his role as an actor in each of the dramas:

> Phèdre conseille à Julien de quitter la vie parce qu'il perd la race humaine.
>   Dr-N. —Quel est donc votre projet? Quel est le fond de votre pensée? Stello s'incline, reçoit quelques mots dans son oreille.
>   —C'est, dit Lamuel, cette passion nouvelle de secourir l'humanité. . . . Ce n'est pas cela, dit le Docteur-Noir. —il se trompe lui-même et sur lui-même.
>   —Lisons . . . *Daphné* suit. (2 : 1059)[33]

In this passage, we can see that the three characters, Julien, Lamuel, and Stello, are identified or confused with each other because Vigny is playing here with mixed diegesis and the instability of the speaking subject. Where is the doctor situated,

in a novel? in a play? outside of plays in a larger epic? Who is
it that hears the voice of Lamuel inside Stello's head and who
is it that "se trompe lui-même"? To whom is this lesson directed and who says "Lisons"? In other words, bivocal utterances allow the speaking subject to move among the positions
of the character, the narrator, and the playwright, demonstrating the textual disruptions of any unified subject of consciousness. Whereas the direct discourse of dialogue fixes two or
more partners as protagonists of a single utterance or *énonciation*, Vigny's inclusion of a narrative instance that is both
separate from and yet privy to the dialogue inside Stello's head
confuses what Benveniste calls the "discursive relations between partners," thereby confusing as well the very integrity
of those characters who speak.[34] Therefore, Vigny's tendency
to conflate dramas and books, as we saw earlier in his discussion of the literary and philosophical axes of art, was not simply a slip in the journal or a decision not yet taken but the expression of an interest in mixing indirect and direct discourses
in order to render interlocutors intentionally uncertain.

Although we are looking at incomplete fragments, we know
that Vigny in his own self-analysis was interested in the problem of form and that the dramatic project itself is an attempt
to represent thought or "intelligence": "Toutes ces Consultations du Docteur Noir aboutiront à la déification de l'intelligence et à la peinture de ses peines" (2:1061; "All these
Consultations of Docteur Noir will end with the deification
of intelligence and the painting of its pains"). We can only
assume, therefore, that elaborate composition and mixed diegesis are related to Vigny's endeavor to represent subjectivity.
That is, the uncertainty of interlocutors exploited in Vigny's
unrealized—and thereby, unrealizable—project for the theater, is a way of recreating, in a reading, the mobility of
thought itself and its propensity to incessantly propose new
self-representations. For Stello and the doctor are not only
characters in literature but surrogates for those earlier discussed double points of view that find themselves theatricalized in Vigny's attempt to write subjectivity:

—Une sensibilité extrême, refoulée dès l'enfance . . . demeura en-
fermée dans le coin le plus secret du coeur. —Le monde ne vit
plus pour jamais que les idées, résultat du travail prompt et exact
de l'intelligence. —Le Docteur Noir seul parut en moi, Stello se
cacha. (2:960)[35]

Stello and the Docteur Noir are clearly roles to play that Vigny finds in the textual configurations of autorepresentation.
For the series of self-representations initiated by these figures
does not stop with them or with Chatterton, Chénier, Julien,
Melanchton, and Rousseau. Indeed, there are other figures associated with Stello, Julien, and *Daphné* that seem to prolif-
erate as we proceed through the journal: Trivulce (2:787–
88), François as of 1840 (2:1129), and, as late as 1859, the
Indian author Cakiamouni, "qui va chasser les castes de
Brahma" ("who will rid the world of Brahmanic castes";
2:1348). In other words, as Vigny looks into what he calls
the "laboratoire intime" where Judgment and Imagination
work together to create art (2:1359), he does not see the logic
of a philosophical system but the endless waves (2:986) of a
textual productivity that constantly proposes new roles to
play in the representation of "Mon cerveau, toujours mobile,
[qui] travaille et tourbillonne" ("My brain, always mobile,
[that] works and turns"; 2:1065).

Although Vigny's strange project of unrepresentable theater is not so surprising insofar as it proposes a history of
religion or of civilization or of the world, it is radically striking insofar as it proposes philosophy as the representation of
subjectivity in theatrical form suggesting that its author conceives of writing or textuality as the inevitably theatricalized
scene of self-representation. Indeed, the notion of an epic
drama about the history of the world complete with its own
spectators and actors is not solely Vigny's concern. Similar
examples or at least a similar desire can be seen in Quinet's
Ahasvérus, Chateaubriand's *Les Martyrs*, Ballanche's *Orphée*,
Lamartine's *Jocelyn*, and even Hugo's *La Légende des siècles*.
In fact, the "épopée romantique" comes to constitute its own
genre.[36] Nevertheless, Vigny's unrealized theatrical project

seems to come closer to German Romanticism's "Ideal Book" and to Diderot's *Neveu* in that it appears to be an attempt to create a literary form adequate to the representation of subjectivity. That is, more crucial than the representation of the history of the world is the problem of representing the world through one's own polyvalent or mobile consciousness and the consequent difficulties of that representation in writing.

Ultimately, this is why both Vigny's idea of theater and his idea of a journal seem much more sophisticated than Hugo's. He not only recognizes theater, as did Hugo, to be the form that will assimilate all the rest, he also makes the connection between theater and the autoanalytic mode of the journal:

> LE THÉÂTRE (SYMBOLE). —Pour Rachel. Le journaliste à com[édienne?]. —La passion du monde est de voir. . . . —C'est pour cela qu'ils ont créé le Théâtre, mais le Théâtre ne parle que du passé ou ne s'explique sur les événements présents que par des allusions très détournées. Il a fallu un théâtre de chaque jour où les grands personnages vinssent jouer le matin leur rôle de la veille ou le soir celui du matin . . . sans que les spectateurs eussent besoin de quitter leur demeure; ce Théâtre a été fait. Ce Théâtre c'est un journal. . . .
>
> Celui qui fait mouvoir chaque jour à son gré ces personnages vivants, celui qui les présente sur son théâtre dans le sens et sous le jour qui lui plaît, celui qui les grandit ou les rapétisse à son gré, c'est le journaliste! ce sera toi demain si tu veux! vois si tu trouves assez vaste cette occupation! (2:974–75)[37]

Here, even if in referring to a "journal" Vigny might mean a newspaper—which elsewhere he claims to despise—the double play on public and private journals seems to operate, for this reference to creating and manipulating characters in a private theater that rivals the actual stage is far too appropriate to his own personal *Journal d'un poète*. Moreover, in his exhortation to write and his suggestion that we each contain our own theater of the mind complete with its own spectators and actors who inhabit multiple roles, Vigny forces us to see the far-reaching implications of the theatricality of his own journal. One writes a journal not only to engage in the philosophical act of self-analysis but to enjoy the dramatic pleasure of watching oneself act out one's own fantasies.

THE THEATERS OF STENDHAL

Je suis arrivé aux derniers confins de ce que la logique peut saisir dans la poésie.[38]

Stendhal is yet another author preoccupied with questions of theater. For years, he dreamed of becoming a great dramatic genius, a second Molière, and of writing the ideal Romantic drama, a "mirror of its times."[39] Unlike Hugo or Vigny, however, Stendhal never realized much more than a theoretical project for the theater outlined in his two pamphlets entitled *Racine et Shakespeare*.[40] Nonetheless, Stendhal's inability to write theater coupled with his fervent desire to participate in the literary debates of his times makes his *Racine et Shakespeare* into one of the most striking manifestations of theatrical theory as a symptom for the growing confusion of literary and philosophical concerns.

The essential impetus of Stendhal's *Racine et Shakespeare* is an attempt to show in what ways current assumptions about the theater—Aristotelian assumptions—are merely a question of "habitude profondément enracinée" ("a deeply rooted [from Racine] habit").[41] He criticizes the tyranny of the unities of time and place, the pretension of presenting universal, timeless truths about humanity and the mania of imitating imitations, that is, of imitating Racine. Whereas Racine himself was Romantic, according to Stendhal, in the sense that his rendering of the dignity and polite language of his time was a reflection of that time as an historically defined social phenomenon (33), Stendhal laments modern society's inability to do the same due to Racine's legacy: spectator preference for good composition according to Jean-François Laharpe's code (19) instead of good drama (7). For Stendhal, theater has become an artificial rite instead of a mirror of the society that produces it.

Indeed, Stendhal's theoretical project for the theater might be defined as a "realist" project since, as Georges Blin has suggested, it is by way of Realism and objectivism that Stendhal distinguishes himself from the classicists and academicians with whose artistic control of the theater he takes issue.[42] For Stendhal, the theater would theoretically represent the "real," as does the novel, by holding up a mirror to life and reflecting that which is "before our eyes" (165). In keeping with this mirror esthetic, Stendhal's idea of the "real" is at best contradictory, ranging from the "inflamed painting of human passions" (252) to the reflection of society's current mores (39), from the presentation of "subjects of national significance" (40–41) to an imitation of nature (172). Paradoxically, Stendhal's theory of the theater with its confused and highly subjective notion of the "real" may explain both why Stendhal was never really able to realize his theatrical project and why he chose to exploit his particular brand of Realist novel.[43]

The ill-defined nature of Stendhal's "real" may make more sense when we consider that his major preoccupation in *Racine et Shakespeare* is not *what* to represent (though Stendhal, unlike Hugo, would prefer subjects of political significance) but, rather, *how* to represent. A Romantic drama should challenge classical conventions: written in prose, it would represent a duration of several months and take place in different locales (159). More important, the Romantic play would insure "dramatic" rather than "epic" pleasure at the theater (6). Stendhal rejects classical conventions because they do not reflect society as it is but he also rejects the Hugolian notion of a Romantic drama whose purpose, as a didactic mode, is to enlighten and educate society. Like Vigny, Stendhal is interested in pleasure.

Epic pleasure, which may be seen as Racine's legacy, is the pleasure of *savoir-faire*. It assumes a knowledgeable spectator who has come to the theater to admire the author's style (16) and the actor's technique (13). It is the pleasure of social interaction and of boastful self-interest: "Connais-tu cet écrit?" (13; "Do you know this piece?"). Dramatic pleasure, on the contrary, produces "profound emotion" (16). It belongs to the domain of the heart and soul, is therefore more easily experienced by women (15), and assumes a total absorption into the fiction. That is, dramatic pleasure requires an absence of self-interest and even of (self-)consciousness. According to Stendhal, this pleasure is more likely to occur, for nineteenth-century audiences, during a play that addresses contemporary issues. He chooses Shakespeare as his model because modern circumstances in France resemble those of the England of 1590 (39).

Stendhal maintains that dramatic pleasure depends upon the frequency of what he calls "moments d'*illusion parfaite*" ("moments of *perfect illusion*"). During such moments, a spectator forgets the actor and sees only the fiction, forgets the conventional distinction between stage and audience or reality and imagination: "Illusion," Stendhal explains, "signifie donc l'action d'un homme qui croit la chose qui n'est pas, comme dans les rêves, par exemple. . . . Mais [at the theater] ces moments durent infiniment peu, par exemple une demi-seconde, ou un quart de seconde" (13−15).[44] The analogy that likens a spectator to a dreamer is perhaps richer than Stendhal himself realizes, as the pleasure of dreaming may be a dramatic or theatrical pleasure. As Freud explains in his *Interpretation of Dreams*, the dream does require the barring of conscious awareness and a belief in the illusion before one's mind's eye as well as a divided or mobile subject who becomes at once the protagonist, the spectator, and the director of his or her own intimate scenario.[45] Although Stendhal does not continue to exploit this analogy, Freud and his critics do.

In his "Psychopathic Characters on the Stage," Freud discusses the possible nature of a spectator's pleasure during the viewing of a tragedy. He argues that it is based on precisely what Stendhal is suggesting, the illusion of belief. This belief, favored by the safety of reality testing—"I know I am at the theater and that it is not I who face the perils of the hero"—relaxes the mind's defenses, allowing an imaginary identification with the hero. As Stendhal proposed, one forgets the actor. Freud then explains that the benefit for a spectator may be to infuse a boring life with the excitement of the hero's exploits without running the same risks. In economic terms, the pleasure of this identification results from a discharge of affective energy, a releasing of the mind's internally energetic tensions (7:305–6). This is also the goal of dreams for which the safety factor is sleep.

Octave Mannoni elaborates upon Freud's discussion of the spectator's pleasure.[46] He agrees that the theater very generally satisfies our desires to "lead another life" but argues that the question of an identification with a hero is too simple. Appropriately for Stendhal, Mannoni uses the example of Tartuffe to show that no one identifies with Tartuffe but that everyone can identify with someone who may take Tartuffe as a role to play. Mannoni is not distinguishing between comedy and tragedy but emphasizing that although spectators may identify with characters or heroes they also identify with the activity of the actor (*Clefs*, 305). That is, contrary to what Stendhal might like, we all go to the theater to see an actor play and we all know that what is represented as true is also presented as false. We know that the stage constructs illusions and that this is an institutionalized theatrical convention. In this sense, we are in concert with the actor (*Clefs*, 164), or, as André Green has suggested, we feel solicited to explore the illusion from his point of view (*Un Oeil en trop*, 14–15). However, at the theater, we all behave as if the illusion on stage could be real, as if there were *someone else* who could believe it. This someone else, who falls prey to the illusion and thus to an identification with a character, not only represents the imaginary aspect of the theatrical effect but that part of our own imaginations—what Mannoni, after Freud and Lacan, calls "l'autre scène"—in which this someone else may represent an instance of our own egos. He likens this instance to the dream agent, that part of the ego that either figures in or believes in the dream (Mannoni, *Clefs*, 165).

According to Mannoni, the theatrical effect requires both that we retain full knowledge of the illusion (theatrical conventions reinforce our defenses) and that we repudiate this knowledge—thus relaxing our defenses (*Clefs*, 166). We consciously know the actor is not the hero but because of this knowledge, which never entirely disappears, the actor may awaken our innate, unconscious tendency toward his vocation: the possibility of playing all kinds of roles in a socially acceptable setting. The source of a spectator's pleasure relies on both epic and dramatic responses to a spectacle. The theater liberates our capacity to identify, as do dreams, but only because it also reinforces our defenses through its conventions (174). Stendhal is then right about the illusion of belief necessary to our pleasure as spectators but wrong to separate it from our appreciation of the actor's skill. Pleasure at the theater is not related to the possibility of vicariously leading a more exciting life by forgetting the illusion but to the possibility of being in two places at once and thereby liberating the mind's potential to propose an infinite number of roles to play (182).

By relating the pleasure of the spectator to his or her identification with an actor and to the liberation of the mind's capacity to propose potential roles, Mannoni seems almost to describe what Stendhal calls his "Beylisme." Victor Brombert defines "Beylisme" as Stendhal's tendency to watch himself playing roles for the world while at the same time hiding or masking his own true sentiments.[47] In other words, Stendhal's "Beylisme" is like the skill of an actor. However, as Jean Starobinski explains, we must distinguish between Diderot's notion of the actor who must keep his own identity at a distance in order to create a believable character and Stendhal's actor whose identity is fundamentally mobile and defined only through the roles he invents for himself to play.[48] It is in order to appear, or to apprehend himself, that Stendhal must dissemble or play roles. There is thus a certain pleasure in Stendhal's celebrated hypocrisy. As Stendhal himself writes, "Je porterais un masque avec plaisir; je changerais de nom avec délices" ("I would wear a mask with pleasure; I would change names with delight").[49]

Ironically, it is because Stendhal might agree with Starobinski or Freud and Mannoni that he would reject the theater in favor of the novel.[50] For whereas the theater allows Stendhal to *analyze* the pleasure of the spectator, the novel allows him to *engage in* that pleasure, the pleasure of "Beylisme," the pleasure of inventing himself as he watches himself play. In this context, Stendhal's concern with a spectator's capacity to experience "moments of *perfect illusion*" forces the mirror esthetic into the background. For it suggests that Stendhal's interest in representing the real is less about the faithful mirroring of an objective reality than about the place and pleasure of a subject in that representation, a spectator's at the theater or, by extension, an author's in his writing. It is less about holding up a mirror to life than about holding up a mirror to oneself and experiencing the pleasurable mobility of being at once the spectator and the actor and the director or author who holds the mirror. Clearly, the availability of these positions on stage, off stage, and in the wings is not possible at the theater but may be in a novel or, as we shall see, in a philosophical treatise.

To understand this displacement of the mirror esthetic, one has only to consider the formal presentation of Stendhal's illusion argument in *Racine et Shakespeare*. The rather unconventional format of Stendhal's original pamphlet is what we might call a theatricalized version of philosophy. Indeed, the most impressive moment in the earlier *Racine et Shakespeare* and probably the moment that crystallizes the form of the second (letters reproducing a debate), is the dialogue between l'Académicien and le Romantique. This dialogue offers a kind of theatricalized version of philosophy since it breaks from an otherwise pedagogical style—the style of the "cours"—in order to dramatize the issues currently at stake in the popular *Journal des débats*. In this sense, the dialogue is an ideal reflection of society's current mores, a "mirror of its times."

In the fiction of *Racine et Shakespeare*, this dialogue takes place during an intermission at the theater. In this way, the dialogue not only performs its own essential argument—that the illusion of time need not conform to classicism's verisimilitude—but it denounces itself as a novelistic fiction. At the end of the dialogue, Stendhal writes: "Ici finit le dialogue des deux adversaires, dialogue dont j'ai été réellement temoin au parterre de la rue Chantereine, et dont il ne tiendrait qu'à moi de nommer les interlocuteurs" (19).[51] The importance of this novelistic intervention in an already "theatricalized" philosophical discourse is to show that just as fiction should resemble life, life already resembles fiction (or politics, theater). It also reveals a triangular structure of theatrical positions available to the speaking subject. Stendhal writes the dialogue (he is holding the mirror), he declares having witnessed the dialogue (he takes up the position of the spectator), and at the same time he is playing the role of the Romantic. Like a real spectator, then, he momentarily identifies with the position of the actor.

To appreciate the subtlety of this identification, we must note the slippery way in which Stendhal inserts himself into the role of the Romantic:

> Pourquoi exigez-vous, dirai-je aux partisans du *classicisme*, que l'action représentée dans une tragédie ne dure pas plus de vingt-quatre ou de trente-six heures, et que le lieu de la scène ne change pas, ou que du moins, comme le dit Voltaire, les changements de lieu ne s'étendent qu'aux divers appartements d'un palais?
>
> L'ACADÉMICIEN. —Parce qu'il n'est pas vraisemblable qu'une action representée en deux heures de temps comprenne la durée d'une semaine ou d'un mois, ni que, dans l'espace de peu de moments, les acteurs aillent de Venise en Chypre, comme dans l'*Othello* de Shakespeare; ou d'Écosse à la cour d'Angleterre, comme dans *Macbeth*.
>
> LE ROMANTIQUE. —Non seulement cela est invraisemblable et impossible; mais il est impossible également que l'action comprenne vingt-quatre ou trente-six heures. (7–8)[52]

In this reproduction of only the bare skeleton of Stendhal's illusion argument, it is easy to see that the Romantic has taken over the point of view of Stendhal's "I." Without insisting upon a somewhat irrelevant distinction, the pamphlet is after all presented more as a philosophical discourse, a statement of its author's ideology, than as a work of fiction. However, it is also apparent that Stendhal would like to underscore his own duplicity. At the very moment that he moves almost imperceptibly into the role of the actor, he also footnotes, as would any good writer, the (probably fictive) source of his argument: "Dialogue d'Hermes Visconti dans le *Conciliatore*, Milan, 1818." Since Stendhal will also portray himself as an innocent bystander or spectator to the dialogue, we can understand the resulting triangular or theatrical structure as a strategy for self-preservation.[53] This is not to say that a reader will not associate Stendhal with the Romantic's point of view, but that his argument is objectified with both his vision and the footnote working as guarantees of Realism. That is, the dialogue is presented as a "mirror of its times" only to protect its sensitive author who "reads in his own heart" (19). This artifice of presentation allows then both the epic pleasure of social interaction (of appearing) and the dramatic pleasure of a total absence of self-consciousness (of dissembling). In this context, a hostile reader could only blame society (or Visconti) for such blatant attacks on the Academy, whereas a benevolent reader (one of the Happy Few) might read through the mirror into Stendhal's heart. In any case, an association has thus been made between the duplicity of the spectator and that of the writer.

The choice of dialogue in Stendhal's pamphlet is particularly significant for my purposes because it introduces a conception of philosophy and a kind of specular activity that links Vigny's notion of pleasure to Hugo's notion of the spectacle of subjectivity. As opposed to Hugo's preface in which the relationship between philosophy and theater had to do with the idea of a "didactic spectacle" and a philosophical mission for the poet, Stendhal allows theater to enter into an otherwise philosophical discourse simply to enable himself to be in two places at once. As was suggested in Vigny's journal and as we can see in the heroes of Stendhal's novels, Stendhal is able here to both play and watch.[54] Therefore, Stendhal's text is like Hugo's in that the author presents ideas and then scrutinizes with his "speculum de génie," but it is like Vigny's in that this scrutiny does not result in self-awareness but in a proliferation of imaginary self-representations. Stendhal has taken pains to let us know that the dialogue is a Realist fiction that both mirrors and hides the intimate nature of its author in much the same way that the theater both resembles and covers up the world it proposes to imitate.

This entrance of fiction into a philosophical discourse is important both in terms of the literary history of the philosophical dialogue and in terms of Stendhal's eagerness to exploit a form that underscores the instability of the speaking subject. Historically speaking, the choice of dialogue carries with it the connotations of hundreds of years of philosophizing and all of the assumptions that that discourse involves.[55] The Platonic dialogue, as an original model, had as its specific purpose to account for truth and/or to induce the listener's representation of it. If truth was not contained in the language spoken, it was to be deduced from it. The passage itself from one voice to the next—*dia-logos* or across language—was intended to render language transparent to truth objectively doubling in visible, audible, material form the invisible and silent essence of being (Lacoue-Labarthe and Nancy, "Le Dialogue des genres" 149–50). It is therefore a discourse that assumes both an ideal of truth and a homogeneous notion of being. However, during its development, the philosophical dialogue would slowly come to terms with its own fiction and begin to question the theatrical nature of a form intended to insure objectivity (Lacoue-Labarthe and Nancy, "Le Dialogue des genres," 152–53).

Though I am not interested in stressing clear historical distinctions, even a cursory review of the history of the Platonic dialogue underscores the ways in which the form itself progressively undermines its original intent. During the Renaissance, imitation of Plato would become an imitation of life and the philosophical dialogue would come to authorize the painting of characters and the use of vulgar language. Therefore, although it remained a mode of theoretical exposition it also came under the auspices of a poet who balanced more openly than Plato between poetry and dialectics, form and content. Furthermore, with the advent of the book came the typical authorial introduction allowing feigned distance from the dialogical scene—now the written imitation of "natural" speech. This both removed the author from the polemics in question and accommodated truth to dissimulation. Obvious examples might include Des Périer's *Cymbalum Mundi* (1537), part of Rabelais's *Tiers Livre* (1546), as well as much earlier texts such as Alain Chartier's *La Belle Dame sans mercy* (1424), or François Villon's *Le Débat du coeur et du corps de Villon* (1461), in which the dialogic form was used to attack and disrupt the conventional value systems with which that form had become synonymous while at the same time protecting the author of those attacks. During the eighteenth-century, as we saw in the case of Diderot, emphasis was in turn placed on the writer of dialogues so that the form once used to insure a sense of objectivity became a more self-conscious investigation of the nature of the speaking subject himself.

With Stendhal's dialogue we can see that Hegel's notion that the presentation of a concept affects the concept itself has become a philosophical dilemma. For the status of language itself is now seen as much more radically subjective, as something that inevitably gets in the way of objective truth. Therefore, the possibility of creating what Roland Barthes calls the "realist effect" is associated in Stendhal's dialogue with an artifice of presentation. In other words, philosophy encounters the problem of its own representation and becomes an esthetic problem giving way to the paradoxical notion apparent in German Romanticism, that the representation of subjectivity can only be presented objectively in literature (Lacoue-Labarthe and Nancy, "Le Dialogue des genres," 168–69, n. 2). As we witnessed in the case of Hugo, the poet and the philosopher have become interchangeable entities. Ultimately, we might say that Stendhal's insertion of a blatantly fictionized dialogue into an otherwise philosophical discourse is representative of a more general crisis in philosophy itself and shows us Stendhal's awareness of the already theatrical nature of dialogue. For although Stendhal never really discusses the dialogue as such, he does speak of Plato. When Lamartine objects to Stendhal's rejection of verse in theater in the name of Plato and "le beau idéal" (*Racine et Shakespeare*,

129–31), Stendhal's response is simply this: "Il y a autant de beaux idéals que de formes de nez différentes ou de caractères différents" (*Racine et Shakespeare*, 108; "There are as many ideal beauties as there are different noses or different characters" [Daniels, 97]). In other words, Stendhal is not only defending prose theater but rejecting the idea of a homogeneous notion of being, not only arguing in favor of "Romantic" expression but questioning the assumption of any discourse about truth. This is why Stendhal opposes Aristotelian notions of drama, why he does not believe in the dramatic representation of a timeless, universal image of humanity, and finally, why he cannot produce actual theater.

Stendhal's fictionizing or theatricalizing of the philosophical dialogue is doubly important because it, like Vigny's *Daphné*, manifests a willful mixing of two different kinds of discourse: one diegetic in which the author speaks in his own voice, the other mimetic in which he hides behind characters' voices. This is of course precisely the distinction Plato simultaneously made and transgressed by writing dialogues. Stendhal was perfectly aware of this transgression:

> Tel est Platon, âme passionnée, poète sublime, poète entraînant, écrivain de premier ordre et raisonneur puérile. Voyez . . . les drôles de raisonnements que fait Socrate. (97–98)[56]

Stendhal clearly appreciates Plato more for his skills as a writer than for his skills as a philosopher, thus underscoring the questionable nature of a discourse designed to lead to truths. However, whereas Plato in dissimulating himself was unfaithful to himself, Stendhal's dissimulation is true to his own nature, providing yet another example to complement the already diverse versions of his theatricalized subjectivity. It is not surprising, then, that Stendhal would engage in the practice of mixing genres, since he seems to be aware that in speaking or writing one is never himself but always a new self-representation.

Ultimately, Stendhal's choice to mix modes of discourse in writing philosophy about the theater shows us his sensitivity to the theatricality inherent in the act of writing itself. He is very different from Hugo who, unaware of this theatricality by which a subject, writing, is always at least double, was caught or displaced by what the text said for him. And whereas Hugo's idea of mixing genres was part of a general fight for literary liberty since all disciplines were subsumed by the poet's mission, Stendhal mixes them in *Racine et Shakespeare* in order to dramatize the way in which any discourse always involves the question of another presentation, the way in which any art in representing, always produces theater.[57] Ironically, mixed literature and philosophy might better describe Stendhal's effort than Hugo's own. So that when the Romantic in Stendhal's dialogue exclaims, "Mais aussi voilà un entracte un peu long qui va finir, la toile se relève" (18; "But also here is a rather lengthy intermission that is going to end. The curtain is going up"), we might take that to mean this dialogue, here, between an Academician and a Romantic, or better, the dialogue itself which as a formal mode of presentation is itself an "entracte" between literature and philosophy, itself caught at that point precisely in which logic reaches its limits in dealing with poetry (17).

THE ONLY THEATER OF OUR MIND, PROTOTYPE OF THE REST

The significance of these three theatricalized versions of philosophy and their redefinitions of theatricality is, as I suggested earlier, that they make Virtual Theater part of a philosophical tradition often seen as unique to Diderot.[58] Indeed, it should be clear from the three examples discussed in the preceding sections that many of Diderot's concerns about the writing of subjectivity and its relation to acting or theatricality became the obsession as well of many Romantic thinkers. Ultimately, while Romanticism's political battles were played out in the social arena of the actual theater, its silent, subjective battles, "entre moi et moi" as Poulet puts it, were played out in the private arenas of personal philosophies and on a stage now conceived as a textual theater. Therefore, the phenomenon of Virtual Theater as it has been discussed in this chapter works as a transition between the philosophical concerns of Diderot's late-eighteenth-century re-reading of Plato and the theatrical concerns of the nineteenth-century French Romantics. For although they appear to belong to two separate traditions—one a reappraisal of Platonic philosophy, the other, a reappraisal of Romantic drama—each exploits figures of theatricality for subjectivity that ultimately anticipate Freud's highly problematic use of a theatrical metaphor.

Like many of the thinkers of the nineteenth-century and certainly like Hugo, Vigny, and Stendhal, Freud's conception of a theatrical metaphor begins with his fascination with the actual theater, in particular, *Hamlet* and *Oedipus Rex*.[59] As Jean Starobinski has shown, Freud's discussions of *Hamlet* always appear in the same contexts as *Oedipus Rex* because both plays define for him the drama of the psychoanalytic subject as a theatrical space.[60] Though the fate of *Oedipus Rex* in Freud's thinking would set aside the question of the theatrical metaphor, as I have already suggested, his discussions of *Hamlet* underscore its significance. As Freud explains in the *Interpretation of Dreams*, whereas *Oedipus Rex* stages the problematic issue of infantile sexuality—what Freud sees as the male child's fundamental and therefore universal desire to kill his father and marry his mother—*Hamlet* only stages the effects of the inhibition of this desire (Starobinski, "Hamlet et Freud," 2118). That is, Hamlet is unable to act because his incestuous desire must remain repressed; it has been defined as criminal by his father's ghost and by his incestuous uncle leaving him unable to surmount a feeling of guilt. Thus, Hamlet invites us to ponder that which may be dissimulated behind his conscious reflections (2123), namely, the way in which the light of consciousness bars the expression of unconscious desires therefore promoting their theatricalized expression in dreams, fantasms, or dramatic scenes. In other words, *Hamlet* presents the dilemma of the divided subject of psychoanalysis who is suspended between an unconscious tendency to desire according to the logic of the pleasure principle and the exigencies of the reality principle. This explains why

Freud will eventually liken this dilemma to that of a spectator at the theater, as we have seen in his "Psychopathic Characters on the Stage."

In their *L'Anti-Oedipe*, Deleuze and Guattari take issue with Freud's theatrical model because it proposes Oedipus as the foremost figure in the theater of "psychic reality," thus substituting classical representation for what they call "desiring production" (31). As a despotic figure based solely on Freud's own autoanalysis, Oedipus then takes over the entire unconscious, subordinating the free-flowing and constantly productive energy of desire—as it is conceived in the theory of the primary processes—to an expressive unconscious, as it is conceived in the theory of wish-fulfillment (65).[61] Hence, both Oedipus and the figure of the theater work to control the productive flows of desire by enclosing it in theatrical scenes: dreams, fantasms, or the universal myth of the Oedipal drama.

Although Jean-François Lyotard would question Deleuze's and Guattari's tendency to replace an idealist ideology with another that is Marxist (Lyotard, *Economie*, 42–43), he would agree that the theatrical metaphor proposed by psychoanalysis is faulty because it supposes a dualistic world of theatricalized signifiers definitively barred from but containing the keys to some hidden, unconscious signified. Lyotard criticizes the dualisms inherent in Freud's metaphor but he also criticizes Deleuze's and Guattari's positing of an ideal "schizophrenic" state of fluid, unbound energy or productivity because it does not account for the ways in which such energy is channeled in a libidinal economy (Lyotard, *Dispositifs*, 46–49). In fact, following a similar line of criticism, Fredric Jameson refers to *L'Anti-Oedipe* as an "overestimation of the Imaginary" and explains that "the instincts, indeed, the libido itself, no matter how energetically boiling, cannot be conceived independently of their representations" ("Imaginary and Symbolic in Lacan," in *Ideologies of Theory*, 1:92, 102). In other words, if we are to understand the means by which any individual human being accommodates his or her own impulses to psychic and/or material fields of reality, some

principle of segmentation, of exteriors and interiors or signifiers and signifieds, must be articulated, even if done with
duplicity.[62]

In this context, I shall argue that the authors of Virtual
Theater offer insight into the means of this ambivalent articu-
lation. In their efforts to examine their own dramas of subjectivity, they discover their own capacity to identify with a
myriad of unconscious or imaginary self-representations but
they are not weighed down by an Oedipal "rock" that fixes
the productions of unconscious thought in universal myths
or familial dramas. Their theatrical models tend, rather, to
elaborate themselves along the lines of those issues momentarily set aside by Freud in favor of Oedipus, to wit, the structure of the fantasm and a theory of identification.

The importance of the structure of the fantasm in its relation to the figure of the theater as it is exploited in Virtual
Theater becomes particularly striking when compared to André Green's definition of the fantasm. In his *Un Oeil en trop*,
Green writes: "Le fantasme serait à la rigueur à rapprocher
d'une certaine forme de théâtre comportant un récitant qui
parlerait d'une action se déroulant en un lieu qu'il désignerait
en lui restant extérieur, tout en n'y étant pas étranger."[63] This
description of the theater of the fantasm renders, most distinctly, the structure common to all virtual plays. As we have
already seen, every virtual play is divided into two separate
theatrical spaces: a dialogical space reserved for characters
made up of potential "lines" for actors, and a narrative space
normally limited to a playwright's stage indications designed
to help guide a potential director. This is precisely the structural phenomenon exhibited by Diderot's *Neveu*, though its
theatrical spaces were more immediately assimilable to those
of Plato's Socratic dialogues than to those of a theater piece
written for actors and directors. Nonetheless, as in Diderot's
Neveu, this narrative space always emits a voice that seems to
belong to an imaginary spectator, to someone "watching"
and discovering alongside the reader. Although the voice thus
establishes a distinction between observer and observed, a
kind of imaginary textual proscenium arch, it also slides over

the border, so to speak, obscuring that distinction precisely as Green's description suggests. Virtual Theater seems to distinguish outsides and insides of an imaginary stage only to demonstrate the mobility of this subject as it finds itself identifying with imaginary self-representations.

The relationships between the two different spaces outlined in a virtual play thus underscore the interaction of literature and philosophy as it has been presented in this chapter. The voice of the narrator/spectator keeps a "philosophical" distance from the self-sufficient dialogical scene—self-sufficient in the same way that a theatrical performance takes place alone, far beyond its textual blueprint. However, because this spectator, in looking, always finds a self-portrait mirrored in the scene before his or her eyes, the possibility of a philosophical discourse, a discourse about ontological truths, is undone. The reader is forced to understand the dialogic scene as the mental production of its "objective" observer. One might say that Plato's assumption about representation through language as a neuter operation remains an ideal of Virtual Theater— the gesture at objectivity suggesting that neuter operation— but that the representation it accomplishes is only always that of subjectivity itself, an "objectivized subjectivity."

Green's description thus proves itself to be remarkably appropriate to the structure of Virtual Theater: a subject, so concretely placed outside the dialogical scene, always manages to play a role in it. As in the fantasm, the speaking subject both creates and watches scenes in which he or she is also the imaginary protagonist. The point seems to be that both subjects and their relation to reality are reorganized by the unconscious energy of desire in its production of obsessive fantasy scenarios. Because subjects can never be sure of mastering their unconscious desires, they can never be sure of apprehending reality nor of knowing where they end and the world begins. In Virtual Theater, both the objectivity of the world and the subjectivity of the subject are put into question as the spectators at first separated from the object of their gaze consistently find themselves oddly confused with it. Moreover, with the structure of the fantasm, emphasis is taken away from the "philosophical" subject matter of these texts and placed onto writing strategies. As in Diderot's *Neveu*, composition in a virtual play comes to borrow its logic from music, resulting in undecidedness and suspended, purely potential connections between thoughts. Writing thus becomes a language performance and, by attempting to dramatize the work of the unconscious in language, it produces a theater that remains on a page. Ultimately then, these theaters are "bookish" not because they attempt to stage history or because they express a Platonic contempt for the social phenomenon of theater but because the drama of subjectivity they want to represent can only be written in the form of a Virtual Theater.

THREE

Liberated Theater

La création aveugle
Hurle, glapit, grince et beugle;
Mais, sous sa main,
L'homme la dompte et la brise;
La forêt grondante est prise
Au piège humain.
—Hugo, *Océan*

In 1854, Victor Hugo con-
tinued to compose journals about his life, amassing records
and documents in the creation of his own personal monument
in writing.[1] Now however, marked by persistent mourning,
disillusionment with politics, and a completely new lifestyle
imposed by exile, Hugo's notion of theater as a didactic, ex-
troverted, social mission was replaced by a notion of theater
that is a personal, inward, philosophical mission: a way to
represent the fragmented mobility of modern subjectivity.
Hugo's *Théâtre en liberté*, a volume of theater pieces begun in
1854 and pursued for another twenty years, is the paradigm
for this modern notion of theater. It is itself fragmented and
mobile and free in many senses. Unrestricted by the demands
of actual representation, it ignores theatrical conventions, the
whims of censors and audiences, and even the logic of *mise en
scène*. To date, its dimensions remain uncertain. There are at
least two separate manuscripts besides the one published in
1886, each containing different entries and a different ordering of pieces.

Speculation on the kind of liberty Hugo was seeking in his

77

"free" theater differs widely. Whereas Jean Gaudon argues that in his *Théâtre en liberté* Hugo made no attempt to confront staging problems and that these plays belong, therefore, to the history of poetry, Georges Ascoli observes that Hugo was looking for "la liberté scénique" in a mixture of fantasy and reality.[2] Charles Affron speaks of "Hugo's renewed interest in the theater" and of a vision that became increasingly personal as "the author examines himself and the genre he so fiercely defended" (83–84). Jean-Bertrand Barrère seems to vacillate. In his early work on Hugo, he calls the *Théâtre en liberté* a failure because Hugo could not decide between the two meanings of its title.[3] More recently, however, Barrère highlights Hugo's desire to free his dramatic conceptions and expressions from the tyranny of logic and of traditional theatrical conventions, arguing that *Le Théâtre en liberté* represents a release of tension from the philosophical anguish of the crisis years.[4] In other words, a question remains as to whether Hugo was still carrying on a Romantic battle to free theatrical representation from its restrictive conventions or whether he was experimenting with new and different kinds of theaters, "jouables seulement," as Hugo would later note, "à ce théâtre idéal que tout homme a dans l'esprit."[5]

I would like to reinforce Hugo's ambivalence about the kind of liberty he was seeking by suggesting that his vacillation or hesitation between two titles for the work, *Théâtre en liberté* or *Théâtre dans l'esprit*, symbolizes the poet's ambivalence about representation in general.[6] *Le Théâtre en liberté* is neither a theory of the theater nor merely a response to Hugo's growing "antitheatrical prejudices"; it may be seen rather as yet another of Hugo's personal journals. Like *Littérature et philosophie mêlées* or the *Journal de l'exil*, it is one more record of the development of Hugo's own mind. But whereas the earlier journals are built on the assumption that thought can be communicated in the first person, that one can look around oneself and objectively reflect upon what one sees, the *Théâtre en liberté* suggests that one cannot be sure to see beyond the walls of one's own imagination. The philo-

sophical subject who once engaged, impartially, in the revolutions of self-examination has now become a fragmented and
mobile subject whose multiple points of view are most appropriately represented as theater. The theater continues, thus, to
be a privileged place in which to envision a philosophy of
representation but, far removed from the scene of social re-
sponsibilities, the didactic spectacle is replaced by a drama of
subjectivity and what was once a social mission is now an
entirely personal philosophical dilemma.[7]

This shift in Hugo's conception of theater from a representation whose goal is to enlighten society to a presentation of
one individual's mind which seeks only to reflect the thoughts
of one subject, ushers in a philosophical shift as well. The poet
no longer strives to understand a human being's relation to
the invisible meanings of a mysteriously animated world;
now, as Hugo will note in his *William Shakespeare*, "Le poète
philosophe parce qu'il imagine."[8] The poet looks into his own
mind to find the world's theaters repeated in it. This is not to
suggest that we should divorce the "Hugo of the people" from
the Hugo of nocturnal metaphysics, as Pierre Albouy cau-
tions,[9] but that we should see the theater as an arena in which
the struggle to reconcile this antithesis and others plays itself
out, an arena whose formal disposition traces, during exile,
the trajectory of Hugo's own personal philosophical concerns.

This redefinition of theater as a philosophical arena occurs
in stages beginning in 1853 with the mystical practice of dia-
loguing with the "Turning Tables." During nightly seances,
Hugo and his circle communicated with the spirits of famous
personages through a painstaking process of questions and
mystical answers.[10] For Hugo, these dialogues and the resulting *Livres des tables* became a means of completing or con-
firming his own personal philosophy. In 1854, Hugo wrote:

> J'avais trouvé par la seule méditation plusieurs des résultats qui
> composent aujourd'hui la révélation de la table . . . j'en avais en-
> trevu d'autres qui restaient dans mon esprit à l'état de linéaments
> confus. . . . Aujourd'hui les choses que j'avais vues en entier, la
> table les confirme, et les demi-choses, elle les complète.[11]

In this passage, an equivalence is suggested between the spiritual dialogues with the tables and the simple meditation that Socrates referred to as a dialogue between the soul and itself. Hugo speaks of meditation as a way of seeing or perceiving his own thoughts as if outside of himself. The spiritual dialogues with the tables stand in relation to meditation then as an outward or material form of the same self-interrogation. Later, in fact, having renounced the practice of the "turning tables," Hugo would admit that they "nous rendent notre pensée, et que c'est tout bonnement un effet de mirage (Levaillant, 301; they "render our own thoughts unto us and that it is quite simply, a mirage-effect"). He thereby intimates that the important factor is not really some spiritual or mystical communication with the other world but rather the scrutinizing of one's own mind and the natural "otherness" or alterity inherent in any philosophical self-interrogation. Nonetheless, it is clear that Hugo used the dialogues with the tables to come to terms with the disquieting issues posed by his own intimate crisis of consciousness.[12]

In April of 1854, the dialogues with the tables reveal a spirit named "Le Drame," the spirit of Shakespeare, who dictates a bizarre, impossible drama subsequently entitled by Hugo *Le Prologue mystique*.[13] This prologue presents *the* drama of the universe, a dialogue between Heaven and Hell during which apparently irreconcilable philosophical dualities such as good and evil, night and day, life and death are reconciled. The essential theme of the drama is not new. Hugo himself noted the analogy to his dialogue of 1853 between Zénith and Nadir, "Deux voix dans le ciel étoilé" (Massin, 9:1366). Barrère has in turn noted its similarity to that dialogue and to two others of 1853 completed too late to appear in *Les Châtiments*, "Sursurrant voces" and "Voix dans le grenier," as well as to "La Bouche d'ombre" of 1854 (*La Fantaisie* 2:42–43,81). Nonetheless, what is new in the *Prologue mystique* is that this reconciling of dualities now takes place within the formal structure of a theater piece.

The prologue opens with an impossible stage setting which tells us first that the dialogue about to begin takes place be-

tween two enormous stars in a darkened sky and second, that
we only know of the dialogue because there are spectators
watching whose opera glasses have been transformed into
magic telescopes:

> Le ciel étoilé. Nuit sereine. Les astres scintillent. Leur scintille-
> ment murmure des paroles mystérieuses. Tout à coup, deux de ces
> étoiles prennent un dévéloppement étrange et deviennent énor-
> mes; et comme si les lorgnettes des spectateurs étaient changées
> en téléscopes magiques, tous ils entendent sortir ces mots de deux
> globes monstrueux. (Massin, 9 : 1363 – 64)[14]

This elaborate narrative stage direction turns an ordinary
dialogue about the drama of the universe into a more interesting dialogue about the relative position of humanity in that
drama. It suggests first that it is one's limited viewpoint and
undoubtedly one's reliance upon arbitrary categories dictated
by language that have divided the incomprehensible universe
into Heavens and Hells. Second, it supposes that the single
poet or philosopher may only know the logic of the universe
if he or she owns a magic telescope, that is, only if he or she
is "voyant" and "entendant" relying not on what the poet or
philosoher actually sees but on his or her own imagination.[15]
Finally, that these philosophical discoveries should find themselves presented in a strange kind of theater implies that philosophy itself is in a precarious position; it looks more and
more like a projected fiction. For as this philosophical theater
piece ends, we see that the dialogue does not finish but that
its voices "comme celles de deux causeurs qui s'éloignent,
n'arrivent plus au spectateurs" (Massin, 9 : 1369; "like those
of two interlocutors who are moving away, no longer reach
the spectators"). As the sun comes up, the merely human
spectators loose their magically charged capacity to hear.

It is not surprising that the spring of 1854 also brings
Hugo's conception of a new kind of literature, an extravagant
theater to be called Le Théâtre en liberté. In fact, Levaillant
proposes that the Prologue mystique may have been intended
as the opening to this project and thus have inaugurated
an entire missing section of the Théâtre en liberté (141).

However, there are many prologues in this theater (Massin, 9:1764, 1786, 1803, 1808) and this quantity of prologues is one good example of why the project is what it hopes to be, a liberated theater with entirely uncertain dimensions, a unity not necessarily constituted by the sum of its parts but one that is created anew with every reader's individual sensibilities.

With *La Forêt mouillée*, the earliest of the plays conceived for the *Théâtre en liberté*, Hugo's personal crisis of 1854 becomes an image of the crisis sustained by modernism itself. This piece marks a shift away from the notion of a *Theatrum Mundi* toward that of the theater of the imagination. Indeed, in this piece, Hugo dispenses with attempts to discover the Theater of the World by showing us that this theater can only be the mental production of its "objective" observer. Though the ordering of the pieces in the *Théâtre en liberté* remains uncertain and we cannot affirm that *La Forêt mouillée* is necessarily intended as its opening, it is the only completed piece composed during the crisis years and it bears a distinct resemblance to the *Prologue mystique*. Like the prologue, it is a theatricalized dialogue between impossible characters, the stones, birds, and flowers of the forest. It also relies upon narrative commentary situated outside of the dialogue itself to both set the stage and to exploit the point of view of an imaginary spectator. This time, however, there is no need for magic telescopes since this spectator is already "voyant," and there is no question of reconciling dualities since the opposites in this drama are already mirror images.

Shortly after the play begins, a stage direction shows us the prose of a narrator intruding into the verse of the play. Though a long narrative intrusion, it is worth quoting in its entirety:

UN MOINEAU FRANC, *sortant de dessous les feuilles et secouant ses ailes.*
Dehors, tous!
Au signal donné par le moineau, un mouvement extraordinaire agite la forêt. Il semble que tout s'éveille et se mette à vivre. Les choses deviennent des êtres. Les fleurs prennent des airs de femmes. On dirait que les esprits des plantes sortent la tête de

dessous les feuilles et se mettent à jaser. Tout parle, tout murmure, tout chuchote. Des querelles ça et là. Toutes les tiges se penchent pêle-mêle les unes vers les autres. Le vent va et vient. Les oiseaux, les papillons, les mouches vont et viennent. Les vers de terre se dressent hors de leurs trous comme en proie à un rut mystérieux. Les parfums et les rayons se baisent. Le soleil fait dans les massifs d'arbres tous les verts possibles. Pendant toute la scène, les mousses, les plantes, les oiseaux, les mouches se mêlent en groupes qui se décomposent et se recomposent sans cesse. Dans des coins, des fleurs font leur toilette, les joyeuses s'ajustant des colliers de gouttes de rosée, les mélancoliques faisant briller au soleil leur larme de pluie. L'eau de l'étang imite les frémissements d'une gaze d'argent. Les nids font de petits cris. Pour le voyant, c'est un immense tumulte; pour l'homme, c'est une paix immense. (*TC*, 2:994–95)[16]

The mixture of narrative, poetic, and authorial voices apparent in this intrusive stage direction is strategically designed to keep the play on the page but also to show that no matter how hard one tries to look at the world and to describe it, one cannot escape the purely illusory perceptions of one's own fantasies. Initially, we notice the voice of a writer who, addressing a prospective director, indicates what should be on stage: movement, quarreling, bending stems, and "pendant toute la scène"—the writer, like a playwright, is clearly informed about what will or should be taking place—the mosses, plants, birds, and flies are endlessly decomposing and recomposing groups almost like a corps de ballet surrounding a principal dancer. Then, there is the voice of a narrator who, addressing the reader, gives the reader at least two ways to look at what is presented as an "objective" scene: for the clairvoyant, this is an immense tumult; for the ordinary person, an immense peace. Finally, there is the voice of a spectator who, apparently addressing himself, proposes purely subjective impressions of what he appears to be experiencing for the very first time: "Il semble que tout s'éveille" ("It *seems that* everything is awakening"), he offers, "On dirait que les esprits des plantes sortent" ("One *could say that* the minds of plants poke out") and the earthworms come up from their holes as if (*comme*) prey to a mysterious heat. (Indeed, one might wonder how this spectator knows how earthworms in heat behave.) In any case, whereas the present tense suggests the objective presence of the scene, the subjective impressions indicated by the "It seems that," "One could say that," or the "as if" imply that the movement of the forest is only activated by a spectator's gaze.

This subjective apprehension of the scene continues. For the spectator also tends to overpoeticize his visions. His choice of verbs interprets the quality of the movement he sees: perfumes and rays *kiss*, the pond water *imitates* the shimmering of silver gauze. He also anthropomorphizes the flowers according to the suggestiveness of both their natural qualities and the words used to name them: "des fleurs font leur toilette, les joyeuses s'ajustant des colliers . . . les mélancoliques faisant briller au soleil leur larme de pluie" ("flowers groom themselves, the happy ones adjusting their necklaces of dew, the melancholy making their teardrop of rain shine in the sun"). In addition, he insists upon an incessant movement and bickering in the forest: The wind comes and goes, birds and butterflies fly to and fro, groups dissolve and coalesce, and everything speaks, murmurs, or whispers. With an almost ecstatic view of the forest, the spectator is "voyant," accomplishing imaginary linguistic metamorphoses before our eyes. Furthermore, because this voice does not correspond to any actor on stage, its presence and the change in typeface used to alert us to its intrusion seem rather to provide a kind of textual proscenium arch behind which an imaginary spectator offers us a model for how to read. This voice is not a mere stage indication. Its poetic language is aimed at a reader and thus might be said to inscribe its own illocutionary force.

The hero of the play, Denarius, plays a role uncannily similar to that of his narrating observer. Denarius, who has renounced the society of women as he has been unlucky in love, comes to the forest to philosophize and announces in what seems to be almost a direct reference to Plato's *Symposium:* "Je blâme / Le bon Dieu d'avoir fait l'homme de deux morceaux / Dont l'un est une femme." He adds, "Aimer! sotte

aventure. / L'homme est fait pour rêver au fond de la nature"
(*TC*, 2:992).[17] As the simple man that he is and as the narrator has suggested, Denarius finds a refreshing peace in the
forest. Unbeknownst to Denarius, however, the forest has already come alive to contradict him with its natural expression
of love and eroticism (*TC*, 2:993). Denarius remains humor-
ously unaware:

LE HOCHQUEUE
Faisons un horrible vacarme.
DENARIUS, **en contemplation.**
Frais silence!

(*TC*, 2:997)[18]

The result is a strange kind of double scene: as the forest characters engage in their own amorous dialogues, Denarius con-
templates silently to himself.

At one point, however, Denarius comes to sense the life of
the forest and like the narrating spectator begins to read and
interpret its messages. Instead of the narrator's "Tout parle,
tout murmure, tout chuchote," we read:

DENARIUS
Tout est énigme et tout est mot
Oh! je sens la forêt pleine de la chimère!
La création, c'est une sombre grammaire
L'invisible, au réel mêlé, change un rayon
En regard, et la fleur et l'arbre en vision.

(*TC*, 2:1003–4)[19]

Like the narrating spectator, Denarius begins to speak of metamorphoses turning his view of the forest into a text to be read:
rays turn into looks and flowers into visions, creation becomes
a grammar. Then, just as magic telescopes helped spectators
to hear murmuring stars, imaginary visions help Denarius to
hear with an invisible ear:

Tout chante un opéra mystérieux ici. . . .
Une oreille invisible entend sortir des gammes. . . .
(S'enfonçant dans sa rêverie)

> Pourquoi pas? Je serais un homme primitif. . . .
> Et je savourerais, seul dans ma stalle verte,
> Force partitions que m'exécuterait
> Le vent musicien dans l'orchestre forêt.
>
> (*TC*, 2:1006–7)[20]

Like his counterpart, Denarius is a spectator sitting in a natural theater, speaking to himself alone while he listens to what he interprets to be the forest's silent concert. His view of the forest is also highly subjective; the wind is anthropomorphized—it has become a musician—and the sounds of the forest have been transformed into a mysterious opera. Moreover, Denarius seems to realize his capacity to make of the forest anything he wants by simply being primitive, that is, by consciously dismissing what he knows to be reality.

Unlike the narrating spectator, however, Denarius becomes aware that he is being carried away by his visions and attempts to control his wild imagination. In what appears to be a surprising forerunner to Mallarmé's *L'Après-midi d'un faune*, Denarius's monologue turns into a discourse about imagination and reality. But whereas Mallarmé's faun has no need for reality as he finds imagination to be infinitely more satisfying, Denarius tries to avoid the illusions of his fertile imagination by becoming a reasoning philosopher, in touch with the "real":

> —Je suis fou. Mon esprit patauge en plein Chompré.—
> Non, restons dans le vrai, dans l'herbe, dans le pré.
> C'est assez d'être un loup, ne soyons pas un faune.
> . . . .
> Le vrai suffit. Soyons un simple philosophe. . . .
> Lorsque l'humanité tétait son pouce, bon,
> La fable avait son prix. Mais l'homme est un barbon,
> Diable! à présent, l'esprit humain porte perruque,
> Et notre raison branle une tête caduque.
> Croire aux nymphes est bête. Il faut être réel.
>
> (*TC*, 2:1008)[21]

According to Denarius, though in its early stages, humanity may have needed fables and fictions in order to learn its lessons—

Greek mythology, for example, was a way of understanding the workings of the world—humanity in its old age is now better equipped to rely upon its powers of reason and no longer needs to see the "real" through mythology. Moreover, since the Revolution, which has literally shaken off the heads of the Old Regime, one is forced to be one's own philosopher. However, for Denarius and as we shall see, for Hugo himself, the philosopher's attempt to assure self-consciousness, to be "real," is continually undermined: the subject "je" is doubled, "restons, soyons," and shakes off its own reasoning head, leaving room for hallucinatory fantasies. In fact, the mere mention of nymphs will send Denarius, like Mallarmé's faun, into erotic thoughts about women. Though Denarius catches himself by remembering that he had rejected the company of women upon entering the forest, he proves that he remains unavoidably (a) "bête" by turning to the flowers and projecting his desires onto them:

> Je veux baigner mon front en feu
> Dans vos seins! me rouler dans vos lits!
> (*TC*, 2:1009)[22]

Feverish with desire, Denarius longs to cool his forehead in what he perceives to be the breasts of flowers and to roll himself up in their "beds." The flowers, however, react with disgust, underlining the distinction between reality and fantasy, between what is there and what Denarius, now desirous, wants to see.

Indeed, the "Forêt" continues to contradict Denarius and to show that no matter how hard he tries, he cannot escape the purely illusory perceptions of his own desiring fantasies. For when finally Denarius decides for certain that "le paradis, c'est la solitude" (*TC*, 2:1012; "paradise is solitude"), an apple falling on his head cries, "Eve". This amusing prediction inaugurates the final scene of the play in which the members of the forest contrive to make Denarius fall in love with one of the women who has entered the scene. By the end of the play, not only does Denarius not really see what is there,

DENARIUS
Cette femme a dans l'oeil la céleste étincelle.
C'est Diane, ou Psyche!
LE MOINEAU
Ça, c'est mademoiselle Balminette, lingère en chambre, rue aux
    Ours
Numéro trois

(TC, 2:1014)

but he also changes his notion of paradise:

Oui, c'est l'idéal, c'est la figure rêvée!
Oh! cette robe blanche un instant soulevée!
L'éclair du paradis!

(TC, 2:1019–20)

And the play closes with the knowing remark by those who
lifted the skirt:

LE CAILLOU, **au ruisseau**
Sans nous, si nous n'avions fait retrousser Goton,
Ce Jocrisse risquait de devenir Platon.

(TC, 2:1020)[23]

An amusing end to a play that began with a reference to
Plato's *Symposium*, these lines suggest as well an ultimate rejection of idealist philosophy as a kind of self-defeating endeavor. Self-consciousness is no longer easily assured since for
all of Denarius's philosophizing, he ends up exactly where he
began. Physically excited, he is unable to get his mind off his
own sexuality. In fact, in this, *La Forêt mouillée* is like the
Théâtre en liberté itself, for it, too, will endlessly repeat itself
in variations on the theme of desire and it, too, seems to finish
by closing itself into a circle, as we shall see.

Given Denarius's inability to distinguish between fantasy
and reality, it is not surprising that neither he nor his narrating
spectator ever really hears the true dialogues of the forest. On
the contrary, each remains outside of them, reading into his
visions much more or at least something very different from

what is actually there. In the case of both Denarius and the narrating spectator, the forest seems to bolster the creative imagination but ultimately only by reflecting back thoughts that originate in the minds of its viewers. *La Forêt Mouillée* works, thus, to create the image of a reality outside of any human perception, but the image of this reality is one of pure fiction.

The fact that we are given a double vision of the forest, the narrator's and Denarius's, neither of which corresponds to what is really there, suggests that one is always mistaken, always unable to apprehend what being really is. This idea is particularly meaningful in the context of this new theater since it represents a rejection of the notion of optimal point of view necessary to actual representation and scenography. Rather, it seems to predict the end of a philosophy of representation on which actual theater must rely and to suggest an attempt to present a multiplicity of points of view among which there can be no one true vision or representation. One might say that the text creates a false sense of presence or being through its use of the present tense—both in the dialogues and in the words of the narrator—but that it is aware of itself as a fiction. Ultimately, the rendering of the immediacy of the viewing experience, and the way in which perceptions can only reflect the mind of the viewer, seems to be more important than any representation. Furthermore, the textual identity established between Denarius and the narrating spectator works to create a *mise en abîme* or nested mirror effect that ultimately keeps the play and its characters from referring to anything outside of themselves. There is no representation of reality, a reality cannot be perceived; the play can only mimic the act of representation itself.

One might indeed argue that the theme of eroticism coupled with the disjunction of material reality and imagination is already suggestive of the disruptive movements of desire. When we further consider that the play relies upon distinctly defined structural positions which separate subjects from objects only to emphasize their subsequent confusion, we might say that the play bears a distinct resemblance to the structure of the fantasm, what Laplanche and Pontalis call the staging of desire ("Fantasy," 17). On one hand, the text takes pains to establish an imaginary proscenium arch that delineates the outsides and insides of an imaginary theatrical space. On the other hand, the mirror effect works against such a delineation, confusing the position of the protagonist with that of the writer. Just as Denarius tries to control his fantasies by philosophizing but ends up being "carried away" by them, the voice of the narrator philosophically distanced from a supposedly self-sufficient dialogical scene creates self-imposed boundaries only to find itself mirrored in that very scene. Denarius's projections have merely replayed those of the narrator for whom the movement of flies became a ballet and the swaying of flowers, an image of women waking to prepare themselves for the day. In other words, both the narrator and Denarius are "turned on" by the forest so that a distinction between what they think and what they see becomes impossible. There is no longer the possibility of a discourse about what *is*, since in their very attempts to seize and describe reality, they can only produce self-generated fictions which, like the fantasm, offer only imaginary, autoerotic satisfactions.

This elaborate structure is not, then, a chance event but a deliberate strategy designed both to render the play unrepresentable and to demonstrate the mobility of a speaking subject. The voice of the writer at first distinctly placed outside of the scene of the play is unable to constitute or maintain a psychological unity in that position; it finds itself repeated or reflected in Denarius, on the inside of that same scene. With the end of a philosophy of representation comes the end of any notion of a stable, unified, philosophical subject and the formal constraints of a written play designed to be "performed" in a reading come to imply that very instability. In fact, Hugo has succeeded in representing what Julia Kristeva describes as a psychoanalytic subject, one whose unity is lost in the very act of speaking or thinking.[24]

One result of this loss of stable identity in theater is that emphasis on character psychology or dramatic logic is displaced onto language. We become attentive, as readers, to various language games. A representative example can be seen in one of the many otherwise meaningless dialogues between the characters of the forest:

> LE MOINEAU, regardant autour de lui
>   Mais palsambleau! c'est la cour
> Que ce bois! C'est Versaille et l'Oeil-de-boeuf . . .
>   (A une touffe de bruyère)
> Bonjour, La Bruyère.
>   (A une branche d'arbre)
> Bonjour, Rameau.
>   (A une corneille sur le rocher)
> Bonjour, Corneille.
>   (Au nénuphar)
> Bonjour, Boileau.
>
> (*TC*, 2 : 1000–1001)[25]

This humorous reference to the seventeenth century may be in part a gesture to the age of great theater in relation to which this theater points to itself as something new. Nonetheless, it is also about another kind of theater, that virtual theater inherent in the space between a writer and his words. For not only does each pun on the great names of classicism play with the disjunction of signifiers and signifieds but each is thereby representative of the way language always creates more than there is, a surplus of meanings. In this passage, each name connotes something more than any simple referent: a tuft of heather is both an object in the world and a pun on a writer's name as are the branch, the crow, and the water lily that drinks water, "boit l'eau." Hugo is not only comically playing with an intended reading experience but also undermining conventional codes of communication. Moreover, this interlude is what Genette calls "dead time" since it has no purpose relative to the dramatic conflict except to illustrate the work of the writer.[26] Instead of language communicating dramatic logic or character psychology, then, this language is a performance. It highlights the theatricality of writing itself, a theatricality based on the mobility of the subject, writing.

DUE to its elaborate structure, *La Forêt mouillée* stands apart from other of Hugo's writings and for that matter, from the other pieces of *Le Théâtre en liberté*. Yet it also serves as a microcosm of the whole. Each of the other pieces also takes place in a forest and each is characterized both by a subtle play of movement on the borders of dramas and by the *mise en scène* of a double perspective, of outsides that become insides. In some cases, the outsides are outsiders who, like Hugo in exile, preach against the perils of political and social tyranny. In almost every case, antithetical points of view are resolved off stage either in *apartés* or in narrative commentary.[27] Moreover, each of the dramas finds its logic as a variation on the theme of love. Whether it be grandmothers and grandchildren, fathers and sons, rulers and their subjects, young couples or illicit lovers, everyone learns to love. In fact, the philosopher-bum Mouffetard sums up his attack on philosophers and theologians with "Mais tu dis: Quelque chose existe. J'en conviens. / Quoi? Le sexe" (*TC*, 2:968; "But you say: 'something exists.' I agree. What? Sex"). As for Denarius, then, ideal questions lead to physical answers until the chronological end of this theater in *Etre aimé* of 1873, the monologue of the aging king who is caught in the endlessness of desiring since he has everything but love.

In the most complicated play of *Le Théâtre en liberté*, *Mangeront-ils?* ("Will They Eat?"), the conflict is situated around an ideal couple, Lord Slada and Lady Janet, who seek refuge in the forest and therefore have nothing to eat (*TC*, 2:855−955). They are fleeing from the king who is in love with the lady and has chosen her for his wife. Separated physically in the ruins of isolated cloisters, the love scene is separated textually from two other groups of couples, antithetical groups: on one hand, we have those tattered but mystical lovers of nature, Aïrolo and Zineb, and on the other, the king and his valet, Mess Tityrus.[28] In fact, three different dramas unfold: one of love, one of power, and one of mysticism. In this way, the drama of the lovers, though the center of the play, proves to be only a foil for a more essential conflict between antithetical poles and their respective relations to the ideal. This more essential conflict takes place between the "insiders," Aïrolo and Zineb, who are really outsiders or "proscrits" like Hugo himself, and the "outsiders" who are in political power. Moreover, until its final amusing reconciliation, this conflict plays itself out off stage in the narrator's stage indications. So although there is nothing so interesting as the constitution of a narrating spectator, the play gains all of its allure through the intrusion of narrative voice and a series of comic *apartés* by Aïrolo.[29] Consequently, we as readers are the only ones who see the interplay of the three groups of couples. It is Zineb who, in dying, resolves the conflict by convincing the king that his fate is tied to Aïrolo's. Unable to ignore or do away with Aïrolo, the king must listen to his advice and accept the hungry couple. This means that the play ultimately comes to a close only because the extreme antithetical groups represented by Aïrolo and the king end up resembling each other.

In *L'Epée*, there is a similar structural phenomenon at work. As the play opens, we see a village in the forest theoretically protected by a certain Prêtre-Pierre and his peace-loving disciple Albos (*TC*, 2:799–854). As the play unfolds, however, we are introduced to Slagistri, an ogre of a man gone to live alone in a cave, who is yet another outsider, another "proscrit". It is Slagistri, this time, who sees all and knows all and who, because of his knowledge, has chosen to flee society. Once again, although the principal scene of the play portrays the happy villagers, their songs and dance, the more essential conflict of the play takes place between Prêtre-Pierre and Slagistri (later surprisingly identified as father and son), between the outsides and insides of the theatrical space. The conflicting perspectives of the two men concerning freedom and political authority are also ultimately resolved off stage when Prêtre-Pierre, on his way to greet the supposedly benevolent king, is beaten and attacked by the king's men. The play ends as Albos

gives up the pacifist teachings of Prêtre-Pierre to accept Slagistri's answer to political tyranny, "l'épée" (*TC*, 2:854).[30]
Like *Mangeront-ils?* then, *L'Epée* uses a theatrical setting
only to emphasize the importance of peripheral conflicts, to
set up outsides and insides, and to show how the outsider and
the insider come, once again, to resemble each other.
La *Grand'Mère* is very different in tone but again bears
a structural and thematic likeness to the other plays. Like
Mangeront-ils? it is constructed around an ideal couple; like
L'Epée, it presents a political conflict. The grandmother, a
margrave, has come to the forest to seek out her son who has
run away with the lower-class woman of his dreams in order
to escape a more personal type of political tyranny. Again the
play revolves around an image of ideal happiness and again,
its conflict takes place outside of that scene. For the grandmother comes to accept her son's unruly ways but not because
she understands ideal love, rather because she spies upon her
grandchildren playing:

> LA MARGRAVE, cachée derrière la haie.
> J'ai la rage dans l'âme.
> **Elle regarde les enfants, et peu à peu les écoute.—Pendant
> qu'ils parlent sans la voir, elle se rapproche d'eux pas à pas.**
>
> (*TC*, 2:793)[31]

In this scene, the grandmother is constituted as an outside
spectator who, like Albos, will be drawn to the other side of
the play's central antithesis. After this scene, the play ends
with the grandmother's surprising exclamation to her previously despised daughter-in-law: "Appelle-moi ta mère!" (*TC*,
2:798; "Call me your mother!").
Finally, a last little scene written much later, in 1873, presents a slightly different version of the same structural conflict. *Sur la lisière d'un bois* presents Léo and Léa, ideal
lovers, and a satyr who, unbeknownst to the couple, examines
them from the outside. Not unlike Aïrolo, the satyr makes
earthy quips in response to the couple's expression of ideal
love in a comic series of *apartés*. As in the other plays, the
outsider knows and sees more than the unsuspecting lovers.

The play begins with Léo's naive respect for his lover, a na-
ïveté signaled by a much wiser satyr:

> LÉO
> ... Tiens ton voile baissé, Léa.
> Je te respecte.
> Ne crains rien de moi.
> UN SATYRE, **dans le bois**
> Phrase absolument suspecte.
>
> (*TC*, 2:957)[32]

The play ends with Léo's seducing Léa into the woods and the
satyr's knowing remark: "Fin de l'idylle: un mioche" (*TC*,
2:964; "Romance over: a crumb"). As for Denarius, then,
ideal questions of love are once again resolved in physical responses, and as in the other plays, antithetical points of view
are reconciled off stage. Here, however, the title already situates the dramatic conflict on the borders or edge of the forest's
theater where in fact all of the conflicts in all of the plays may
be said to have taken place.

Ultimately, then, in each of the plays, though in different
ways, the theme of love or eroticism coupled with the logic of
the fantasm seems to repeatedly occur. Each play constitutes
textual outsides and insides only to confuse those distinctions
and each takes place on those imaginary borders where outsides come to resemble insides. In other words, though each
of the plays may stand on its own—indeed, many have become very popular on the stage—it is important to remember
that they were initially conceived as parts of a whole, pieces
of theater intended to form a volume. Therefore, whether the
Théâtre en liberté was conceived of at the same time as the
Forêt with the crisis of 1854, or rather, later, with the major
portion of the plays, closer to 1865, the volume remains an
important concept. In fact, what appears to be a gap between
the composition of the *Forêt* and the remainder of the pieces
intended for this volume is really an explosion of interesting
investigations into writing theater. Though most of these writing investigations are only fragments or incomplete projects,
many of them manifest structural problems similar to those

explored in the other plays. All of the fragments can be thematically classified as a confusion or mixing of two types of natural theater: that of human beings and their imagination and that of nature itself.

In what seems to be an exploration into theories of animism, for example, there are some wonderful fragments about the inherently playful theater of nature. One example conflates nature's play with child's play:

CONVERSATION DES FLOTS

Sous l'eau

La scène se passe à la Porte-Saint-Martin, en pleine mer, pendant le drame: *La Bourrasque.*

GAMINS:

FLOTS: { Romarin   Filasse
Boilu   Popard
Grimebodin   Bigaru
Talotte   Quine-au-lièvre

Bigarreau

PREMIER FLOT

Dis-donc, Titi, tu m'as marché à même sur la main.

DEUXIEME FLOT

M'sieu, tu m'embêtes.

The superimposing of childlike dialogue onto the waves continues until the narrative comment at the end:

(Ceci vient après un dialogue sérieux et terrible des vents dans une tempête du pôle. Les deux scènes sont dans la même pièce.) (Massin, 9:978–79)[33]

In this project, we have not only an impossible play but also a demonstration of the way Hugo expanded and explored his own sense of theater. This scene may be said to extend an interest already present in *La Forêt mouillée*, for not only is natural theater a result of mental production, but the reader's imagination is provoked by narrative commentary. This is a significant interest. With the only necessary material element being, as it is here, the stage of the reader's imagination, not only is a volume of theater a conceivable project, but the number of theaters in it is infinite and, in that sense, purely potential. The notion of a volume which, like Baudelaire's *Petits Poèmes en prose*, would be made up of movable parts, is further attested to by suggested links between many of these fragments. In one series of fragments which appear to prolong the *Forêt*, for example, we see Denarius and Balminette (the ideal woman in the last scene of *La Forêt mouillée*) as a couple dealing with conjugal love (Massin, 9:980–81, 952–64). Pierre Albouy has suggested that these fragments may have been intended for an unfinished project entitled *Homo*, but the characters are not limited to specific plays and seem to suggest places of conflict rather than psychological unities.[34] Denarius, for example, appears in dialogue with Vaugirard and is therefore linked to the project *Les Gueux* (*TC*, 2:1683–1707). He also plays the role of a student in one fragment called "Le Spleen" (*TC*, 2:1732–42) and in yet another called "Les Étudiants" (*TC*, 2:1743–53). In still more fragments, Balminette appears with child and is thus related to the various projects on children including *Les Mômes* (Massin, 9:971–79). On a more sinister note, she also finds herself in a scene with her friend, Balmusette, in which she commits suicide (Massin, 9:977). This scene thus serves as a link between *Le Théâtre en liberté* and all of the fragments on suicide. Indeed, the fact that the characters are not conceived of as psychological unities but rather as links between ideas might suggest an explanation for the incompletion of these many projects.

Hugo himself mused about this problem in a notebook dated 1867:

> Est-ce un tort à un auteur d'être auteur au point de faire complètement vivre au fond de sa pensée les types plus ou moins réels dans lesquels il incarne ses idées? L'auteur a-t-il le droit de pousser la création jusqu'à faire exister les personnages de son drame en dehors et au delà du drame même? Quand le jeune homme enthousiaste, *qui chantait*, quand l'enfant misérable et joyeux, quand ces deux êtres qui souffraient et chantaient sont tombés, est-il permis d'entr'ouvrir leurs tombes, pour en laisser sortir leurs

voix, comme des souffles de l'ombre? Si le lecteur répond oui, il
ne rejettera pas ce livre. (*TC*, 2:1788)[35]

We see here a specific reference to theater conceived as a book
meant to be read. We can also infer from this passage that the
characters intended for this book are an incarnation of the
author's thoughts moving inside and outside the borders of
dramas. This may explain why such characters as Denarius
and Balminette can disappear and reappear in the fragments
for various different projects. It also suggests that Hugo's volume of theater is intended neither as a representation of the
real world nor as one concerned with revealing those "seven
or eight philosophical truths" to which the didactic dramaturge felt himself limited. On the contrary, the volume is a
presentation of ideas, of those "breaths from the shadow," a
purely potential set. Furthermore, the characters represent not
only ideas but these ideas appear to be themselves like characters playing on the stage of the author's thoughts. That is,
they may be materialized in fragments of theater or they may
simply live on in the author's imagination. Therefore, Hugo's
experimentation with theater not only seeks to represent the
theaters inherent to nature but goes so far as to suggest that
theater is inherent to nature because it is also inherent to
thought. The mind is already its own kind of theater.

That the representation of this theater of thought should in
turn appear as fragments shows us a profound modernity in
Hugo's notion of the subject thinking. Indeed it proposes a
subject who, in thinking, is never quite a fixed entity but always a collection of fragments of characters, an unfinished
volume of theatricalized ideas. Perhaps this is why Hugo's
Théâtre en liberté was fated to remain unfinished and why the
various projects intended for it seem to be less and less devel-
oped until, finally, there is nothing but a formidable repertory
of names (*TC*, 2:1806–19). In this context, this repertory
suggests that, given names as the material of ideas, a writer
or reader could virtually create any theater he or she could
imagine.

This progressive movement toward thought as a theater of the imagination finds a rather more theoretical setting in Hugo's *William Shakespeare*. Written in 1863 at a time when the insomnia, uncertainty, and general crisis conditions of 1854 seem to be repeating themselves (Barrère, *La Fantaisie*, 2 : 372), the work's completion marks the beginning of a period of composition during which the remainder of the plays intended for the *Théâtre en liberté* are created. It is as if the discoveries made while writing fragments caused a return to a more analytical or philosophical mode of thinking which in turn gave way to an even more creative notion of theater.

In this theoretical tome, Hugo seems to explain the idea of a volume of theater when he notes that Shakespeare's entire works can be seen as "une pensée colossale et un caprice immense" (*WS*, 160; "one colossal thought and one immense caprice"). As this statement suggests, it seems that Hugo's renewed interest in completing a volume of theater pieces, in 1865, coincides with his understanding of Shakespeare's works as one great theater of ideas. We have already seen that Hugo's own characters are the incarnation of his ideas, and on the subject of one of the plays intended for this volume of theater, Hugo noted: "Je ne publierai pas ce drame. Je l'ai fait pour me délivrer de l'obsession d'une idée" (Barrère, *La Fantaisie*, 2 : 372; "I will not publish this drama. I wrote it in order to deliver myself from the obsession of an idea"). In other words, whether or not the idea of not publishing the drama is pure rhetoric, it suggests that the *Théâtre en liberté* is a kind of therapeutic exercise conceived as a way of exorcising or externalizing ideas. Furthermore, since the *Théâtre en liberté* can be read as the story of one lifetime—it begins with Denarius, the impetuous youth who has come to the forest to find solitude, and finishes with the aging king who, also unlucky in love, regrets his solitude—it seems that Hugo's theater of ideas, like Shakespeare's complete works, represents one colossal thought and one immense caprice, the development of one man's thoughts on love.

In this light, we could say that the volume of theater pieces that make up *Le Théâtre en liberté* proposes a very modern version of this one immense, capricious thought. For what begins in *La Forêt mouillée* and ends in *Etre aimé* of 1873 (*TC*, 2:987–89) is the circular fantasy production of unrequited desire.[36] Each of the plays and/or fragments contained in this unwieldy volume does indeed find its logic as a variation on the theme of love but only because love is itself emblematic of the disruptive movements of desire. It is the movement of desire, and of its constantly renewable fantasy scenarios, that produces and is reproduced in the disrupted fragments of Hugo's liberated theater. In it, anecdotes of love and storytelling become secondary to structured movements inside and out of plays, to language games and misdirected dialogues, and to a plurality of points of view, all of which bring an end to the possibility of objective perceptions and to the very notion of a stable or unified philosophical subject. On the contrary, the volume affords the perfect setting for a modern subjectivity in which the poet's caprice becomes a variety of truth (*WS*, 160).

With its evocation of the antithetical poles of Shakespeare's work, *William Shakespeare* also offers an explanation for Hugo's repetitive *mise en scène* of a double perspective, of outsides and insides, and of obsessive conflicts between those who see or know and those who do not. For in his study of Shakespeare's theater of ideas, Hugo discovers an essential esthetics of antithesis (*WS*, 162–63). Though the concept of antitheses necessary to art was touched on much earlier by Hugo in the doctrine of the sublime and the grotesque, the question of mixing tones becomes, in the case of Shakespeare, a description of the movement of thought itself. This association of thought and antithesis in turn leads to the much more modern theory that art does not *represent* but rather *repeats* life by repeating thought.

In his introduction to the life of Shakespeare, Hugo uses the image of the ocean to show that the great mind, the mind of the poet-philosopher, is analogous to the workings of nature:

Ces ondes, ce flux et ce reflux, ce va-et-vient terrible . . . ce niveau
après ce bouleversement, ces enfers et ces paradis de l'immensité
éternellement émue, cet infini, cet insondable, tout cela peut être
dans un esprit et alors cet esprit s'appelle génie . . . et c'est la
même chose de regarder ces âmes ou de regarder l'océan. (WS,
12–13)[37]

According to this passage, the mind of the genius both resembles and contains the drama of the universe. To look inside the mind is to see the ocean, outside, so that a look at the
ocean apprehends the movement of thought. More radically,
however, what were once conceived, in the *Prologue mystique*
for example, as irreconcilable antithetical poles—Heaven and
Hell, the calm and the storm—have now become pluralized
points in an endlessly moving immensity. That is, the paradises and infernos of the ocean or of the mind are designated
only to emphasize the incessant movement that both divides
and joins them, movement that constantly folds in upon itself.
This explains why Hugo's representation of the theater of
thought repeatedly produces opposites that come to resemble
each other and fragments that ebb and flow with the turbulence of a storm.

The analogy, however, does not stop there. If the mind resembles the drama of the universe with its extreme poles of
mobile opposition, thought itself is like a promontory on
which only the genius steps and from which the genius can
only perceive the blackness of the abyss of uncertainty:

Qu'est-ce que la sonde vous rapporte, jetée dans ce mystère? Que
voyez-vous? Les conjectures tremblent, les doctrines frissonnent;
les hypothèses flottent; toute la philosophie humaine vacille d'un
souffle sombre devant cette ouverture. . . . On presse l'abîme de
questions. Rien de plus. (WS, 140–41)[38]

This is a startling image of Hugo's uncertainty regarding philosophy; conjectures, doctrines, hypotheses, all of philosophy
is set afloat in the contemplation of the ocean (or, we may
assume, of the mind). Yet, this may also be an image of the
role of philosophical interrogation in Hugo's efforts to write.

That is, this vacillation of philosophy may help us to see Hugo's volume of theater as the representation of the movement of this uncertain interrogation—the ebb and flow of nature, the ebb and flow of the mind. The passages themselves move with a certain dramatic quality in their own rhythmic fluidity. The ocean in the first and the questions in the second seem to perform the vacillation of philosophy. This is undoubtedly because "tout songeur a en lui ce monde imaginaire. Cette cime du rêve est sous le crâne de tout poète comme la montagne sous le ciel. C'est un vague royaume plein du mouvement inexprimable de la chimère." [39] Ultimately, this means that what began for Hugo in dialogue with the tables as an attempt to apprehend the invisible theaters of the world ended in the understanding that the recording of the movements of one man's inexpressible fantasies is the only way to represent that potentially infinite number of theaters.

===

FOUR

The Dynamic Universe of Flaubert's *Tentation*

Au milieu de mes chagrins, j'achève mon *Saint Antoine*, c'est l'oeuvre de
toute ma vie, puisque la première idée m'est venue en 1845, à Gênes, devant
un tableau de Breughel, et depuis ce temps-là, je n'ai cessé d'y songer et de
faire des lectures afférentes.

—Flaubert, *Correspondance*

*L*a Tentation de Saint An-
toine exploits the figure of the theater in order to dramatize
the structure and functioning of the mind.[1] A mixture of dramatic dialogue and narration, the play is an ideal example of
Virtual Theater insofar as it anticipates several of the strategies outlined by Freud's dream work which characterize the
interaction of conscious and unconscious thinking. Although
Flaubert himself noted, "J'ai été moi-même dans *Saint Antoine* le saint Antoine" (*C*, 1:91; "I was myself in *Saint
Anthony* the saint Anthony"), in much the same way he had
offered the much more popular "Madame Bovary, c'est moi,"
literary criticism has been infinitely less concerned, as a rule,
with understanding the ways in which *La Tentation* prob-
lematizes and informs the question of subjectivity in Flaubert's writing.[2] Therefore, by making *La Tentation* part of the
"history" of Virtual Theater, I intend to highlight its transformation of a personal philosophy into a psychoanalytic drama
of subjectivity. For like philosophy, *La Tentation* takes as its
subject matter the question of philosophical consciousness,
but, like psychoanalysis, it assumes a consciousness or ego

always out of touch with the inner life of the mind and a reality destabilized by the procreative interplay of memory and desire, a reality transformed into a dynamic universe. Though the uniqueness of its form has been noted on occasion, the theatrical nature of *La Tentation* has received surprisingly little attention.[3] This is undoubtedly because it disrupts those generally accepted categories of literature that Flaubert might have called the "idées reçues" of literary history. Whether it be a distinction between genres (theater and novels), between disciplines (literature and philosophy), or between literary movements (Realism and Romanticism, Structuralism and post-Structuralism, or modernism and postmodernism), criticism's concern with separating fields of expertise has reduced the theatricality of *La Tentation* to questions of narrative and character. In other words, criticism associates *La Tentation* with the evolution of Flaubert's evasive Realism rather than seeing it as the elaboration of a psychical apparatus whose interdisciplinary form has a precedent in Romantic theory.[4]

Those who study theater recognize the place of *La Tentation* in or in relation to a history of Romantic drama. El Nouty notes its participation in the subgenre called "ideal" theater and its particularly unique use of "scénographie verbale," a technique that belongs neither to narrative nor to dramatic discourse but which has the effect of keeping the play inevitably glued to the page (El Nouty, 251, 254–55). Katherine Singer Kovács notes Flaubert's general interest in "féeries" and suggests a vital link between many of the techniques at work in *La Tentation* and Flaubert's other unsuccessful projects in that genre. She also notes Flaubert's growing interest in psychological studies.[5] However, Kovács does not discover the unique mixture of the psychological and the theatrical in *La Tentation*. In this way, although both of these critics underscore the theatricality of Flaubert's *Tentation*, they miss its theory of the theater and the way in which its elaboration of a metapsychology of the spectator harbors insights into the author's notions of both esthetic reception and textual production.

Looking from what we might call the opposite point of view, that of the history of the novel and of Flaubert's Realism, the neglect of the formal dimensions of Flaubert's "novel" is most evident in those studies that see *La Tentation* as part of a Romantic ideal. Victor Brombert's study of Flaubert's novels, for example, does seem to almost unconsciously suggest that *La Tentation* and, in particular, its saint create a kind of skeleton for the interaction of dream and reality in all of the novels, as Baudelaire once suggested.[6] Moreover, Brombert sees this interaction as part of the "pivotal dialectic conflicts of Romanticism" (*The Novels of Flaubert*, 193). However, his study of the "Romanticism" of this "novel" seems to displace what we can identify as the psychoanalytic aspects of dreaming—subject/object relations (201), autoerotic pleasures of sublimation (209), cinematic impressions or "fade-ins" (206), and past desires enacted in an imaginary future (188)—in favor of a study of four antithetical "Romantic" themes (193). So although Brombert's conclusion and many of his readings suggest that Flaubert stands at the threshold of modern literature, they also emphasize the thematic nature of this modernity: "And *La Tentation de saint Antoine*, a book he carried in his mind for over thirty years, is a true summa of Romantic themes and tensions" (288). This is not to suggest that Brombert's thematic study is not insightful but rather that his lack of attention to *La Tentation*'s theatrical framework causes a shift away from the more interesting philosophical dimensions of Romanticism provocatively illustrated in this play.

A more recent example of a misconstrued notion of Romanticism appears in Jonathan Culler's *Flaubert: The Uses of Uncertainty*, in a telltale section of the book entitled "'Beyond' Romanticism."[7] Though the quotation marks surrounding "Beyond" reveal a certain hesitation, Culler notes in that section that Flaubert could not have been a Vigny or a Hugo who "looked down on the world from the posture of a dispossessed monarch" nor could Flaubert have been Sartre's "poète maudit" for he was too willing to laugh at the spectacle of the world (32–33). So although he experimented with what Culler refers to as "derivative Romantic forms" (36) and faced what Geoffrey Hartman calls the "basic problem of Romantic literature: whether the mind can find an unselfconscious medium for itself" (69), these Romantic endeavors are dismissed in light of Flaubert's modern sense of the ironic vulnerability of self-display. Indeed, according to Culler, capturing the individuality of artistic vision in a form that transcends both the irony of the solipsistic and the vulnerability of the subjective is impossible or at least impossible to gauge, unless one interprets it in a peculiarly Hegelian way as "the state of a spirit without a self to be true to" (69).

Certainly the question of that "self to be true to" has already proven to be highly problematic in Flaubert's work unless one resorts to the biology of the "family idiot" or to the psychology of the psychopath/epileptic.[8] However, I am far less interested in discussing the problematic question of personality than in pointing out that Culler's description of this unattainable Romantic ideal uses terms that carve out a place for Flaubert's Saint Antoine in the "history" of Virtual Theater. Indeed, Culler continues his description of that "spirit without a self to be true to" in the following terms:

> This would be not precisely the condition of Rameau's nephew, whom Hegel cites as a case of freedom in and through alienation, but of a dialectical successor who can mimic without playing the buffoon, who is not himself present in every objectification, and who therefore is defined only as an absence which lies behind the forms that are presented. . . . a consciousness which does not define itself by taking a position but tries to receive everything into itself by, as he [Flaubert] says, describing it. (69)

Ironically, the dimensions of this impossible Romantic project provide a perfect description of *La Tentation*. It is clearly a dialectical successor to *Le Neveu de Rameau* and its staging of the drama of subjectivity does rely upon the point of view of a subject who cannot be located. Perhaps more important, the Romantic ideal of objectivizing subjectivity by making the world a corollary to its subject is quite openly exploited by the theatrical framework of *La Tentation*. Therefore, Culler's dismissal of this project in favor of the more mature ideals of Realism—"far better for Flaubert to take as his subject a country doctor and his adulterous wife or two aging autodidacts" (74)—becomes noticeably ironic. Indeed, the questionable tendency to describe Flaubert's maturation as a movement away from efforts to find a setting for philosophical concerns in *Smarh* for example, or *Rêve d'enfer*, and toward the Realist endeavors of later novels has been noted by Michal Peled Ginsberg (4–5) and by Leyla Perrone-Moisés.[9] However, this tendency becomes particularly spurious in light of the lifelong rewritings of *La Tentation de Saint Antoine* that follow and complement each of Flaubert's "more mature" endeavors, making his Realism into part of that Romantic struggle and not the opposite.[10]

The strange, formal contours of *La Tentation* as well as Flaubert's constant return to it may have something to do with its author's appreciation of his own era as a period of transition. In 1850, Flaubert wrote:

> Nous sommes venus, nous autres, ou trop tôt ou trop tard. Nous aurons fait ce qu'il y a de plus difficile et de moins glorieux: la transition. Pour établir quelque chose de durable, il faut une base fixe; l'avenir nous tourmente et le passé nous retient. Voilà pourquoi le présent nous échappe. (C, 2:34)[11]

Flaubert's notion of transition is striking in part because, in retrospect, it offers quite an apt commentary on the literary history of the nineteenth century. It is true that the first half of the century in particular is characterized by a dynamic upheaval in genres and disciplines that can be understood, in light of the Romantic theory I have been promulgating, as the symptom of a crisis in the history of subjectivity. In this context, Flaubert's evocation of the lack of any fixed or durable base, of an ephemeral present, which leaves him suspended between an uncertain future and a tenacious past, underscores his philosophical, rather than political, obsession with transition. It suggests a concern with the tenuous relationship that one entertains with one's field of reality and an uncertainty regarding the role of art or representation in this constantly shifting and elusive interaction. Insofar as Flaubert's notion of transition can be thus primarily understood as a description of the nature of human subjectivity, *La Tentation* can be seen as the representation of this transit.

Certainly in terms of Flaubert's own maturation, *La Tentation* may suppose a transition away from the poetic transcription of a personal philosophy toward the staging of the dynamics of any philosophical inquiry. Many have noted that the author's early "philosophical years," greatly influenced by Spinoza, have been marked or contaminated by readings of Kant and Hegel and by an avid interest in scientific, psychological studies.[12] Though I am not interested in discussing this contamination in terms of stylistic changes from version to version, these kinds of studies do suggest a transformation of Flaubert's own philosophical concerns into a more impersonal, more theatrical representation of universal doubt.[13] In the final *Tentation* we are exposed to many divergent philosophical points of view, but all of them come, ultimately, to resemble each other. The respective proofs and documents of each philosophical system expose themselves as fictions in what Laurence Porter has referred to as the inevitable relativity of all religious beliefs (Porter, 158). Indeed, the dramatic format of *La Tentation* keeps us from assigning any one opinion to the author. As Flaubert himself noted, "La forme dramatique a cela de bon, elle annule l'auteur" (C, 2:181–82; "That's what's good about dramatic form, it invalidates the author").

La Tentation best illustrates Flaubert's philosophical transition, however, by situating its events in fourth-century Alexandria—a period of transition between paganism and the birth of Christianity—and by making these events into the hallucinatory revivals of Antoine's own memories. Indeed, the only real character in the play is the saint whose quest for truth ultimately brings to life the entire history of humanity. On the private stage of his own imagination, Antoine witnesses the earliest burgeoning of Eastern mythologies, the troubled birth of Western metaphysics, and the origins of life as they are defined by modern science. Yet, the fact that each of these explanations for the origins of life both repeats and replaces one that has come before proves that although the logic of the *Tentation* is one of philosophical probing and historical evolution, this theoretically linear progression is doomed to a structure of epistemological revolution. For each stage in the saint's mental recapitulation of the history of humanity's development is presented not only as an elaborate fiction designed to satisfy humankind's basic desire to believe but also as a product imaginatively synthesized out of Antoine's memories and his insatiable desire to know. Moreover, as we move forward in the book, Antoine delves backward into his memories, making the *Tentation* into a dynamic symphony of themes and variations built entirely upon the very small amount of material Antoine recalls in his opening monologue. In this way, the play is indeed a successor to Diderot's *Neveu* in which a series of opening themes formed the basic skeletal structure of the dialogic fugue to come. In *La Tentation*, a similar opening monologue produces endless waves of philosophical variations in what can only be called a textual symphony. As a result, Antoine becomes a very literal representation of humanity's suspension between a tenacious past and an uncertain future.

Antoine's opening monologue is an addition to the final version that constitutes itself as a microcosm of the entire play. It begins at the end of the day with Antoine's "Encore un jour! un jour de passé!"—a sigh that suggests not only the boring monotony of every passing day but also the inescapable circularity or renewability of both Antoine's hallucinations and of the play itself.[14] For as the book ends, the sun comes up and Antoine resumes his prayers, having learned, one can infer, nothing from the events of the night and having in no way altered his monotonous existence. In fact, Flaubert uses what Proust referred to as his "éternel imparfait" ("the eternal imperfect")[15] to evoke the inevitable repetitiveness of Antoine's life: "Autrefois . . . je commençais mes oraisons; puis je descendais vers le fleuve . . . je remontais par le sentier . . . je m'amusais . . . je prenais . . . je sentais comme une fontaine de miséricorde qui s'épanchait du haut du ciel dans mon coeur. Elle est tarie, maintenant. Pourquoi?" (*Tentation*, 2).[16] It is this repetitiveness which plants, each night, the seeds of doubt, for this first questioning of his unchanging existence initiates a philosophical inquiry which will push Antoine further back into his memories and ultimately further away from both himself and his sense of reality.

A second set of memories, embedded more deeply in his mind, allows Antoine to enumerate his various past identities always in search of the answer to that question, "Why?" This second set of memories is touched off by the only decisively finished action in the text: "Tous me blâmaient lorsque j'ai quitté la maison. Ma mère s'affaissa mourante . . ." (2–3; "They all blamed me when I left home. My mother collapsed, dying . . ." [Mrosovsky, 62]). His mother's death is left suspended but the act of leaving is a fact. This is important because as Antoine enumerates his various past existences and identities, it becomes clear that the only thing they have in common is the fact of leaving, each departure cemented in a *passé composé*. First he chose a Pharaoh's tomb, but the paintings on the wall began to live and speak so, "j'ai fui jusqu'au bord de la mer Rouge dans une citadelle en ruines" (3; "I fled to a ruined citadel on the edge of the Red Sea" [ibid.]). But among the ruins Antoine was assailed by scorpions and eagles' wings and horrible demons. "Alors, j'ai voulu m'instruire près du bon vieillard Didyme" (3; "I then decided to study under good old Didymus" [Mrosovsky, 63]), but there he found heretics and fighting in the streets and a barrage of discourses by those hoping to convert. Thus, "Je me suis réfugié à Colzim" (4; "I took refuge at Colzim"). In Colzim, though he gained disciples, he became afraid. People were torturing confessors and "la soif du martyre m'entraîna dans Alexandrie" (4; "a thirst for martyrdom attracted me to Alexandria" [ibid.]), where he encountered, among others, his favorite disciple, Hilarion. In this conglomeration of past existences, we see Antoine's repeated attempt to flee the ephemeral contingencies of identity in a continual self-abnegating search for that nonidentity that the martyr's life promises. But each set of contingencies is really only an imaginary obstacle—paintings coming to life, horrible demons, fear—ultimately no different from that original "Why?" insofar as they are merely functions of his own mind. Therefore, no matter how hard Antoine tries to become a blank page of nonidentity, all his past experiences remain inescapable: "Engourdies ou furieuses, elles demeurent dans ma conscience. Je les écrase, elles renaissent, m'étouffent . . ." (48–49; "Sleeping or rampaging they persist in my consciousness. I stamp them out, they reappear, smother me . . ." [Mrosovsky, 99]).

Flaubert insists upon the inescapable nature of these past experiences by turning each successive chapter in *La Tentation* into an aggrandized representation of each of these places. Each personage or experience barely mentioned in the monologue reappears in infinitely multiplied and transformed visions. As I suggested earlier—and I shall return to the formal dimensions of this question again—the progression is nothing but a symphonic working back into these memories Antoine so hoped to escape.[17] In Chapter II of *La Tentation* those tortured confessors appear; Chapter III brings Hilarion; Chapter IV is made up of discourses designed to convert the saint, the ruins come back as do the Christian heretics; the paintings on the walls of the Pharaoh's tomb reappear in Chapter V; the Devil creates the shape of Chapter VI but he is really only an image of Hilarion transfigured; Didymus comes back as the source of knowledge for Chapter VII, and at the very end of the book, Antoine's mother reappears reclothed in the image of death. Though a cursory review of *La Tentation*, it is clear that each of Antoine's initial memories becomes more elaborate and confused in order to demonstrate the way in which Antoine's mind not only obliterates both the origins and the temporalness of anything present in it but uses those originally subjective impressions to move further and further away from reality, deeper and deeper into precisely those thoughts the saint would like to forget.

Due to this fertile productivity of Antoine's mind, his continual search for nonidentity makes him, at the same time, all identities. That is, his conscious desire to liberate himself from his own individuality allows him to identify himself with all possible imaginary self-representations. Though this tendency is repeatedly illustrated throughout the play, it occurs for the first time in this same opening monologue as a paradigm for Antoine's capacity to propose new identities to inhabit. Out of the description of his actual past, Antoine begins to recreate a fantasmatic one: "Mais j'aurais mieux servi mes frères en étant tout simplement un prêtre. . . . D'ailleurs, les laïques ne sont pas tous damnés, et il ne tenait qu'à moi d'être . . . par exemple . . . grammarien, philosophe. . . . Mais il y a trop d'orgeuil à ces triomphes! Soldat valait mieux. J'étais robuste et hardi . . ." (6).[18] In this list of imaginary identities, the use of the past conditional suggests a conscious thought process something like, "If I had not chosen to be a nonidentity, I could have been anything"; but it suggests an unconscious thought process something more like, "I want to be a non-identity so I can enjoy the pleasure of imaginary identifications." That is, the conditional off-screen "if" supposed by Antoine's list of possible past lives reveals the work of desire which turns his memories into a potentially infinite collection of hallucinatory self-representations. Later, in fact, the oft-cited words of Hilarion will accuse him of precisely this kind of sinful, if imaginary, pleasure: "Hypocrite qui s'enfonce dans la solitude pour se livrer mieux au débordement de ses convoitises! Tu te prives de viandes, de vin, d'étuves, d'es-claves et d'honneurs; mais comme tu laisses ton imagination t'offrir des banquets, des parfums, des femmes nues et des foules applaudissantes! Ta chasteté n'est qu'une corruption plus subtile" (42).[19]

Logically, the work of desire that alters Antoine's conscious identity also always alters his conscious perceptions. That is, Antoine absorbs the realities around him only to recreate mental equivalents. Out of a red sky, the narrator tells us, "tout à coup, passent des oiseaux formant un bataillon trian-gulaire pareil à un morceau de métal, et dont les bords seuls frémissent. Antoine les regarde" (5; "suddenly a battalion of birds is seen passing in triangular formation, like a slice of metal quivering at the edges only. Anthony watches them" [Mrosovsky, 64]). This metaphoric altering of the flight of birds (into a metallic, triangular battalion) is contagious, for interrupting his monologue of memories, Antoine begins to desire:

Ah! que je voudrais les suivre!

Combien de fois, aussi, n'ai-je pas contemplé avec envie les longs bateaux, dont les voiles ressemblent à des ailes et surtout quand ils emmenaient au loin ceux que j'avais reçus chez moi! . . . D'où vient mon obstination à continuer une vie pareille? (5–6)[20]

In this passage, the work of desire is quite obvious: wings suggest sails and flight suggests escape, echoing the already obsessive leitmotif of the monologue. The way in which the real image of wings combines with the metaphoric wings of sailboats implies a process similar to what Freud calls the dream work: perceptions and imagination become confused only to allow the expression of an unconscious wish. In this case, it is Antoine's desire to flee which, once expressed, is immediately displaced onto a less painful memory of being left.[21] The desire is thus expressed outside (or to the side) of its original setting and source which was related to leaving (or losing) his mother. More important, the all too easy sliding of real images into imaginary ones implies that it is impossible for any perception to avoid alteration by the inner life of the mind. Looking outward, Antoine really only sees himself in another place.

Another example comes up a few lines later when Antoine turns to the scriptures in an effort to quench the thirst of his desire to flee. Once again, however, perceptions become confused with imagination and re-reading results in re-writing. As Antoine reads the saints' lives, choosing passages by chance, each one he turns to offers him, not by chance, the opposite of what he consciously seeks but the perfect image of what he unconsciously seeks. For each one evokes one of those seven deadly pleasures Antoine has rejected by choosing his ascetic lifestyle. In a passage on Peter, killing and eating suggests gluttony (8); the Jews slaughtering their enemies seems to condone vengeance; Nebuchadnezzar exalts pride (9); Hezekiah justifies the accumulation of riches; and the Queen of Sheba proposes the temptation of enigmas (9–10). Brilliantly staged in the text itself, the silent dialogue between Antoine and the reproduced passages of the scriptures shows us not the meaning or usefulness of reading the saints' lives but the way in which reading calls upon unconscious associations. For Antoine essentially re-writes the scriptures, transforming and disfiguring the images he reads in the same way he reinterpreted the birds or his own past. In this case, it is because these pleasures are forbidden that they become desirable, and it is because any real satisfactions are impossible that Antoine can create imaginary ones.[22] Each passage describes a desire that echoes one of the past lives Antoine never lived: grammarian, philosopher, soldier, toll-gatherer; and each one will in turn result in imaginary wish-fulfillments that come to life before Antoine's very eyes. It is interesting to note in this context that Flaubert, beginning to conceive of his final *Tentation*, wrote in a notebook of 1863: "Différencier autant que possible les Entrées dans le commencement faire que St. Antoine [penche] [pense] les péchés plutôt qu'il y ne les voit—ou mieux avant de les voir" (quoted by Kovács, 91).[23] Certainly the episode in Bible study has this effect, for not only do the sins appear as projections of Antoine's previous thoughts, but the entire play can now take place on the imaginary stage of Antoine's mind where the same old satisfactions will continue to circulate in constantly renewed scenarios.

Logically, then, in order to turn Antoine's sinful thoughts into a personal imaginary drama, these inner representations of sinful pleasures are subsequently projected before the saint, materializing the inner life of his mind into voices at the end of the monologue (14–15), into momentary wish-fulfillments in Chapter II, and then into characters throughout the rest of the text. Though they are the purely fictive products of his own inner drama, these voices and characters come to share, as Michel Foucault has demonstrated, the same degree of stage reality as the saint himself ("La Bibliothèque fantastique," 18–19). This means that the Freudian analogy does not stop with the likening of mental productivity to the laws of the dream work. Flaubert's project also anticipates what we can identify as the structure and functioning of the fantasm in a pattern of regression. In *La Tentation*, any perception always combines with memories and the unconscious desire to flee in order to replace the reality of Antoine's boring existence with visual representations emanating from the unconscious which appear to the subject to be real.[24]

This may be why Antoine becomes, at the end of the opening monologue, a very passive actor but a very active spectator. The regressive pattern requires sleep or at least a state of immobility in which a subject's conscious awareness is cut off from the world around him so as to promote the productivity of inner or virtual representations.[25] Of Antoine we read:

> Malgré le vacarme de sa tête, il perçoit un silence énorme qui le sépare du monde. Il tâche de parler; impossible! C'est comme si le lien général de son être se dissolvait; et, ne résistant plus, Antoine tombe sur la natte. (15)[26]

Here, Antoine, the only actor on stage, is clearly also a spectator. Outside of the turmoil of noise and images in his head, "le vacarme," he perceives, paradoxically, an enormous silence. He is literally in two places at once. His physical being is separate from the world both of reality and of his own mental hallucinations, and at the same time, that same being is as if dissolved in them. In this way, Antoine offers an ideal image of both Freud's dreamer and of Flaubert in transition between the tenacious past of memories and the hallucinatory productivity of desire's tendency to create imaginary, uncertain futures.

As this association of Antoine and Flaubert implies, Antoine's situation is a perfect description of Flaubert's notion of the pleasure of writing:

> Voilà pourquoi j'aime l'Art. C'est que là, au moins, tout est liberté dans ce monde des fictions. On y assouvit tout, on y fait tout, on est à la fois son roi et son peuple, actif et passif, victime et prêtre. Pas de limites; l'humanité est pour vous un pantin à grelots que l'on fait sonner au bout de sa phrase comme un bateleur au bout de son pied (je me suis souvent, ainsi, bien vengé de l'existence; je me suis repassé un tas de douceurs avec ma plume; je me suis

donné des femmes, de l'argent, des voyages), comme l'âme cour-
bée se déploie dans cet azur qui ne s'arrête qu'aux frontières du
Vrai.[27]

In this passage, the pleasure of art is related, by Flaubert,
to the possibility writing affords of forsaking reality in favor
of the temptations of imaginary satisfactions and of finding
oneself in two places at once. There may also be an echo of
Baudelaire's idea that the imagination is evil because it is mor-
ally ambiguous allowing one to be both the king and the
people, both victim and priest.[28] In any case, like Antoine
whose nonidentity allowed all identities and whose total immobility at the end of Chapter I allows the imaginary satisfactions of women, money, and travels, Flaubert, writing, prefers
art's world of fictions to the realities of existence. He, like the
saint, is at once active, creating fictions which like puppets
can be manipulated by their strings, and passive in that he
offers these imaginary satisfactions to himself. His insistent
use of reflexive verbs is exemplary of the way in which Flaubert is both subject and object, mobile and immobile, actor in
and spectator to his own fantasies. In this light, Antoine's
character looks very much like that of the writer's insofar as
he is caught in the act of conceiving and projecting imaginary
models. That is, Antoine is the kind of writer described by
Diderot's theatrical theory, one whose writing involves the
preliminary stage of becoming an imaginary spectator and
actor.

Flaubert's description of the pleasure of writing may explain why his final version of *La Tentation* is designed to be
an imaginary theater. Conceiving of writing as the work of
imaginary spectators and actors puts the question of representation into the realm of theater. It implies that outside of an
age-old concept of theatrical representation as a real performance in an actual theater, there exists an earlier or primary
representation which may be understood as a virtual performance taking place in the mind itself. Given that Flaubert
himself describes this kind of virtual performance as a theatrical pleasure, the pleasure of watching oneself inhabit limit-

less imaginary roles, we are justified in examining this pleasure from the point of view of psychoanalysis. Indeed, in
Freudian thought pleasure is related to wish-fulfillment in
dreams, that fantasmatic organization of an imaginary scene
in which desire reenacts a memory of past satisfaction.[29] The
pleasure of these scenes is in turn associated with the theatrical metaphor for unconscious functioning insofar as it
involves the elaboration of a dramatized visual scenario in
which the subject is always present both as an observer and
as a participant (Laplanche and Pontalis, *Vocabulaire*, 156).
This subject is at once an imaginary spectator who watches a
scene of satisfaction and an imaginary actor who enacts the
scene of satisfaction but who, in so doing, disrupts the unity
of his or her wakeful, conscious identity. Referring in particular to Freud's "A Child Is Being Beaten," Laplanche and
Pontalis emphasize Freud's notion that such fantasy scenes of
satisfaction do not represent an object of desire but a sequence
in which the subject himself may inhabit many possible roles
(156), a structure in which the subject moves between various
identifications. Therefore, both Flaubert's and Freud's pleasures are based on a mental liberating of self-representations
that is only possible because of a certain physical immobility
or removal from the real dangers of existence. In fact, there is
a striking resemblance between the active/passive, mobile/
immobile nature of Flaubert's writer and what Freud and
more recent scholars understand to be the nature of the
dreamer.

In *The Interpretation of Dreams*, fantasy scenes are associated by Freud with both the unconscious phenomenon
of dreaming and the conscious phenomenon of daydreaming (Laplanche and Pontalis, *Vocabulaire*, 153–54). Though
this indistinction has been problematic for some, notably
Laplanche and Pontalis themselves,[30] it has been very useful
for those theorists who are interested in articulating a metapsychology of the spectator at the theater. For like the daydreamer but unlike the dreamer, the spectator is an intermittently conscious and unconscious subject who is positioned
both inside and outside the scenes of his or her fantasies.

Theories relating the spectator to the daydreamer thus help to articulate Flaubert's apparent preoccupation with the interaction of conscious and unconscious thought processes.

In "The Fiction Film and its Spectator," Christian Metz distinguishes among dream scenes, fantasy scenes, and filmic or theatrical scenes, while at the same time outlining their points of intersection. These scenes are primarily distinguished by the nature of their images—mental or real—and by the degree of belief they engender, that is to say, by the relative involvement they require on the part of the subject. Following Freud's dream theory, Metz argues that in dream scenes a dreamer does not generally know he or she is dreaming and is therefore subject to total belief in the mental images furnished by the dream. The daydreamer or spectator, on the contrary, is consciously aware of either fantasizing or being at the theater and is therefore subject to only partial belief in the images before his or her eyes.[31] Though the analogy is not perfect in that daydreamers face mental perceptions in which they see themselves acting out desires and film spectators face real perceptions in which they see others acting, the daydreamers' and film audience's situations are similar in that they are both caught in a state of intermediate wakefulness and reduced motor activity which can promote a subtle overlapping of mental and real perceptions. For just as the mental images of a fantasy may be influenced by real perceptions, the real images of a film may be influenced by mental perceptions that momentarily interrupt the spectator's conscious attention to the film. In this way, the situation of the spectator may fleetingly approach that of the daydreamer in that the spectator may find himself or herself both inside and out of a scene built on both real and purely mental perceptions which he or she partially believes.[32]

This notion of belief in dreams or fantasms has been contested by Mikkel Borch-Jacobsen who argues that there is no subject of the unconscious who believes or not, belief being a conscious activity.[33] He stresses that dreams are less a question of belief than of a subject's capacity to identify with a dream agent or protagonist in the dream. As he puts it, "L'essentiel est plutôt qu'à chaque fois le moi mêle ses traits avec ceux d'un étranger, et qu'en cette indistinction du *je* et du *il* réside la condition nécessaire de toute *Wunscherfüllung*" (31; "The essential thing is rather that each time [he dreams], the ego blends its character traits with those of a stranger, and that it is in this indistinction of the *I* and the *he* that the necessary condition of every wish-fulfillment resides"). In other words, for Borch-Jacobsen, who would do away with the specular nature of the theatrical metaphor, the pleasure of dreaming is based on an identification with imaginary roles and a concomitant disruption of any unified subject rather than in the viewing of a scene of satisfaction (56). It is not an object of desire that satisfies but the subject's identification with another subject (50), the possibility of an exchange of an "I" for a "he" (or a "she"). We could say, then, that those brief interruptions of the spectator's conscious attention to which Metz refers may be precisely those moments during which Borch-Jacobsen's pleasurable indistinction of the "I" and the "she" or "he" is enacted. Metz's fleeting fusions of mental and real perceptions may be thus better understood as partial identifications.

It is these partial identifications which seem to explain the peculiar behavior of Flaubert's saint. For Antoine is clearly caught in an intermediate position between his conscious attention to the ascetic reality of his existence and his unconscious attention to those outright hallucinations (those purely mental perceptions that actually replace and transform reality) that will shape the contours of the remainder of the book. Indeed, the entire book is marked by Antoine's oscillation between his hallucinations and his conscious awareness of the actual situation. It is not surprising that this vacillation is introduced by a wakeful conscious fantasy in which Antoine first exhibits his capacity to partially believe in the new roles he invents for himself to play.

The second chapter opens with the following oft-cited dream sequence:

Antoine, les yeux toujours fermés, jouit de son inaction; et il étale ses membres sur la natte.

Elle lui semble douce, de plus en plus, si bien qu'elle se rembourre, elle se hausse, elle devient un lit, le lit une chaloupe, de l'eau clapote contre ses flancs.

A droite et à gauche, s'élèvent deux langues de terre noire que dominent des champs cultivés, avec un sycomore de place en place. Un bruit de grelots, de tambours et de chanteurs retentit au loin. Ce sont des gens qui s'en vont à Canope dormir sur le temple de Sérapis pour avoir des songes. Antoine sait cela; et il glisse, poussé par le vent, entre les deux berges du canal. . . . Il est étendu au fond de la barque; un aviron, à l'arrière, traine dans l'eau. . . . Le murmure des petites vagues diminue. Un assoupissement le prend. Il songe qu'il est un solitaire d'Egypte.

Alors il se relève en sursaut.

Ai-je rêvé? . . . **c'était si net que j'en doute. La langue me brûle! J'ai soif!** (16) [34]

Antoine's reaction following his daydream shows us his confusion as to what is real and what imaginary and, therefore, his partial belief in the images he has just seen. It also shows us that his thirst or lack of water has resulted in a water fantasy. The relation between the water fantasy and his thirst supposes the interruption of mental images by real perceptions but also demonstrates the way in which dreams can be built on the residue of daytime thoughts. In both cases, Antoine's intermittently conscious and unconscious behavior is underscored.

Though the water fantasy may represent an unconscious satisfaction for Antoine's thirst, it also proposes a momentary fantasy satisfaction for his more deeply embedded desire to flee. For not only do the instantaneous metamorphoses of the mat offer Antoine a literal mental voyage as if charged by the energy of this same desire to flee, but he has projected himself into another place. This "solitaire d'Egypte" is an image of himself that Antoine perceives outside of himself as if on an "other stage". That is, he has not necessarily viewed a scene of satisfaction in which he would either drink or leave.

Rather, he enacts Borch-Jacobsen's indistinction of an "I" and a "he": the characteristics of his own ego are indeterminately mixed with those of the represented others. His own situation in which the pleasure of inactivity results in dreaming is reproduced before him in the image of others departing to sleep and to dream.

At the same time that Antoine identifies with those who are going to Canopus in order to sleep and dream, however, he also identifies with the lives of others in a condensed version of two separate memories. Indeed, Flaubert has quite carefully prepared this sexualized reenactment of a memory of past satisfactions by condensing in this scene two memories of other lives with which Antoine now identifies. First, Antoine appears in this scene to be embarking in a boat similar to the one that once carried away those friends whose company he now regrets. Second, these travelers also recall Antoine's memory of the merchants in Alexandria who, "naviguent les jours de fête sur la rivière Canope, et boivent du vin dans des calices de lotus, au bruit des tambourins qui font trembler les tavernes le long du bord!" (6–7; "sail on feast-days down the Canopic river, and drink wine from lotus chalices to the sound of tambourines that force the taverns along the banks to tremble!"). Though I shall have more to say about Flaubert's own "dream work" later, it is clear from this dream fantasy that whereas earlier Antoine showed us his tendency to displace memory traces from more to less painful images, in this scene, he shows us his mind's capacity to condense these memories into a single fantasy.

The striking thing about Antoine's pleasure, then, is that it seems to be a result of mobilizing his own identity. That is, this first hint of the slippery nature of Antoine's identity makes us attentive to the way in which it foreshadows all the identities Antoine will yet inhabit. For he will make many imaginary voyages outside of himself, each propelled by the mobilizing energy of desire. The next time Antoine desires to flee, expressing his exasperation with "Il y a trop longtemps que je me contiens!" (20–21; "I've been containing myself much too long!"), we read, "Il se croit à Alexandrie sur le Paneum" (21; "He believes he is in Alexandria on the Panium"). There, surrounded by a group of wild heretics performing violent acts, Antoine's belief in the scene again causes a split into the roles of spectator and actor: "Antoine retrouve tous ses ennemies l'un après l'autre. Il en reconnaît qu'il avait oubliés; avant de les tuer, il les outrage. Il éventre, égorge, assomme, traine les vieillards par la barbe, écrase les enfants, frappe les blessés" (23).[35] Immobile before this image of himself acting out a fantasy, it is clear that he first scrutinizes—"il retrouve, reconnaît" ("he finds them, recognizes them")—then identifies with the wild crowd around him, reliving a past satisfaction described in the passage on the Jews. After this, Antoine desires to contest the powers of the hated Council of Nicaea and we read, "Le voilà devenu un des grands de la Cour, confident de l'Empéreur, premier ministre!" (26; "Here he has become one of the magnates of the Court, the Emperor's confidant, the prime minister!"). Then, meeting the admirable, if frightening, Nebuchadnezzar, "Antoine lit sur son front toutes ses pensées. Elles le pénètrent et il devient Nebuchodonosor" (27; "Anthony reads all his thoughts on his brow. They penetrate him and he becomes Nebuchadnezzar"). In short, each time Antoine desires, he literally becomes what he wants to be and each time he is left with growing doubts about who he really is both inside his fantasy scenes—"Il souhaite l'occasion de répandre sa vie pour le Sauveur, ne sachant pas s'il n'est point lui-même un de ses martyrs" (78)—and outside of them: "Je deviens fou. Du calme! où étais-je? qu'y avait-il? (88).[36] In other words, Antoine never ceases to act out an indistinction between his I and a whole series of imaginary he's.

Flaubert underscores the fact that this pleasurable mobility of identity is only a fantasy satisfaction by showing us that desire is, by definition, always insatiable and therefore always proposing renewed and renewable satisfactions. For Antoine's only real desire as expressed in the monologue and restated throughout, is to escape himself. The pleasure of his many identities derives thus from imaginary self-destructions acted out in those indistinctions of subject and object. The content of each new identity is thus subordinate to the circular structure of fantasy itself by which Antoine continues to act out his singular wish. This is why, at the very end of the book, Antoine's ultimate, shocking desire to "penetrate every atom" and to "be matter" (200—201) is really no different from the original. Like Flaubert's desire to be everywhere and nowhere in his writing, Antoine's desire is to be no one and thus everyone. But even in the end, fantasy self-annihilation is only a tentative escape. For, at the end, Antoine will merely start over again, as always.

FLAUBERT'S evocation of the imaginary pleasure of the daydreamer is not, however, exhausted in a discussion of Antoine, the actor. Indeed, Antoine's mental activities are doubled on the outside of this imaginary mental stage by the work of the Flaubertian narrator. That is, *La Tentation* is not an actual play but a virtual play for it does not relegate the playwright's voice to an off-stage or hidden position. On the contrary, the textual voice responsible for setting scenes and describing characters also becomes an integral part of the performance in a unique mixture of novelistic (or narrative) and theatrical (or dramatic) techniques.

When the play opens, the setting is described by what initially appears to be a playwright merely addressing a prospective director. One cannot say, however, that the stage is set. Rather it is set in motion as simple stage indications give way to the presence of a narrator attempting to describe to the reader the subtle metamorphoses already taking place before Antoine begins to speak or think. As the opening to *La Tentation* is representative of the problematic nature of narrative voice throughout, it is worth citing at length:

> C'est la Thébaïde, au haut d'une montagne, sur une plate-forme arrondie en demi-lune, et qu'enferment de grosses pierres.

La cabane de l'ermite occupe le fond. Elle est faite de boue et de roseaux, à toit plat, sans porte. On distingue dans l'intérieur une cruche avec du pain noir; au milieu, sur une stèle de bois, un gros livre; . . .
   A dix pas de la cabane, il y a une longue croix plantée dans le sol; et à l'autre bout de la plate-forme, . . . le Nil semble faire un lac au bas de la falaise.
   La vue est bornée à droite et à gauche par l'enceinte des roches. Mais du côté du désert, comme des plages qui se succéderaient, d'immenses ondulations parallèles d'un blond cendré s'étirent les unes derrière les autres, en montant toujours. . . . En face, le soleil s'abaisse. Le ciel, dans le nord, est d'une teinte gris perle, tandis qu'au zénith des nuages de pourpre, disposés comme les flocons d'une crinière gigantesque, s'allongent sur la voûte bleue. Ces rais de flamme se rembrunissent, les parties d'azur prennent une pâleur nacrée; . . . tout paraît dur comme du bronze; et dans l'espace flotte une poudre d'or tellement menue qu'elle se confond avec la vibration de la lumière.

SAINT ANTOINE
qui a une longue barbe, de longs cheveux, et une tunique de peau de chèvre, est assis, jambes croisées, en train de faire des nattes. Dès que le soleil disparaît, il pousse un grand soupir, et regardant l'horizon:

Encore un jour! un jour de passé! $(1-2)$[37]

This brilliant opening passage is full of writing strategies designed to mobilize the setting before any action takes place. Yet, there is an odd combination of stabilizing and mobilizing elements, an insistence upon anchoring the setting in the presence of reality so as to emphasize the process of reality's destabilization. Stabilizing elements are those one might find in the text of any play. First, the playwright's position is distinctly separated from the setting of the play through the typographical differentiation of boldface, capitalization, and varying type size. Second, Antoine, his props, and the lighting effects are all described in the present tense of any stage indication addressing a director or an actor. However, the distinct boundary drawn between the writer and his play is dislodged by narrative elements that situate the stage setting within a novel and change the playwright into a narrator—"But out in the desert, like beaches that *would unfold*, immense parallel ash-blond undulations stretch out one after the other, gradually rising" (my emphasis). Not only is there no need for the conditional verb in scenic indications but the metaphoric movement of the continually mounting sand dunes is a purely narrative technique.

This narrator, however, does not seem to be in control of his descriptions. His remarks contain a sense of uncertainty and discovery which make him appear to be a spectator: *one* distinguishes a pitcher and a loaf of black bread; the Nile *seems to* form a lake; and the clouds are disposed in the sky *like* tufts of a giant mane. Instead of an omniscient narrator—I see it therefore it is true—this one gives only the subjective impressions of a spectator: I see it therefore it may not be true. In addition, as El Nouty argues, the present tense of the introductory "C'est" ("It is") turns a novelistic description—*C'était* ("It was")—into an instance of "verbal scenography" (250). For it is as if the vision of the Thebaid is called into being by someone already looking. In this way, the playwright's distance from his play is undermined by the narrative inclusion of metaphors and the narrator's distance from his novel is undermined by the subjective gaze of a spectator whose descriptions are either imprecise or entirely imaginary.

This paradoxical coexistence of novelistic and theatrical elements works on one hand to imply a metapsychology of a spectator at the theater: any spectator, the play suggests, will always establish an affective relation to the stage, insuring that the spectator's gaze will always effect a subjective confusion of real and imagined perceptions. On the other hand, it also implies the impossibility of constituting the supposedly objective narrator of Realist fiction for it shows that any observer of nature will also always establish a similar affective relation. Vision marks both the guarantee and the complete undermining of Realism. Like the natural amphitheater of the

Thebaid mountains, nature, when observed, is always like a theater not because humans are players but because they are first and foremost spectators. Likewise, a narrator, no matter how indifferent, will always be a spectator. Though this setting is natural and appears to be a presently existing phenomenon, its presence is as hallucinatory as the images of a dream because one constitutes one's relationship to reality as an observer. To call the scene into being with that initial "C'est" is both to set the scene in reality and to deny its natural existence. As a result, one's sense of being conscious is no longer determined as a conflict between the self and the world but as Lacan proposes in his "Stade du miroir," a conflict between the self and the self as other.[38]

However, unlike any real spectator at the theater or any real observer of nature, this spectator cannot be located. Both the object of his scrutiny and he himself are moving. That is, we know that he is not positioned outside of what Stanislavski called the "fourth wall," since his field of vision encompasses an entire 360 degrees. Initially, the spectator looks into the hermit's cabin but the fact that his view is cut off to the right and the left supposes the position of an actor. In fact, the sands on the desert side are behind any theoretical spectators and are therefore seen from an actor's point of view. However, "en face," that is, facing these sands, the sun is going down, the rays are turning brownish, parts of the blue are becoming nacreous, and what appears to be as hard as bronze is actually a mass of tiny particles of floating space becoming confused with the vibrating light. Not only is this a lovely description of a setting sun and its natural movement, but the weighty materiality of all scenic elements disappears in the constantly changing lighting effects that some ubiquitous individual is presently experiencing. In a sense, then, even before Antoine begins to act, or, more precisely, to think and to hallucinate, someone else is already doing it. Amusingly, like the negative equivalent to an Aristotelian day, the sun is going down and at the end it will come up, inscribing the events of the play in a most classical unity of time but one that is slightly askew.

This is the mirror opposite or virtual image of a classical play. Flaubert's creation of dramatic movement is not, however, limited to the narrator's tendency to move on and off stage. Indeed, one of the crucial changes in the final version is that the narrating spectator is not only both inside and outside the imaginary stage but both inside and outside the confines of Antoine's mind. We have seen examples of this movement in the passage concerning the metaphoric altering of the flight of birds and in Antoine's daydream at the opening of the second chapter. In this opening monologue, the narrator's metaphoric approximations—"comme" or "comme si" ("as" or "as if")—attest to the presence of a speaking subject caught somewhere between the playwright's objectivized descriptions of characters and props, the spectator's subjective impressions of events on and off stage, and the narrator's rendering of Antoine's inner and outer perceptions. From a seemingly objective stance of a camera placed distinctly outside the stage of the play, the point of view moves onto the stage, and then in and out of Antoine's head, creating images that are as present and as real for the spectator as they may be for Antoine.[39] In this way, not only has the "I" of the off-stage playwright become a mobile eye, but it is capable, like Antoine, of shifting identities. The playwright is also a narrator, the narrator a spectator and the eye of the spectator is confused with that of the actor.

Much like the problems posed by Vigny's intentional mixing of direct and indirect discourses in *Daphné* (see chapter 1), Flaubert's use of free indirect discourse creates bivocal utterances that allow the speaking subject to take the positions of both a narrator and a character.[40] One might say that the free indirect discourse of *Madame Bovary* or of *L'Education sentimentale* is here formally rendered and problematized in a structural rather than linguistic demonstration of this phenomenon. For the voice of this playwright renders the thoughts of a narrator and those of the characters but it also emits the slippery, ubiquitous sounds of an unconscious thought process of its own. In her study of Flaubert's free indirect discourse, Ginsberg argues that the Flaubertian narrator can have a surrogate who either sees or acts but who cannot do both (70). But the narrator of *La Tentation*, like the one in Vigny's *Daphné*, is both active and passive even before finding himself replicated in the supposed surrogate, Antoine. That is, his activities as a spectator are already one kind of a surrogate operation for his role as narrator. This means that Antoine is not really a surrogate for the narrator but a mirror double who, like a real spectator, is active only because he is passive. As Mannoni might put it, "they *know full well* that they are only spectators *but even so* they enter the illusion."

It is not then surprising that the identity of the playwright/narrator/spectator resembles Antoine's fluid identity. Just as Antoine's dissolving subjectivity relied upon his forced immobility, the narrator's slippery ubiquity is also made possible by physical immobility, assured by those distinct textual boundaries set up and then obliterated between the outsides and insides of the Thebaid stage setting. Again, contrary to Ginsberg's notion that the use of free indirect discourse is only possible in a novelistic narration because it marks a "dissolution of the dramatic form" that separates characters and narrators (64), I am proposing that it is precisely the dramatic form's capacity to separate both narrators and characters from a field of reality that cannot be satisfying which promotes the either metaphoric or hallucinatory alteration of that reality. The "search for fusion" may well be a "fundamental feature of Flaubert's writing" (ibid.), but it is enacted in *La Tentation* only because characters and their spaces are decidedly distinct. The dramatic form serves the narrative goal, creating separate spaces across which (and because of which) spectators can fuse.

We can say, then, that there is a kind of proscenium mirror placed between Antoine and his narrator. Just like Antoine, the narrator is mentally active because he is also physically passive and just like Antoine, he cannot ever get outside of his own mental projections. Each is both a spectator and an actor because these activities, insofar as they are purely mental activities, are merely sides of the same coin. In both cases, the result is that theatrical pleasure of liberated self-representations because each subject is always doubled on an "other stage," because behind conscious thought or description, there always lies an "other subject." Every actor is also a spectator and every spectator an actor, because desire always theatricalizes both one's sense of reality and one's sense of self. Both Antoine and his narrator demonstrate the impossibility of remaining self-conscious since the work of desire always distorts their conscious thoughts and displaces their conscious identities. Neither ever escapes his own personal drama; they are separate but equal. In this light, it seems that the theater Flaubert sought to reproduce in a virtual play was indeed the theater of subjectivity itself in which the subject thinking can never be constituted as a concrete entity since he is always in transit between his work as a spectator which makes him an imaginary actor and his work as an actor which, like Diderot's actor, requires the input of an imaginary spectator.

THIS proscenium mirror placed between the outsides and insides of the stage makes *La Tentation* into a virtual play, a play or book about nothing but its own mechanics. This mirror catches whatever appears on either side of it in an endless cycle of reflection. This mirror means that just as Antoine can never get outside of his own mind, *La Tentation* can never get outside of its own elaborate structure. In fact, I propose that the larger structure of the play forces it to enclose itself into an image of the dynamic but inescapable prison that is Antoine's mind.

Several critics have noted that the construction of Antoine's new opening monologue creates a psychic reality for Antoine which transforms the cultural history of the world into Antoine's own personal story.[41] Though a reductive psychoanalytic reading searches, in this configuration, for the original "events" in the monologue that underlie all future hallucinations, thus psychoanalyzing Antoine and/or Flaubert, I am more interested in showing the strategies at work in *La Tentation* which invite us to discover the laws of psychic representability responsible for the dynamism of the inner workings of the mind, laws that illustrate a Flaubertian-style "dream work".

Therefore, although the opening monologue does serve as the source of all of Antoine's future hallucinations, what is of interest is not the way in which it provides a secret or hidden identity for Antoine but the structural patterns that arise from it to show us how his identity is continually mobilized. For just like Antoine, who appears to travel but never really escapes, the play also appears to progress but without ever really reaching outside of itself. Rather, it circles back incessantly to the original material of the monologue, creating a symphonic structure of theme and variations. As I have already suggested in the case of Diderot's *Neveu*, musical metaphors are the most appropriate way of accommodating the highly structured fluidity of a virtual play. In the case of *La Tentation*, they may also explain why, according to Flaubert, musicians rather than painters were attracted to it (*C*, 7:136).

Indeed, the episodes of *La Tentation* do not move forward but rather multiply indefinitely in a pattern of repetition and progression. This symphonic pattern clearly proceeds by way of metonymical or contiguous associations that are halted or repeated in a metaphoric circling back. This makes Flaubert's play into a remarkable anticipation of the laws of representability characteristic of Freud's dream work, for the play moves according to the syntactical laws and logic of displacement by association and condensation of disparate but similar images. It is the tension between these two structural forces that creates the dynamic universe of the book at the level of both its general structure and the form and content of its narrative techniques.

In terms of general structure, it is clear that although each new chapter appears to progress, each in fact consists of a working back into the events of the monologue. The second chapter of the book is nothing but a more visual, aggrandized repetition of each of Antoine's readings of passages from the saints' lives. In massive quantities, Antoine sees materializing before him food, gold and jewels, and opportunities to exalt and avenge himself (17–27). Then, at the end of the chapter, the Queen of Sheba arrives to tempt Antoine exactly as she had tempted Solomon and, in this way Antoine's thirst for knowledge is associated with his tendency to lust or desire. This means that Chapter II is a hallucinatory revival of each of Antoine's readings and that each one offers imaginary satisfactions that conform to Freud's description of regression: a shift from thoughts and words to visual representations produced in present-tense fantasy scenes to which belief is attached (*The Interpretation of Dreams*, 572–73). This visual representation of Antoine's inner perceptions then continues throughout the remainder of the play.

Chapter III introduces Hilarion, whom Antoine had remembered just before reading the saints' lives. In terms of the logic of conscious memory Antoine is thus moving backward, delving more deeply into his past. However, the third chapter associates itself to the second by way of a displacement forward from more to less painful representations of Antoine's secret desire to flee—from the erotic Queen of Sheba to the faithful disciple Hilarion. Nonetheless, just as she represents the temptation of knowledge or science through her posing of enigmas and asking of questions, Hilarion's role is similar. He tempts by asking and answering enigmatic questions about Antoine's belief system. This interrogation includes the nature of miracles, of scriptures, of God, and of dogma in general. But whereas the Queen's tempting is painful or uncomfortable because it is associated with lust, Hilarion's tempting represents the intellectual curiosity of a faithful disciple. Similarly, however, when Hilarion's negating of Antoine's dogma becomes insufferable—"Te tairas-tu vipère!" ("Will you be quiet, viper!")—these same issues are in turn displaced onto the discourses of heretics in Chapter IV, alternate systems of belief in Chapter V, and then the Devil's enigmatic solution for all doubts in Chapter VI. Though each of the chapters, beginning with Chapter IV, merely reproduces Antoine's past lives in reverse order, it is this displacement toward less and less emotionally charged personages—from characters Antoine actually knew toward mythological creatures and symbols—that creates a sense of progress in the book.

In other words, at the same time that personages displace, furnishing what appears to be new food for thought, their progress is punctuated by the circling back of condensed images. Hilarion, for example, can be seen as a repetition of Antoine's very first "Pourquoi?" thus becoming an aggrandized version of his initial philosophical inquiry. In the same way, each of the arguments Hilarion uses to counter Antoine's dogmatic beliefs comes to life in the following chapter as we witness a prodigious number of miracles, scriptures, and dogmas, each as (il)logical as the next. Not only were the discourses of these heretical alternatives already mentioned in the monologue (4) but each represents one of those seven deadly sins Antoine has already thought while reading the saints' lives. Some believe in sloth, others, gluttony or fornication. Similarly, the Eastern or pagan Gods in Chapter V are merely remembrances of the drawings on the walls of Héliopolis's tomb. In the monologue, Antoine had noted that he left that tomb because the drawings came to life to frighten him and in Chapter V they do exactly the same thing. It is simply that Antoine is no longer fleeing, but delving more deeply into his memories. It is his curiosity, his unending desire to know, that brings them all on the stage.

This reenactment of past memories—hallucinated or real—means that although Antoine appears to be expanding his field of knowledge, progressing by way of displacement, he is really only circling back within the walls of that prison that knowledge ultimately is. As he says in dialogue with Hilarion, "Oui! oui! ma pensée se débat pour sortir de sa prison. . . . Quelquefois même, pendant la durée d'un éclair, je me trouve comme suspendu; puis je retombe" (49; "Yes! yes! My thought struggles to leave its prison. . . . From time to time even, for a lightning moment, I find myself as if suspended; then I fall back!"). This exclamation supposes that Antoine's thoughts form a prison because he is suspended between his hope for progress—the possibility of escape through knowledge—and the regressive pull of memories that bring him back to where he began. And indeed, at the end of the book, Antoine is back where he began, caught between the backward pull of memory and his insatiable desire to escape, between the suggested death of his mother and a supposed lust for Ammonaria, between his desire to end it all and his unwavering belief in dogma.

This pattern of progression and regression or displacement and condensation can also be identified at the level of narrative technique. I cannot reproduce all the instances in which the pattern occurs, but I can note two different examples that include the movement of narrative point of view and the theme of the prison as an image of Antoine's mind. The association of the mind and the prison appears to originate in dialogue with Hilarion at which time Hilarion, the viper, comes to represent a way out. Yet this association is already a replay of Antoine's initial frustration at being enclosed in an unchanging existence at which time his first "Why?" also represented a way out. In this way, knowledge is ambiguously identified as both the limited space of the prison—those memories that circulate and recombine indefinitely—and the limitless expansion of tempting hallucinations. Clearly Antoine is a bit like Faust in that he has chosen his ascetic lifestyle because he is too knowledgeable but he is also tempted each night to escape this lifestyle precisely because he is knowledgeable.

This paradoxical description of the enclosure and expansion of thought becomes an image of the regressive/progressive structure of the novel as the snake once associated with Hilarion condenses with the image of the prison. The result is a gigantic, expanding python whose coils enclose Antoine: "La tête d'un python paraît. Il passe lentement sur le bord du pain . . . puis se développe, s'allonge; il est énorme. . . . Ses anneaux se dédoublent, emplissent la chambre; ils enferment Antoine" (76; "The head of a python appears. It passes slowly along the edge of the bread . . . and then stretches, uncoils; it is enormous. . . . Its coils multiply, fill the room;

they enclose Antony" [Mrosovsky, 124–25]). Then, a moment later:

> Cette commotion lui fait entr'ouvrir les yeux et il aperçoit le Nil, onduleux et clair sous la blancheur de la lune, comme un grand serpent au milieu des sables.
> Puis, la voûte d'une prison l'environne. Des barreaux, devant lui, font des lignes noires sur un fond bleu. . . .
> Et il aperçoit en face, derrière les barreaux d'une autre loge, un lion qui se promène. . . . Au delà, des couronnes de monde étagées symétriquement vont en s'élargissant depuis la plus basse qui enferme l'arène jusqu'à la plus haute. (76–77)[42]

This series of scene changes is an ideal example of what some have called Flaubert's poor transitions.[43] But, the logic of these scene changes are best understood as an impressive example of Freud's condensation: the prison = the snake = a snake prison; then, the serpentine Nile (a real perception that invades an otherwise mental fantasy) = the prison = the circular, symmetrical tiers of an arena. The growth of the snake thus supposes that temptation may lead Antoine out of his prison just as Hilarion's appearance and subsequent growth will suppose. But this is only an illusion; the prison is in fact expanding. Antoine has not progressed but only multiplied versions of his own prison of thought in constantly renewed self-representations. Indeed, from its relation to the Nile and the original stage setting, it is clear that the growth of the snake stands for the development of the book in general: any progress is only an illusion of regression, a moving back into the monologue or a delving more deeply into Antoine's memories.

Given the association between the snake and the arena in Chapter IV of *La Tentation*, it is significant to note that at the opening of that chapter, this delving process is reproduced through the movement of point of view, thus creating a different kind of regressive tension. For the arena at the opening of Chapter IV appears to be the image of an expanded mind into which Hilarion as *metteur en scène* invites Antoine with his

"Entrons!" (49; "Let's go in!"). However, by way of a cinematic zooming or delving of point of view, we move in this
opening from generals to specifics, from the arena-like basilica of a crowd of wild heretics to particular groups, then to
details of their costumes, then to their eyes, then to the faces
of those who will speak. We finally come to rest on the face
of Manès, yet another character already introduced in the
monologue (4). In other words, the image of an expanded
mind or of the progress of knowledge is only an illusion of the
senses, only an intensification or elaboration of old, forgotten
memories. Yet the zooming of the narrator's camera-like eye
does not stop with the evocation of the original memory; on
the contrary it introduces new, if old, material on which to
build the illusion of progress. Of Manès we read, ". . . à sa
main gauche un livre d'images peintes. . . . Les images repré-
sentent les créatures qui sommeillaient dans le chaos. Antoine
penche pour les voir" (51–52; ". . . in his left hand a book of
painted images. . . . The images represent the creatures who
lay sleeping within chaos. Antony leans over to see them"
[Mrosovsky, 102]). These sleeping creatures are undoubtedly
the ones who will parade before Antoine at the opening of
Chapter V or come to life to inhabit the contours of Chapter
VII, born out of the chaos of successively crumbling civilizations. In either case, these relatively tiny images will come to
impress themselves upon the screen of Antoine's memories,
furnishing material on which to circle back in the further symphonic development of the play.

These formal examples of Flaubert's dream-work writing
strategies are repeated at the level of the play's content, thus
commenting on the evolution of the cultural history of humankind. The most dramatic example occurs in Chapter V, a thorough review of the rise and fall of Eastern civilizations. Although the chapter represents an historical progression from
Asian and Indian belief systems to those of the Etruscans, the
Greeks, the Romans, and finally to the God of the Jews, this
progress is undermined by the similarities drawn between
each belief system and by the fact that each one builds then

crumbles only to give rise to the next. The supposition is that religions, like Antoine, are constantly proposing new self-representations while repeating in difference the same essential myths. Each has martyrs, prophets, and disciples; each has gods who manifest themselves in many forms and each is born out of the ashes of its predecessor's destruction. In other words, though civilizations, like the *Tentation*, appear to progress, cultural history is really cyclical. Each civilization only offers a new set of answers in response to humanity's insatiable, unchanging desire to know. In fact, *La Tentation* can be read as a remarkable staging of Flaubert's notion of the history of religions: "Pourquoi a-t-on cette manie de nier, de conspuer son passé, de rougir d'hier et de vouloir que la religion nouvelle efface les anciennes? . . . Le coeur dans ses affections, comme l'humanité dans ses idées, s'étend sans cesse en cercles plus élargies" (C, 2:120–21).[44] Religions, like the scenes of *La Tentation*, do not erase each other in a linear path of progress. Rather, they repeat each other indefinitely developing in ever-enlarging concentric circles. In this light, the regressive/progressive pattern of *La Tentation* comes to imply that neither thought nor cultural history is a cumulative working toward truth, but that they are incessantly enlarging fiction-producing processes. In its representation of this process, *La Tentation* shows us that the movement of thought itself propelled by the theatricalizing energy of desire can never progress but only circulate among past and future fictions in what the Devil finally calls "un flux perpétuel des choses" (176; "a perpetual flux of things").

Ultimately, through its representation of these ever-expanding, repetitive circles, Antoine's inescapable prison of thought is recreated in the larger structure of the play. For in addition to its condensing and displacing of associated images that work to create a musical structure of theme and variation, the text itself is also constructed with a mirror at its center. This imaginary mirror folds the play in half, forcing its two extremities to meet. That is, at the center of the book, between the fourth and fifth chapters, the book folds over to create a reverse image of its opening, or, in the vocabulary of optics, its

virtual image. This visual model best approximates the resulting structure of the play if it is read as a three-dimensional
image whose end-points converge, locking the whole into a
circle.

I & II   III   IV   V   VI   VII

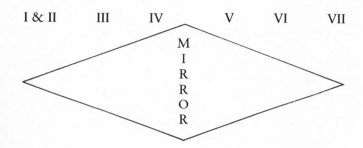

M
I
R
R
O
R

I shall read this model from its end-points toward its center.
The opening monologue and its revival in Chapter II show us
Antoine caught between memory and desire, perception and
imagination, reality and hallucination, creating fantasy escapes
from his boring existence. Likewise, in the final chapter, Antoine finds himself where he began. He regrets his past (178),
remembers earlier voyages (179), and oscillates between fantasy and reality. These two poles are personified respectively
by the return of his mother and of Ammonaria (180−84),
who are in turn transformed into Death and Lust and, then,
into the Sphinx and the Chimera (187−91). Near the very end,
having witnessed the very origins of life in matter, Antoine's
ultimate wishful escape is to become one with that matter. But
this ultimate manifestation of the wish is really like all of the
others in that it returns him to his boredom and to his dogmatic will to believe. He is therefore ready to relive the events
of the play anew. In Chapter III, Hilarion enters the scene as
the voice of reason or conscience. He tempts Antoine through
his questioning of dogma and fuels his quest for knowledge.
Likewise, the penultimate chapter, Chapter VI, introduces the
figure of the Devil, another voice of reason who further tempts
and questions dogma (176). At the opening of Chapter IV, Antoine's enters the basilica to witness a kind of cinema of Chris-

tian history, and in Chapter V there is another cinema, this time of Oriental history.[45] (It is the wide visual scope of these two cinemas that inspires the shape of my structural model.) Notably, in this center of the book where East meets West, Antoine encounters two figures who simultaneously mirror each other and Antoine himself. The Gymnosophiste (85–87), on the Western side, and the Buddha on the other (122–24), are each martyrs who resist temptation by living in solitude and by spending their time contemplating God. Like Antoine, both are imprisoned in their thoughts, for they have renounced all earthy pleasures and physical sensations. Through this elaborate game of reflections, the book reproduces the specular prison that is Antoine's mind, holding itself suspended through its progressive and regressive tensions.

The interest of this specular structure is that it reproduces Lacan's "poinçon" ($\Diamond$), the lozenge which functions at the center of his formula for the fantasy:

$$\text{\$} \qquad \Diamond \qquad a$$
(the divided subject desires an object)[46]

Like *La Tentation*, this formula assumes a circular process which both includes and excludes the subject from the scene of his fantasies. However, as Elisabeth Lyon explains it, the lozenge also signifies "the circulation among positions of subject and object in the fantasy, where the subject plays a role not only as an observer but as a participant in his own fantasy."[47] Given that the circulation of subjects and objects or spectators and actors is already accented in Antoine's and in his narrator's relation to the scenes of the play, it is striking to see that the structure of *La Tentation* reproduces this lozenge. It suggests that we, as readers, are being called upon to reproduce the subject's mobilized positioning in and around fantasy scenes. And just as Antoine's monologue does away with any particular self or subject whose psychology would ground the images of the text, *La Tentation*, through its *mise en scène* of cultural history, keeps us from grounding it in the history of its author. On the contrary, every strategy in *La Tentation* is designed to turn our attention away from the writer and onto the writing so that we might become "players in the game." It is for this reason that *La Tentation* exposes its own mechanisms like a broken toy but this is also why it turns away from the linear logic of drama or of narrative, inviting us to read it in all conceivable directions.

Due to its elaborate specular activity and its precisely defined structured fluidity, *La Tentation* seems to realize one of Flaubert's dreams of an ideal style of prose, a style conceived with a reading effect in mind. In a passage from his correspondence of 1852, Flaubert explains this ideal prose as a kind of music that lets us float:

> Je reviens à *Graziella*. Il y a un paragraphe d'une grande page tout en infinitifs: "se lever matin, etc." L'homme qui adopte de pareilles tournures a l'oreille fausse; ce n'est pas un écrivain. . . . J'en conçois un, moi, un style: un style qui serait beau, que quelqu'un fera à quelque jour, dans dix ans ou dans dix siècles, et qui serait rhythmé comme le vers, précis comme le langage des sciences, et avec des ondulations, des ronflements de violoncelle, des aigrettes de feu; un style qui vous entrerait dans l'idée comme un coup de stylet, et où votre pensée enfin voguerait sur des surfaces lisses, comme lorsqu'on file dans un canot avec bon vent arrière. (C, 2:129)[48]

In this passage, Flaubert's ideal style is musical, rhythmic, and precise in order to create a particular experience for the reader. By means of a "thrusting stiletto" (or a "cutting style") that would penetrate deeply into the mind of its reader, that same reader would benefit from a pleasure not unlike Antoine's. The chance to glide on smooth surfaces—the pleasure of the movement of thought itself—would be for the reader like the saint's own fluid mental voyages. This pleasure would result from a mixture of scientific precision or detail and musical undulations, a description that echoes *La Tentation*'s precise historical details which glide and undulate in a symphonic structure of theme and variations. The music of this ideal style, like the music of *La Tentation*, describes the new kind of logic and the new kind of reading that Virtual Theater inevitably displays. For *La Tentation*, like all virtual plays, demands a tremendous attention to writing strategies and to complicated structural games, only to, paradoxically, mobilize its readers and to offer them an imaginary voyage "with a good tail wind behind."

In light of Foucault's theory that *La Tentation* invites us to become spectators ("La Bibliothèque fantastique", 17), conserving in its interior everything necessary to an eventual representation (13), one might speculate that in its representation of the structure of the fantasm, *La Tentation* demands that we become its subject. Like the spectator at the theater or, indeed, like Flaubert himself, conscious attention to the details of textual construction may open up unconscious sources of pleasure and potential identifications on one's own imaginary stage. In other words, Antoine and his playwright/narrator become a model for how to read. And just as they rely on theatrical structures—the complementary activities of the spectator and the actor—in order to demonstrate their mental mobility, Flaubert relies upon signifying processes similar to those of Freud's dream work in order to demand of us that very same mobility. He thereby recreates, in one "thrust of style," the theatricality inherent in the very act of reading and writing. With this in mind, it is striking that Maurice Béjart chose to actualize Flaubert's virtual play in dance, a highly complex visual and physical structuring of space which allows a fluid and musical experience for both the audience and the performers.[49] In its re-reading of Flaubert's *Tentation*, Béjart's ballet does not limit the flow of individual associations but realizes the mobility both of Flaubert's writing style and of the reading experience that such a mobile performance demands. To theorize this mobile and musical writing style, Mallarmé speculates about an association, by way of virtuality, between dancing and writing, between being and seeing theater.

FIVE

Virtuality, Actuality, and Stéphane Mallarmé

Un théâtre, inhérent à l'esprit, quiconque d'un oeil certain regarda la nature
le porte avec soi, résumé de types et d'accords; ainsi que les confronte le
volume ouvrant des pages parallèles.

—Mallarmé, *Oeuvres complètes*

When Mallarmé redefines his *L'Après-midi d'un faune* as "non possible au théâtre mais exigeant le théâtre" ("not possible at the theater but requiring theater"), he opens an inquiry into his own fundamentally ambivalent fascination with the virtuality of theater.[1] What is this theatricality that is not possible at the theater but required by the *Faune* in 1865? And how is it that this same theatricality seems to become so eminently stageworthy and fascinating in those later essays of the 1890s which discuss actual performing arts? One answer is that Mallarmé, like the other authors of Virtual Theater, speculates about the negative and positive aspects of actual performance and its metaphorical or virtual equivalents in writing. Indeed, in his later experiences as a spectator at the theater, the poet will admit that although it is often rendered banal for the general public or simply not fully exploited, the theater is by nature a "sublime milieu" (OC, 313) because it invokes what he calls the "paradox of the superior writer": his desire to both watch and recreate the "essential principles" of the theatrical in a writing style that would both replay and replace its original indefinitely (OC, 295).

This paradox explains how those critics who see Mallarmé's theater as a step in the development of symbolist drama as well as those who see his theater as the metaphor or figuration of consciousness and/or writing can have equally viable positions.[2] Throughout the poet's writings, there is a preponderance of references to a virtual theatricality that can describe nature (OC, 299), the mind (OC, 300, 345), the act of writing and/or reading (OC, 328), the gaze of the competent observer (ibid.), and the effect of a good performance in language or on stage, each theater resulting both in and from the others. The virtual or figurative need not therefore be divided from the actual; the ambivalence that associates them need only be clarified. Mallarmé is fascinated by the virtual dynamics of actual theater and by the ways in which the dynamics can be reappropriated through the writing and reading of poetry. As Derrida has suggested in his essay "La Double Séance," Mallarmé's theater is not exclusively a mental scene (264–65), and as this chapter will propose, it is not exclusively a writing scene but the evasive elaboration of a theatrical apparatus that finds itself repeated both on and off stage.[3]

It is the pervasive but ill-defined theatricality of this apparatus, this metaphoric sliding of replays and replacements, that I would like to trace through the study of the poet's virtual plays, Hérodïade and L'Après-midi d'un faune. Ultimately, Mallarmé's reconciliation of a virtual with an actual theatricality creates an important link between the metaphor of the theater to describe the functioning of a psychical apparatus and the relationship of this apparatus to actual performing arts.[4] My goal in this essay is therefore to play Mallarmé's early virtual theaters against his later theories of the theatrical to show that these plays already shape the contours of his fascination with certain performing arts—notably dance and music—by virtue of the fact that his writing already proposes virtual equivalents for them. My analysis will thus proceed with a view toward Jacques Scherer's idea that for Mallarmé, the figurative theaters of writing rival the actual theater in almost every instance.[5] I would not say that the figurative theaters of writing are better or more fully representative of Mallarmé's notion of the theatrical. However, I would argue instead that both the virtual and the actual, when successful, perform the same essential functions or "principles."

Like Hugo's *Théâtre en liberté*, Mallarmé's reconception of *L'Après-midi d'un faune* and of *Hérodiade* as virtual rather than actual theater pieces coincides with his own personal philosophical crisis and with the onset of his desire to write an Ideal Book that can be seen as the end product or summa in that history of Virtual Theater first inaugurated by the idealistic dreams of the German Romantics.[6] Though this crisis as it is presented in Mallarmé's correspondence and its relation to an Ideal Work or Book have been thoroughly discussed elsewhere, I am interested in examining just one passage from that famous correspondence which authorizes an inquiry into the theatrical nature of this Ideal Book.

In a much-cited letter of 1866 that enthusiastically describes the poet's first conception of *Hérodiade*'s "Ouverture musicale" and at the same time his painful encounter with Nothingness, Mallarmé writes:

> Oui, *je le sais*, nous ne sommes que de vaines formes de la matière, mais bien sublimes pour avoir inventé Dieu et notre âme. Si sublimes, mon ami! que je veux me donner ce spectacle de la matière, ayant conscience d'être et, cependant, s'élançant forcenément dans le Rêve qu'elle sait n'être pas, chantant l'Ame et toutes les divines impressions pareilles qui se sont amassées en nous depuis les premiers âges et proclament, devant le Rien qui est la vérité, ces glorieux mensonges!
> Tel est le plan de mon volume lyrique. . . . (*Correspondance*, 207–8)[7]

Mallarmé begins this commentary on the limitations of human nature by underscoring our only sublimity: a capacity for creative thought evidenced by our invention of God and of our own souls. According to his logic, though we are only vain forms of matter, our intellectual inventions make us into a spectacle of glorious lies worthy of representation. He then goes on to detail what will be required in order to offer this spectacle to himself: while remaining conscious of being, of existing here and now, one must at the same time, nonetheless, throw oneself wildly into a dream or fiction that consciousness knows does not exist in order to sing (of) the soul and all similarly inspired divine impressions amassed within us since the earliest times. Against the Nothing that *is*, such a spectacle constitutes Being. It appears, then, that a representation of this spectacle that is Being or subjectivity demands at once the elimination of a conscious self so as to get at those amassed inner impressions of sublime thought and the harnessing of that same consciousness in order to watch them or sing of their unfolding.

In psychoanalytic terms, this spectacle or drama of subjectivity requires a divided subject who is both the subject and the object of his or her own creative thoughts. Much like Freud's dreamer, one becomes a spectacle unto oneself. Moreover, those impressions and the dream or fiction into which consciousness must throw itself are strikingly similar to Freud's description of the unconscious as a collection of introjected perceptions recorded throughout our waking lives and the fictive fantasy scenarios we create while dreaming or daydreaming which alone make those impressions available to consciousness. In this context, this "spectacle of matter" may be said to demand an almost impossible task: a conscious observation of those mechanisms of unconscious thought only put into motion or made accessible during the quiescence of conscious awareness. Despite the difficulty of this task, it is precisely this theatricalizing of a subject engaged in an attempt to understand the spectacular source and/or workings of creative thought that is recorded in the virtual drama of Mallarmé's *Hérodïade*.

HÉRODÏADE

Like Flaubert's *Tentation de Saint Antoine*, Mallarmé's *Hérodïade* spans almost the entire creative lifetime of its author, beginning with the "Scène" of 1864 and continuing to obsess

him until the last days of his life (OC, 1440–46). *Hérodïade*
is therefore made up of an indefinite number of scenes or
parts. The three parts of it published during the poet's own
lifetime and recorded in the Pléïade edition of his complete
works have since been complemented by Gardner Davies's
Les Noces d'Hérodïade.[8] Though I am not interested in entering into a discussion concerning which of these parts should
or should not be included in *Hérodïade*, I am interested in
briefly examining certain questions related to the whole before looking in detail at its "Ouverture ancienne." I believe
that each of *Hérodïade*'s parts may be understood as different
versions of the same "spectacle of matter," variations on the
theme of a theatricalized subjectivity. That is, although the
formats and the anecdotes change in each part of the play,
they each offer the representation of this spectacle. In this way,
dramatic logic which would require a linear unfolding of
events is replaced, in *Hérodïade*, by a repetitive structure
made of movable, compositionally self-sufficient but dissimi-
lar parts. In fact, if *Hérodïade* was reconceived as a virtual
rather than actual performance, it was due undoubtedly in
part to the necessity that its characters occupy several positions at once, sliding among locations and identities in what,
taken as a whole, appears to be a continually renewed and
renewable fantasy scenario.

Even a cursory review of *Hérodïade*'s "Scène" and its
"Cantique" demonstrate this remarkable repetition. Hérodïade in her "Scène" is the perfect image of Mallarmé's mar-
velous spectator, a divided subject who gazes in her mirror
only to feel the potential fiery movements of memory and its
fragmented thought processes beneath the cold, frozen exterior of her virginal self:

O miroir!

. . . .

. . . désolée

Des songes et cherchant mes souvenirs qui sont
Comme des feuilles sous ta glace au trou profond,

. . . .

> ... dans ta sévère fontaine,
> J'ai de mon rêve épars connu la nudité!
>
> (OC, 45)

And later, addressing her mirror image:

> Et ta soeur solitaire, ô ma soeur éternelle
> Mon rêve montera vers toi: telle déjà,
> Rare limpidité d'un coeur qui le songea. . . .
>
> (OC, 48)[9]

As both of these passages suggest, Hérodïade presents an image of Mallarmé's theatricalized subject who throws herself into the fiction proposed by her mirror in order to get at the "rare limpidity" or "nudity" of a heart that dreams.

Similarly, Saint Jean in his "Cantique," though written much later, quite literally mimics this phenomenon: "Et ma tête surgie / . . . S'opiniâtre à suivre / En quelque bond hagard / Son pur regard / Là-haut . . . (OC, 49; "And my head surging up / . . . Stubbornly follows / In some haggard bound / Its pure look / Up there . . . [Cohn, 83–85, modified]). Though this poem involves a more sophisticated notion of subjectivity—amassed impressions become a kind of rhythmic bouncing—it is clear that a divided subject "throws himself wildly into a fiction that cannot be" since the saint's discourse emanates from a body whose severed head is propelled outward to follow the look of a speaking "Je." In both the case of Hérodïade and that of her saint, the theatrical dynamics of a self-conscious investigation bear a striking resemblance to the child in Lacan's mirror phase. Like that child, they both confront and then identify with the fiction of an ideal, "pure," or "eternal" "I" in the alienated image of themselves in the mirror ("Le Stade du miroir," 91). Though the mirror stage represents, for Lacan, that moment in the history of the subject at which an ego or "I" is constituted or frozen despite the turbulence of heterogeneous psychic realities that animate that subject (ibid., 92–94), we could say that for Mallarmé, the process is as if reversed in an attempt to get at the scattered impressions of a fragmented subjectivity. (Our attention to the Nurse in the "Ouverture ancienne" will further clarify the dynamics of this procedure.) Nonetheless, as this brief review supposes, each part of *Hérodïade* presents what we can call a repetition in difference of the same fictive spectacle.

And yet, at the same.time that each part of *Hérodïade* offers a renewed version of this same essential spectacle, each is also linked to the next by a suggested continuity or by what Roland Barthes would call a narrative lure (*S/Z*, 82). These parts can thus be read accordingly as both separate illuminations and as derivative moments that take place in an unspoken narrative progression. Indeed, the temporal configurations of each part of *Hérodïade* work to create the spatial configurations of a place outside of time, a place we can liken to a purely psychic reality.[10] For each part gestures toward a possible future event while ruling out the possibility of anything ever taking place. Each thereby locks itself into a single self-contained entity, beginning as if already finished. The "Ouverture" or "dawning" of the play begins with an abolished dawn (*OC*, 41) that may be a sunset: "De crépuscule, non, mais de rouge lever . . . on ne sait plus l'heure . . ." (*OC*, 43; "Of dusk, no, but of red dawn . . . one no longer knows the hour . . ." [Cohn, 60]). Similarly, the "Scène" opens with Hérodïade's entrance but undermines its own credibility by making this return the possible figment of the Nurse's imagination: "Tu vis! ou vois-je ici l'ombre d'une princess?" (*OC*, 44; "You are alive! Or do I see here the shade of a princess?" [Cohn, 67]). Is the princess alive or is she only a shade? The "Cantique," in the same manner, begins with a stroke of life-giving death (*OC*, 49). In addition, while each of the openings begins at an end, each of the endings finishes in expectant beginnings: "La rougeur de ce temps prophétique . . ." (*OC*, 43; "the redness of this prophetic hour . . ."); the awaiting of "une chose inconnue . . ." (*OC*, 48; "an unknown thing . . ."); and "un salut" (*OC*, 49; "a *salve*") which is either a salvation that is also a baptism or a simple "hello" indicative of commencement (Bersani, *The Death*, 78–80). The possibility of actual performance is thus clearly undone, in *Hérodïade*, by the linguistic creation of imaginary scenes which cannot take place in real time and space and which have only potential relationships between them.

The temporal configurations of this play caught somewhere between an already past future and a past that may not yet be announce Mallarmé's later theory of theater as a potential event taking place between opposing antagonistic forces, reality and imagination, memory and desire. In his celebrated essay on *Hamlet*, though written much later than *Hérodiade* in 1886, Mallarmé outlines the theoretical implications of these temporal configurations. Associating the tension produced by the antagonistic forces of dream and reality with the very essence of Hamlet's drama, Mallarmé explains that this drama repeats the structural dimensions of an actual theatrical space:

> Son solitaire drame! et qui, parfois, tant ce promeneur d'un labyrinthe de trouble et de griefs en prolonge les circuits avec le suspens d'un acte inachevé, semble le spectacle même pourquoi existent la rampe ainsi que l'espace doré quasi moral qu'elle défend, car il n'est point d'autre sujet, sachez bien: l'antagonisme de rêve chez l'homme avec les fatalités à son existence départies par le malheur. (*OC*, 300)[11]

Hamlet's personal drama seems to explain the very existence of theater because it describes an essential antagonism between dream and reality or expectations and fatal disappointments inherent both in the nature of the mind and in the spatial layout of a theater. Just as nineteenth-century theaters were constructed as a double scene, a golden space separated by footlights from the real life of the spectators, the mind is also constructed as a double scene: a labyrinthian unconscious whose prolonged circuits may or may not result in a conscious act. Hamlet's dilemma is thus emblematic of that drama which describes the divided subject of psychoanalysis, the same drama that furnishes floor plans for the design of modern theaters: "le seul théâtre de notre esprit, prototype du reste" (ibid.). This means not only that the drama of subjectivity is like a theater but that both the physical theater and the well-constructed play repeat the structure and functioning (or fictionizing) of this psychical apparatus.

This idea that the mind's figurative theater finds itself repeated in Shakespeare's play and in actual physical theatrical space can also be seen in *Hérodïade*. For, without exploiting the obvious likeness of Hérodïade and Hamlet—she too is a double hero ("Hero/dyade") and she too walks in a labyrinth of troubles prolonging the circuits of a suspended sexual act—it is evident that the play works to create that doubled theatrical space characteristic of Virtual Theater. Though I shall limit my remarks to the "Ouverture ancienne," this indeed is what each of *Hérodïade*'s parts has in common. For the "Ouverture ancienne," while remaining a self-sufficient totality, also stands in relation to the whole as a model for how to read. For the work of the narrating spectator of the "Ouverture" finds itself endlessly repeated or mirrored in each of the play's inconclusive parts.

Like the opening of all virtual plays, this "Ouverture" opens or introduces the whole by presenting itself as a kind of narrative stage setting. Offered as an "Incantation" delivered by Hérodïade's Nurse, it tells us what time it is (sometime between dawn and daylight); it tells us where the scene is set (in a room in a castle bordered by the forest); we are informed that the protagonist is a princess (her father, now gone, is the king); we know that the princess has been out all night (the bed is empty, the candle blown out) and that she is still out now: "elle erre" ("she wanders"). The Nurse is thus constituted as some kind of narrator or playwright who is setting the scene for a proposed action to come, creating an atmosphere of prophecy and doom. Moreover, most of these facts are presented in the past tense, establishing a background and setting for events about to take place.

Like all narrators of Virtual Theater, however, the Nurse is also a spectator. Her past-tense narration is contaminated by present-tense description. The Dawn "a . . . choisi / Notre tour," the beautiful bird/princess "a fuie" ("the Dawn *has chosen* our tower," the princess "*has fled*") but "L'eau morne

se résigne" and "l'eau reflète l'abandon" ("The dreary water
is resigning itself," "the water *reflects* abandonment"). In this
way, the facts reported in the finished past tense by a theoretically objective narrator are confused with the subjective
present-tense impressions of a spectator. As in all virtual
plays, the text works to insure the distance of narrative objectivity so as to illustrate the mobility of subjectivity across that
distance. For, on one hand, the Nurse is not present in the
scene except to direct and watch it. This setting is presented
as through the eye of a camera that sweeps across a crimson
sky and the tower of the manor house to the still waters of
an empty pond, and then through an open window to "La
chambre singulière en un cadre" (*OC*, 41; "The singular
room in a frame"). As in Flaubert's *Tentation*, the camera's
point of view zooms, becoming more and more specific. On
the other hand, however, the Nurse cannot remain objectively
behind the camera lens. That is, although the text makes a
point of creating a doubled theatrical space by separating the
outside from the inside of a room and placing a window
frame between them, the Nurse's looking turns this window
frame into an imaginary proscenium arch by projecting an
imaginary performance into the stillness. Curiously, (and again
like the *Tentation*,) though the entire "Ouverture" opens
with a point of view that appears to gaze from inside the
manor house out to the dawn and still waters, the second
strophe begins with the image of the room in a frame, that is,
with a point of view that now moves from the outside in. The
Nurse's point of view thus turns an entire 360 degrees, locat-
ing her both inside and outside the window frame.

In relation to this window frame, the Nurse is like that
conscious subject who "throws herself wildly into a Dream or
fiction consciousness knows is not." For, like all narrators of
Virtual Theater, the Nurse, in looking, mobilizes the scene as
her point of view repeats the mobility of the camera. From the
window frame across the goldwork of the bedroom to folds
of tapestry hanging in that room, the Nurse's eye lights on a
sibyl supposedly woven into the tapestry. As Leo Bersani has
shown, this sibyl is an ideal example of all of the unstable

designations in the "Ouverture," sliding identities as well as "casual and unexplained shifts in the register of being" (*The Death*, 11). The sibyl also draws our attention to a more general shift away from semantic logic towards what may most appropriately be called a semiotic logic.[12] For the location of the sibyl, like the logic of Mallarmé's writing, slips and slides along channels of metonymic association. She is at once caught in the tapestry, "plis / Inutiles avec les yeux ensevelis / De sibylles" ("useless folds / With the buried eyes / Of sybils [sic]" [Cohn, 60]), and embroidered on a dress enclosed in an ivory armoire: "Une d'elles, avec un passé de ramages / Sur ma robe blanchie en l'ivoire fermé" ("One of them, with a past of flowery vines / On my bleached dress in the closed ivory" [ibid.]). In addition, this sibyl seems to be flying off, possibly in the form of an aroma:

Une d'elles . . .
. . . .
Semble, de vols partis costumée et fantôme,
Un arôme qui porte, ô roses! un arôme . . .

(OC, 42)[13]

The sibyl is thus woven into a tapestry, embroidered on a faded dress enclosed in an ivory armoire *and* flying off in an imaginary prolongation as an aroma of roses or, later, of cold bones (or gold).[14] In this very still and faded setting, then, the only performance is the one inaugurated by the Nurse's gaze that shifts both her perspectives and those of the objects at which she looks, lending to the sibyl the characteristics of her own mobility. Given this identification of the Nurse with the sibyl, one might point out that the sibyl is already an equivalent for the Nurse insofar as both are "bearers of prophecy."

This identification of the subject looking with the object of her regard anticipates Mallarmé's later discussions of the work of an actual spectator before an ideal performance. This ideal performance, for the poet who would rather read, write, and think, is one that solicits the involvement of one's own fantasies—"le bizarre luxe de sa propre chimère" (OC, 316; "the bizarre luxury of his own fantasy")—in order to result in an esthetic experience.[15] The perfect description of such an ideal esthetic experience is therefore best illustrated in Mallarmé's own attempts to understand ballet, though it is important to note that at the end of this passage Mallarmé equates this experience at the theater with the essential operation of poetry. He writes:

> Quand s'isole pour le regard un signe de l'éparse beauté générale, fleur, onde, nuée et bijou, etc., si, chez nous, le moyen exclusif de le savoir consiste à en juxtaposer l'aspect à notre nudité spirituelle afin qu'elle le sente analogue et se l'adapte dans quelque confusion exquise d'elle avec cette forme envolée—rien qu'au travers du rite, là, énoncé de l'Idée, est-ce que ne paraît pas la danseuse à demi l'élément en cause, à demi humanité apte à s'y confondre, dans la flottaison de rêverie? L'opération, ou poésie, par excellence et le théâtre. (OC, 295–96)[16]

The potential multiplicity of meanings that ballet may evoke takes place by passing through the eye of the beholder: "le regard." Like the dance, thought fuels itself: a flower becomes a wave, becomes a cloud, becomes a jewel, and so on, so that the spectator's associations are as mobile as the dance itself. Here, however, a duplicity is necessary to the production of these constantly shifting and reproductive meanings. First, as spectators, we look at the dance. We are clearly separate from the theatrical space, passive spectators. Then, we appropriate the object of our gaze, feeling it analogous to ourselves and causing an imaginary identification or "exquisite confusion" between our own minds and the dancer's unidentifiable flight. The implication is not only that it is the antirepresentational nature of those movements that allows and requires this identification but that the spectator's own mind or "spiritual nudity"—the mind not yet contaminated by the logical categories of conscious thought—is itself constituted by similarly meaningless movements: scattered signs, "forms in flight," "amassed impressions," or the prolonged circuits of Hamlet's labyrinthian troubles. In other words, Mallarmé intimates that mental productions, like the movement of dancers, are not logical and coherent but rhythmic and mobile

much like the semiotic designs of *Hérodïade*'s verse. Therefore, the dance performance creates meaning only by making
the spectator's thoughts into a double of its own mobility. In
this case, the scattered signs of dance evoke associative (if illogical or unconscious) links between the poet's favorite recurring images: flowers, waves, clouds, and jewels.

Furthermore, at the same time that the dance performance
sets the subject in flight, suspending him—like Hamlet or the
Nurse—somewhere between passive appreciation and active
participation, the dancer herself becomes a kind of paradigm
for this confusion of the subject and the object of his look.[17]
For she is both an object or representational element on stage
and a real human being or subject always potentially lost in a
role which is constantly shifting. In the same way, the sibyl is
both fixed on the tapestry or enclosed in the armoire and flying off, that is, mobilized in a series of possible locations. The
sibyl and the Nurse, like the dancer and the spectator, are
caught in that indistinction of subjects and objects to which
Mallarmé, like Laplanche and Pontalis, refers as the floating
of daydreams. The dance is then a form of theater which cannot fix representations on one side of the footlights and a
spectator or subject on the other but one which promotes a
mobile interchangeability of subjects and objects. The strategies of the dance performance as Mallarmé reads them are
thus reminiscent of what Borch-Jacobsen calls indistinctions
of the "I" and the "she" or "he" and what Jean-François
Lyotard envisions as a kind of rotating proscenium arch that
simultaneously distinguishes and confuses the audience and
the stage, the theater and the world, reality and fantasy, catch-
ing a spectator somewhere between the intensities of his or
her own unconscious desires and those emanating from bodies and signs on stage (Lyotard, *Dispositifs*, 102–3).[18]

This mobile interchangeability of subjects and objects or
spectators and performers explains why the Nurse's gaze establishes identities not only between herself and the sibyl but
between the separate spaces inscribed in the "Ouverture" itself. For just as the Nurse seems to have both an objective and
a subjective point of view, the room itself, though distinctly

separated from the outside owing to the presence of that window frame, is only the double of the landscape outside it. The abolished dawn is repeated in the room's extinguished gold-work and snuffed candle. The empty, resigned water reflecting abandon, "que ne visite plus la plume ni le cygne" ("that is visited neither by the feather [or pen] nor the swan"), is repeated in the useless folds of tapestry and the empty bed which Hérodïade, "comme un cygne" has also abandoned. Likewise, the stems of flowers which "trempent en un seul verre à l'éclat alangui" ("dip into a single glass with a languished bursting") seem to mirror the wing of the abolished dawn as it dips into a single basin also, we might say, "à l'éclat alangui." This makes the outsides and the insides of the room both separate and equal, divided mirror images.

Remarkably, this division of outsides and insides created only to highlight the rhythmic sliding that links them offers the perfect image of a *mise en abîme* or embedded mirror structure since the two spaces catch whatever is between them—in this case the Nurse—in a similar play of reflections. That is, the division of the theatrical space of the "Ouverture" into two separate but equal realities is repeated in the Nurse herself. To put this another way, the landscape is to the room as the room is to the Nurse as the Nurse is to the dawn, and so on. In following a pattern of cinematic zoom effects from general to specific, the Nurse's attention moves, according to the logic of displacement, from the folds of tapestry into the folds of her own thoughts. As a result, in this "incantation" or inner, silent singing, the Nurse hears a voice but is not sure whether it comes from outside or inside herself. We could say that "having consciousness of being, the Nurse has already thrown herself into a dream or fiction she knows is not," so that she may now "sing of those divine impressions amassed within her from the beginning of time."

In the third strophe, the Nurse describes the potential movement of this unlocalizable voice:

Ombre magicienne aux symboliques charmes!
Une voix, du passé longue évocation,

Est-ce la mienne prête à l'incantation
Encore dans les plis jaunes de la pensée
Traînant, antique, ainsi qu'une étoile encensée
Sur un confus amas d'ostensoirs refroidis,
Par les tous anciens et par les plis roidis
Percés selon le rhythme et les dentelles pures
Du suaire laissant par ses belles guipures
Désespéré monter le vieil éclat voilé
S'élève: (ô quel lointain en ces appels celé!)

(*OC*, 42) [19]

The Nurse is unsure whether or not the voice she hears is her own, and if it is, whether it is still enclosed within the yellow folds of thought, dragging among the confused masses of her inner mind like an aromatic star or whether it is already rising up beyond those hidden depths. In this way, the incantation is potential and, like the drama, about to begin, but it is also already in progress, having begun at the opening of the "Ouverture" with the poet's silent stage indication:

LA NOURRICE
(Incantation)

In other words, the Nurse's reading of her own incantation doubles the poet's with its semantic gaps and uncertain syntax, as an image of the silent music of thought and the scattered forms of its rhythmic flight. In fact, in the same way that the sibyl is mobilized by that distance which separates her from the look of the Nurse, in this passage, flight or movement is suggested not by the predicate "s'élève" but by the distance filled by tangential, rhythmic qualifiers that separate this predicate from its subject, the voice. Moreover, this confused accumulation of ancient contents through which the energy of thought moves before surfacing might be likened to what Freud calls mnemic traces, that material made of introjected impressions from the past which is reorganized and represented in dream and fantasy scenes (*The Interpretation of Dreams*, 578). For the Nurse's voice is a potentially mobile energy caught somewhere between the ancient contents of those mnemic traces and her consciousness of them. It is as if the shroud that separates preconscious or unconscious thoughts from consciousness were allowing a rhythmic, uncertain seepage, just like the window frame or, indeed, the closed armoire.

In fact, this inner mind with its "ancient holes" and "stiffened folds" is clearly made up of previously introjected perceptions since it repeats both the room and its surroundings. It is old like the "aurore ancienne" and stiff like the resigned water; it is faded like the coloration of the room with its "ancienne teinte" and immobile like the "plis inutiles" of its tapestry. And like the deserted outside and inside of the room, the stiff and frozen inner mind is only mobilized by the distant yet attentive gaze of the Nurse. We may speak of an impersonal or anonymous appropriation of the external world or of a projection of the mind's theater onto that world.

Moreover, like the entire "Ouverture" itself, both prophetic and abolished, the Nurse's voice is both not yet enclosed in language or conscious thought, not yet bursting out and, at the same time, already returning back to its hidden and distant origins. It is thought caught in what Mallarmé repeatedly refers to as a state of "spiritual nudity":

> Le vieil éclat voilé du vermeil insolite,
> De la voix languissant, nulle, sans acolyte
> Jettera-t-il son or par derniers splendeurs,
> Elle, encore, l'antienne aux versets demandeurs,
> A l'heure d'agonie et de luttes funèbres!
> Et, force du silence et des noires ténèbres
> Tout rentre également en l'ancien passé,
> Fatidique, vaincu, monotone, lassé,
> Comme l'eau des bassins anciens se résigne.
>
> (OC, 42)[20]

There is very little difference here between what is outside the Nurse and what is inside her. Her voice is vermilion and tenebrous like the crimson and blackened dawn. It is potentially throwing out its gold in a last splendor just as the autumn's golden light is both "fustigeant" and already "éteignant . . .

son brandon." And like the dawn of this last day which is also a sunset, the "veiled bursting" of the voice is both rising to the surface in a last refrain and ("Et"), like everything else in this both expectant and abolished setting, already returning to its ancient past, to the silence and darkness of memory. Indeed, the potential bursting begins already veiled.

This gesture toward a futurity which is somehow already too late not only mirrors the opening of the "Ouverture" with its both abolished and prophetic dawn but calls to the remainder of the piece with its repeated inquiries about a future that can never be. In fact, the larger structure of the piece, which Mallarmé called symphonic (*Correspondance*, 161), may be said to repeat this tension with its themes and variations. For if the camera eye moves forward, in the beginning, from the outside to the inside of Hérodïade's room, the text repeats its opening lines at the end of its first strophe, causing a backward pull and a renewed beginning: "Une Aurore traînait ses ailes dans les larmes!" ("A Dawn dragged its wings in the tears!" [Cohn, 61]). Then, as the object of the Nurse's attention moves from the room to the inside of her own mind, this progressive development is also pulled back at the end of the second strophe, by another variation on an opening theme: "Comme l'eau des bassins anciens se résigne" ("As the water of ancient basins grows resigned" [Cohn, 64]). In both cases, the musicality of this symphonic overture is established by the repetition of words now placed in slightly varying syntactical relations, creating rapports between separate spaces. Finally, in the third strophe, the absent swans of the opening reappear as an equivalent for the absent princess, and that star which in the first strophe had never shown and in the second strophe appeared to drag aromatically, now, at the very end, "ne brille plus," no longer shines. In this way, Mallarmé not only has encircled the entire "Ouverture" into an impossible or virtual time slot caught in an "exquisite confusion" between night and day, dream and reality, past and future, looker and looked at, but he has literally borrowed back the positive values of music.

Indeed, this symphonic structure of the "Ouverture" along

with the potential bursting of the Nurse's preconscious inner voice may be seen as a significant step toward Mallarmé's future notion of music as a silent set of rhythms that describe the very nature of being. These rhythms constitute both the "being" of the individual subject—"Toute âme est un noeud rhythmique" (OC, 633; "Every soul is a rhythmic knot")— and the intrinsic nature of all things: "l'ensemble des rapports existant dans tout" (OC, 368; "the totality of relationships existing in everything"). Therefore, music understood not as sound but as rhythm explains why one *sings* (of) amassed inner impressions in the writing of a drama of subjectivity. Rhythm is the knot across which human nature and the universe are tied; it is the only conception of mind or of nature one can ever have (OC, 345). Therefore, as the Nurse's evocation of an hour of agony and funereal struggles suggests, writing must respond in a like performance.

This rather radical notion that the rhythms of thought can reflect or repeat the rhythms of being further explains how Mallarmé's own efforts to represent subjectivity in writing could have been conceived of, originally, as a Romantic project for an Ideal Book, an impersonal reflection of the universe realizable only through the study of the individual subject.[21] As Mallarmé wrote in 1867, "je suis maintenant impersonnel . . . une aptitude qu'a l'Univers spirituel à se voir et à se développer, à travers ce qui fut moi" (*Correspondance*, 242; "I am now impersonal . . . an aptitude of the spiritual Universe to see itself and develop itself across what was once me"). Theoretically, if one could reproduce those purely rhythmic impressions that constitute thought, one might both eliminate the particular personality of the author and re-create a mirror reflection of the essential nature of all things. Writing would then be a kind of two-way mirror not unlike the mirror we find in *Hérodïade*.[22] In fact, this notion of rhythm as a description of being pulls together a number of isolated but fascinating phrases which suggest that because the mind itself is nothing but a collection of rhythms or energies, words in a book must find rhythmic or energetic equivalents for them.

Answering in "Crise de vers," a rhetorical, really unposed, question concerning just what the magic of literary art is, Mallarmé continues, "Son sortilège à lui, si ce n'est libérer, hors d'une poignée de poussière ou réalité sans l'enclore, au livre, même comme texte, la dispersion volatile, soit l'esprit qui n'a que faire de rien outre la musicalité de tout" (*OC*, 366).[23] Writing, then, might begin in a relationship with reality but rather than representing that reality, it encloses, in a book, only the imaginary prolongation of its musicality or rhythms. In the same way, the palace or the flower in that essay are removed, leaving only their musical evocations (*OC*, 366, 368). The real magic of literary sorcery is to liberate the inherent musicality of all things and insert into the textual surface of a book ("*même comme texte*") that volatile dispersion which is also the mind.

This explains why, according to Mallarmé, the book can rival a Wagnerian opera:

> Oui, en tant qu'un opéra sans accompagnement ni chant, mais parlé; maintenant le livre essaiera de suffire, pour entr'ouvrir la scène intérieur et en chuchoter les échos. Un ensemble versifié convie à une idéale représentation. . . . Telle portion incline dans un rhythme ou mouvement de pensée, à quoi s'oppose tel contradictoire dessin. (*OC*, 328)[24]

In this passage, the ideal representation of the rhythmic or musical nature of the mind's inner scene is best rendered in the silent movements of verse with contradictory designs. Indeed, from Mallarmé's notion of poetry's intellectual music, it is easy to deduce that writing stands in relation to music as a silent and therefore ideal representation of the inner rhythms of both nature and of thought. However, the origins of these rhythms remain suspended. Do these rhythms echo the writer's interior scene or do they actually half-open the reader's interior scene? Are the movements of thought inclined into contradictory designs through the work of the writer or that of the reader?

In *Hérodïade*, the unresolvedness of this dilemma seems to

be expressly maintained since the Nurse appears to play both roles. She is the narrator who envisions and creates the scene before her, thereby mimicking the work of the writer, but she is also the spectator who mobilizes the scene, thereby mimicking the work of the reader. As a result, the Nurse's incantation is like a musical score that both awaits the interpretation of an individual performer or "acolyte" (. . . le livre tarde tel qu'il est, un déversoir, indifférent, où se vide l'autre" [OC, 379]) and creates vibratory, rhythmic dispersions on its own, as a self contained, ideal entity—"Le Livre, où vit l'esprit satisfait . . . ne réclame approche de lecteur. . . . il a lieu tout seul: fait, étant. . . . Le sens enseveli se meut et dispose, en choeur, des feuillets" (OC, 372).[25] In either case, it is the formal representation of the mind's inner rhythms that makes writing musical. Hérodïade, like the Ideal Book, both repeats and elicits (or elicits because it repeats) the echoes of the interior scenes of both readers and writers.

For the reader, Hérodïade's evocation of the mind's musical energies shows us that Mallarmé has created an intellectual concert only potentially realizable in a reading. Inner repetitions, echoes, reflections, enjambments, unsettled rhythms, and phrases without rests or which must be arrested artificially, tend to blur narrative continuity and obscure semantic relations in much the same way as the inner mind might do. The reader is thus asked to repeat the gaze of the Nurse. We must retrace our steps and dance among a confused mass of rhythmic associations between signifiers, mobilizing the object of our gaze according to our own inner designs. This may be an exercise in what Thibaudet referred to as "technical virtuosity" but it is also a way of inscribing within the surface of the text a potential mobility that reflects the Nurse's point of view.[26] Ultimately, the tensions between a stable setting and a mobile point of view or an apparently stable surface and the latent imaginations it may unfold are maintained in the narrative and in the means used to express it, creating a mirror for the spectator or, in this case the reader.[27] For this textual virtuosity becomes very much like the mirror in Hérodïade's "Scène" which opens up scattered dreams or the dancer in

Mallarmé's theater who "écrira *ta* vision à la façon d'un Signe, qu'elle est" (*OC*, 307, emphasis mine; "will write *your* vision like a Sign, which she is").

In this context, I would like to recall Mannoni's discussion of the double spectator whose conscious attention to characters allows an imaginary identification with the work of the performer, that is, with the possibility of playing multiple roles. Not only do these multiple roles echo Mallarmé's concept of how our internal mental spaces double the space of the theater, but as Mannoni points out, that part of our egos that plays these multiple roles can be likened to the credulous child we once were and who, in some sense, we never stop being.[28] In other words, our unconscious identification with the performer relies upon a momentary liberation from adulthood or conscious identity and the reliving of childhood's fantasy play during which multiple self-representations are easily elicited. One can recognize in this childhood fantasy play a liberated consciousness that throws itself into fictions that cannot be.

In the following passage, Mallarmé intimates that this kind of identification can be solicited both at the theater and at home, while reading:

> La danse seule, du fait de ses évolutions, avec le mime me paraît nécessiter un espace réel ou la scène.
>
> A la rigueur un papier suffit pour évoquer toute pièce: aidé de sa personnalité multiple chacun pouvant se la jouer en dedans, ce qui n'est pas le cas quand il s'agit de pirouettes. (*OC*, 315)[29]

Mallarmé's juxtaposition of these two paragraphs draws an analogy between reading and attending a dance or mime performance. In both cases, the performance relies upon its capacity to elicit its observer's own mental acrobatics. Although the observer cannot perform physical pirouettes, his or her mind contains all the elements necessary to mental pirouettes, that is, to the creation of imaginary representations. With an intrinsic capacity to play multiple roles, the reader or spectator can become both the spectator and the actor in an intimate performance on his or her own personal stage: "*on se* la joue," one plays it for oneself. This potential suggests that reading functions like a performance insofar as it doubles in an internal space the duplicity of, for example, Hamlet's stage space by calling into play the possibility of an identification with multiple positions available on a mental stage. It is this desire to recreate in writing the duplicity of actual stage space that explains in retrospect the Nurse's relation to her own mind as well as the reader's relation to the Nurse. For it is through the potential interaction of audience and stage or reader and text that theater, virtual or actual, both represents and reenacts the drama that subjectivity is.

Mallarmé's "Ouverture" clearly does just this by presenting us with a text that describes and inscribes a theatrical apparatus. The reading of *Hérodiade* requires extraordinary attention but, as the myriad of critical re-readings of *Hérodiade* supposes, that attention only helps us to write our own thoughts. One never accomplishes the unfolding of *Hérodiade*'s layers but moves between them invoking a silent, inner song. Just as the Nurse's conscious attention to the surroundings mobilizes unconscious associations with what she sees, we can only read by matching that mobility. Instead of attending to a description of folds of tapestry, the Nurse slips from those folds to the folds of thought; and instead of describing a sibyl embroidered on those folds, her attention shifts from the sibyl to its aromatic prolongation. Likewise, I have moved from the folds of the pages to a description of the inner mind and from the movements embroidered on those pages, I have embroidered a theory of unconscious identification. In other words, the Nurse is the perfect image of an intermittently conscious and unconscious spectator or reader: looking outward, she finds her own mind written before her.

At the same time that the Nurse offers a model for the potential work of the reader, she nonetheless also provides the image of a theatricalized writer. In "L'Action Restreinte," Mallarmé portrays this theatricalized writer in terms reminiscent of the Nurse's performance:

> L'écrivain, de ses maux, dragons qu'il a choyés, ou d'une allégresse, doit s'instituer, au texte, le spirituel histrion.

Plancher, lustre, obnubilations des tissus et liquéfaction de mi-
roirs, en l'ordre réel, jusqu'aux bonds excessifs de notre forme
gazée autour d'un arrêt, sur pied, de la virile stature, un Lieu se
présente, scène, majoration devant tous du spectacle de Soi; là, en
raison des intermédiaires de la lumière, de la chair et des rires le
sacrifice qu'y fait, relativement à sa personnalité, l'inspirateur,
aboutit complet ou c'est, dans une résurrection étrangère, fini de
celui-ci: de qui le verbe répercuté et vain désormais s'exhale par
la chimère orchestrale.

Une salle, il se célèbre, anonyme, dans le héros. (OC, 370–71)[30]

Most striking in this passage is the theatricalized mobility of
the writer himself. First, he is a "spiritual histrion," a kind of
imaginary performer who inscribes himself within the text.
Then, he appears as an "inspirateur," who, like an orchestra
conductor, directs a performance from which he is absent. He
is both sacrificed to this performance and strangely resurrected in the prolonged repercussions of his words. In fact,
the use of "étrangère" to describe this resurrection echoes that
strange rising of the Nurse's own voice. Indeed, like the Nurse
who believes she hears a voice but is not sure whether it is
hers, this author is both disengaged from an enunciating subject (he is not an actor but a spiritual performer partly because he is sacrificed and resurrected) and, at the same time,
expressed or exhaled in a kind of imaginary music.[31] At the
end, however, the writer also appears to be outside of his text,
an anonymous audience to the performance of his own subjectivity. He celebrates himself anonymously in the hero but
appears to become, as well, "Une salle," a place for an audience: "As an audience, he celebrates himself anonymously in
the hero." One could argue that this is also the Nurse's relation to the "Scène" during which she may be said to "celebrate herself anonymously" in Hérodïade since the princess
will merely repeat in different terms the Nurse's own theatricalized drama. As a result, the writer's identity is not only
excessively mobile like that of the Nurse but writing itself becomes an image of that fictive space both presented and elicited in a dance performance, a double of the theater complete

with floor boards, chandelier, lighting, flesh and laughter, obscured fabrics, and liquefied mirrors. In relation to this theater, the writer appears to be not only both on and off stage,
but a spectacle unto himself: actor, director, and spectator
or audience. It is as if writing becomes a performance space
because its author occupies these sundry positions in and
around it. This is the key to *Hérodïade*'s theater and, as we
shall see, the key as well to *L'Après-midi d'un faune*.

Writing, moreover, is here displayed as a kind of pirou-
ette—an ideal evocation of the essential mobility at stake
here—a whirling verticality sustained between its opposing
centripetal and centrifugal forces, a plumb-line or center maintained only by excessive leaps away from that center. Logically, between those opposing aerodynamic pressures, an imaginary Place is carved out, a place or more precisely a fictive
theatrical space defined as the scene or spectacle of subjectivity itself, an objectified, anonymous "spectacle de Soi."
This is not a "spectacle du Moi," the writer does not stage
himself; his own ego or personality has been sacrificed to
the performance. It is the unanchored spectacle of a kind of
reified subjectivity, an event, in which, theoretically, both
readers and writers are joined. Writing, like dancing, becomes
a source of latent drama by eliciting a fantasmatic performance on either side of the page.

This is why *L'Après-midi d'un faune*, written during summer months as a playful respite from the painful *Hérodïade*
(*Correspondance*, 166), may be seen as yet another version of
Mallarmé's ideal theater, for it, too, involves an imaginary
spectacle of subjectivity in which the subject is constituted
as a collection of theatrical positions. In fact, the *Faune* is a
remarkable *mise en scène* of the fantasm that repeats the
structure of *Hérodïade*'s parts but, in so doing, also does
away with its weighty, metaphysical ambiance. The drama of
subjectivity merely shifts its register or tone, reconciling the
more serious with the more frivolous Mallarmé, the searcher
for an Orphic explanation of the Earth (*OC*, 663) with the
painter of Easter eggs (*OC*, 139–40). The *Faune* exploits
more openly what *Hérodïade* only supposes: a significant re-

lationship between the theater and the creative performances of spectators who write. For the faun repeats the work of the Nurse but he analyzes as he proceeds.

THE AFTERNOON OF A FAUN

Like *Hérodïade*, the *Faune* was originally conceived for actual representation complete, in its first version, with copious scenic indications that instructed the faun-actor to stand, sit, pace, and address the décor. However, in its final posh edition of 1876, both the scenic indications and the presence of nymph-actresses have been completely eliminated.[32] In this way, whereas the monologue had originally opened with notations according to which a faun would release two nymphs from his arms and declare, "J'avais des Nymphes! / Est-ce un songe? / Non . . ." (OC, 1450; "I had Nymphs! Is it a dream? No . . ."), the new version opens with a doubt as to whether or not the faun ever possessed any nymphs at all:

LE FAUNE
Ces nymphes, je les veux perpétuer.
Si clair,
Leur incarnat léger, qu'il voltige dans l'air
Assoupi de sommeils touffus.

(OC, 50)[33]

The result of this change is that the reality of any "original scene" of satisfaction is put into doubt. It no longer matters whether the nymphs were real or imaginary, the faun is really content to perpetuate them fantasmatically; their reality is happily replaced by imaginary revivals. In fact, in this new version, the absence of nymphs is, paradoxically, the condition for the faun's erotic pleasure and the creative source of the eclogue itself. The entire eclogue is now nothing but the faun's repetitive "perpetuating" of this lost or nonexistent "original scene," a perpetuating based solely on his wanting to do so, a fantasmatic activity fueled by desire. In this way, the faun's monologue begins with a dismissal of reality, the removal of any real object of desire and, therefore, the possibility of autoerotic fantasy scenarios. The proof is that this play, like *Hérodïade*, also ends in a beginning that closes it into a circle. As a kind of reverse image of Flaubert's *Tentation*, the faun begins by waking up and ends by going to sleep, thus suggesting that his activities take place in the same way every day.

Indeed, the faun, like the Nurse, reproduces Mallarmé's ambivalence toward the theater by making himself into a curious spectator suspended somewhere between passive appreciation and active participation. In his attempt to describe the constantly receding origins of this pleasurable memory in which he ravaged two nymphs, the faun wonders whether the nymphs he recalls were only a dream or the memory of an illusion derived from the setting around him and fueled by his desires. Consciously attentive to this dilemma, the faun becomes a bit of a philosopher who dialogues with himself, thereby splitting himself into the double position necessary to the functioning of the fantasm. He wonders:

> Aimai-*je* un rêve?
> Mon doute, amas de nuit ancienne, s'achève
> En maint rameau subtil, qui, demeuré les vrais
> Bois mêmes, prouve, hélas! que bien seul *je m*'offrais
> Pour triomphe la faute idéale de roses.
> Réfléchissons . . .
> ou si les femmes dont *tu* gloses
> Figurent un souhait de *tes* sens fabuleux!
> (*OC*, 50, my emphasis)[34]

As the personal pronouns multiply in this passage, the faun, like Mallarmé, reading, realizes that he is performing dramas for himself. The subject, "I," takes itself as an object, "to myself," becoming a collective subject in the tacit "we" of "let us reflect," only to finish as a new, externalized subject, "you." He then looks for proof of this autoerotic phenomenon and finds it, initially, in the real trees around him. He proves to himself that his doubt about the nymph's reality is appropriate because of the facility with which his point of view seems

to glide from uncertainty (that mass of ancient nights or collected dream images in his mind) to the subtle, intertwined
branches before him. He is thereby convinced that he cannot
be sure to distinguish dream from reality or the images of his
inner mind from those of the external world. As in a daydream, real perceptions are invaded by imaginary perceptions
that repeat them metaphorically: branches of doubt are also
real branches; the mass of ancient nights is renewed in the
mass of subtle branches. In this way, a circularity is created to
link external and internal perceptions as we saw in both the
"Ouverture" and in Mallarmé's reading of the ballet. This is
why the faun is assured only momentarily that his pleasurable memory or dream was something he created for himself
based on the "ideal absence of roses," an absence or lack filled
by desire. For it is equally possible that these women he is
already glossing, already re-writing, are nothing but a wish in
disguise.

Indeed, the faun is caught, like Hérodïade's Nurse, between
memory or memory traces (his "amas de nuit ancienne" is like
her "confus amas") and those potential futures his senses re-
create everywhere. As a result, the more the faun seeks to fix
his memory of the nymphs in a description, the further away
he moves from ever finding any certain answer. More analytical than the Nurse, the faun proceeds to ask himself whether
he is not merely confusing his desires with a wish inspired by
the surrounding landscape. Was his visual impression of a
blue-eyed nymph purely illusory, the re-translation of a "crying spring"? And the tactile sensation of the other, sighing,
was it merely an effect of the "warm summer breeze?" (OC,
50). Just as the confused images of his mental uncertainty
found their equivalent before him in subtle branches, the
flowing water of the spring and the warm breeze around him
renew his associative inner perceptions of nymphs.

Realizing, however, that there is neither spring nor breeze,
the faun shows us that the only mobility in this suffocated and
immobile landscape is a metaphoric sliding between internal
and external equivalents:

Ne murmure point d'eau que ne verse ma flûte
        . . . et le seul vent

. . . .

C'est, à l'horizon pas remué d'une ride,
Le visible et serein souffle artificiel
De l'inspiration, qui regagne le ciel.[35]

Like the Nurse's empty and still room, there is no movement in this quiet marsh other than the actual music exhaled through the faun's own flute and the inner, silent music of his own inspiration—that artificial double of some other perhaps natural spring. The faun has, then, not only proven that he cannot distinguish the nymphs as real or illusory, a memory or a desire, he has also proven that he cannot apprehend the world around him. To reflect consciously upon the world is to unconsciously re-create it in a mental equivalent.

Frustrated, in fact, by his inability to solve this enigma, the faun dismisses the analytic mode of this search for origins in favor of fantasy reenactments of the supposed rape. In three modulated versions of this now lost original scene, the faun circulates among the positions of a director, a spectator, and an actor only to discover that his pleasure is not related to the objects of his desires but to the pleasurable mobility of a consciousness in transit in a constantly renewable fantasy scenario. In the text itself, the faun's various positions in and around the scenes of his scenarios are now emphasized by typographical differences. These differences underscore the separation of those two distinct theatrical spaces typical of Virtual Theater: that of the faun as a narrating spectator and that of his orchestrated fantasy scenario. In this way, the conscious dialogic thought process of the faun-philosopher is separated from the fantasy scenes that constantly displace it. As always, however, this graphic securing of positions in the text only demonstrates the faun's mental mobility in and around them. Like the fantasm as it is described by Laplanche and Pontalis, the faun's scene is staged within a fixed structure that allows the fluidity of the faun's subsequent identifications. To occupy theatrical positions is to give up the conscious identity of the

philosopher but only, paradoxically, because conscious awareness is secure.

In the first of his fantasy scenes, the faun takes on the roles
of Mallarmé's writer in "L'Action restreinte" in the creation
of his own "spectacle de Soi." Initially, the faun appears as a
kind of backstage director, or "inspirateur," who addresses
the silent and still shores of the marsh. In so doing, he transforms them into an imaginary proscenium arch, complete
with artificial lighting and action:

> O bords siciliens d'un calme marécage
> Qu'à l'envi de soleils ma vanité saccage,
> Tacite sous les fleurs d'étincelles, CONTEZ
> *"Que je coupais ici les creux roseaux domptés*
> *"Par le talent; quand, sur l'or glauque de lointains*
> *"Verdures dédiant leur vigne à des fontaines,*
> *"Ondoie une blancheur animale au repos:*
> *"Et qu'au prélude lent où naissent les pipeaux*
> *"Ce vol de cygnes, non! de naïades se sauve*
> *"Ou plonge . . ."*
>
> (OC, 50–51)[36]

The capital letters of the imperative " CONTEZ" ordered here
by the faun as director and playwright create an objective theatrical space. The faun directs the spectacle from the outside,
telling the marsh shores to recount a tale in which he was
cutting reeds. However, in his telling to tell, the scene materializes before him, turning a past-tense narration into the immediacy of a present-tense description. His personality, like
Mallarmé's, is sacrificed to the performance then resurrected,
"strangely," in an orchestrated scene. A desirous prelude to
the ravishing finds its equivalent in a musical prelude of pipes
and the nymphs perform a kind of ballet in which they appear
first as an undefined but undulating animal whiteness, then as
swans flying or as water sprites diving. In fact, this uncertain
identification of the imaginary characters makes the faun into
a kind of unsuspecting spectator who, like the Nurse, can now
"celebrate himself anonymously in the hero." The verb "on-

doie" is essential to this strange, celebratory resurrection insofar as it is cleverly and ambiguously imbued with two different functions. As a subjunctive mode it supposes that the scene does not really exist and that the faun knows it, but as a present-tense indicative it supposes that the faun actually sees the scene coming to life before his own eyes. That is, the verb "ondoie" suggests that it is both despite and because of the faun's distance from the self-contained scene that he, like all spectators, begins to be necessarily drawn inside it, fantasmatically. The scene is "musicalized" and comes to life as a vision in which the faun participates through his desiring look upon it.

Curiously, this imaginary fantasy, which is only the prelude to a desired ravishing, extinguishes itself at the precise moment of the faun's potential approach. This not only leaves him immobile but desirous—"Inerte, tout brûle dans l'heure fauve" (OC, 51; "Inert, everything is burning in this hour of the wild beast")—it also suggests that he is not really interested in a fantasy replay of satisfaction, but rather in suspending himself in the mounting prelude of desire itself. Again, he does not want nymphs, he wants them perpetuated. In fact, this is only the first in a series of three fantasy scenarios which both progress and repeat, differently, the same rape scene. The *Faune* offers, in this way, a condensed version of *Hérodïade* in that it is built on a series of scenes that begin at the end and end in new beginnings.

Realizing his power to create memories at will in the same way that he can blow into empty grape skins and then gaze upon their luminosity only to find in them "d'idolâtres peintures" (OC, 51)—the world re-organized according to his own designs—the faun addresses the nymphs: "O nymphs, regonflons des SOUVENIRS divers" ("O nymphs, let us reinflate some diverse MEMORIES"; Cohn, 24). Again the capital letters separate the faun's thoughts from his body as he orders the nymphs to revivify his own memories. Memories are by now "diverse" because whether or not there was ever any "original scene" no longer matters; the faun can create (and already has created) new memories as he pleases. Therefore, a new, if old, fantasy begins as the faun's distance from the scene of his desires allows an even more emphasized inability to remain outside it. A past-tense narrative is once again interrupted by a present-tense gaze that forces the spectator into the scene:

> "Mon oeil, trouant les joncs, dardait chaque encolure
>
> . . . .
>
> "Et le splendide bain de cheveux disparaît
>
> . . . .
>
> "J'accours . . .
>
> (OC, 51–52)

He runs after the nymphs and finding them entwined at his feet:

> "Je les ravis, sans les désenlacer, et vole
> "A ce massif . . .
> "Où notre ébat au jour consumé soit pareil.
>
> (OC, 52)[37]

This time, the fantasy scene has gone further. The faun precipitates himself into the narrative scene—"J'accours"—and he rapes the two imaginary nymphs entwined at his feet. We could say that the faun has penetrated the nymphs in the same way his eye penetrated the reeds. Oddly, however, the satisfaction of the rape is less important than the faun's realization that satisfaction only renews lack of itself. Having accomplished the desired rape, the faun's fertile imagination is once again off and running. His struggle with the fading daylight is *the same as* his ravishing of nymphs. Satisfaction thus becomes a memory of satisfaction which in turn becomes a fantasy that creates a new memory of satisfaction, and so on. Desire is endless and circular as is *L'Après-midi d'un faune*. This is why the faun prefers the angry evasiveness of the nymphs to their submission: "Je t'adore, courroux des vièrges, ô délices . . . qui se glisse / Pour fuir ma lèvre en feu buvant" (ibid.; "I adore you, wrath of virgins, O delight . . . which slides / To flee my fire-drinking lip"). This is also why the very end of the eclogue is a gesture toward a new beginning of the same afternoon activities: "Couple, adieu; je vais voir l'ombre que tu devins." (*OC*, 53; "Couple, adieu; I'm going to see the shadow you became"). The nymphs become a shadow or (past) memory of satisfaction which the faun is eternally going to see in those present-tense scenes he is unconsciously willing to believe.

In his theatricalized recreations of a scene of satisfaction, the faun anticipates Freud's use of the figure of the theater for a description of a psychical apparatus. But Freud remains caught in the search for an original model or scene, that "Oedipal rock" back to which fantasy scenarios can be traced, whereas the faun echoes the work of contemporary French revisionists who dismiss the search for origins in order to theorize the mechanics of a "desiring production" that offers pleasure by mobilizing consciousness. In the essay cited several times and whose French title best approximates these revisions, "Fantasme originaire, fantasmes des origines, origine du fantasme," Laplanche and Pontalis argue that the fantasm is first and foremost a structure that stages desire and that it produces pleasure not by replaying an original scene of satisfaction but by allowing a subject to circulate indefinitely both inside and outside the scenes of his fantasies ("Fantasy," 8–14). That is, this pleasure, like the faun's, results from the potential to move among theatrical positions: director of, spectator to, and actor in imaginary scenarios. As a result, whereas Freud looks back across a "history" of the subject to understand and uncover the source of subsequent fantasy scenarios, the faun, like Laplanche and Pontalis, looks forward to the fantasies produced by unconscious desire to discover the ways in which they endlessly move away from any notion of a centralized self.

Since the pleasure inscribed in the structure of the fantasm has also been linked, as we have seen, to that of an actual spectator at the theater and since it appears to reflect as well Mallarmé's own pleasure as a spectator, the faun's enactment of this structure outlines a theatrical apparatus that ultimately reconciles Mallarmé's ambivalent thoughts about theater. Behind the faun's own virtual theaters lies the poet's own specific affective subject-response articulated in his essays on the theater. And this response is in turn programed for readers, in those antirepresentational yet theatrical plays that both present and demand readers who will become spectators of Mallarmé's ilk. In fact, the reason for the faun's intense interest in suspending himself in an imaginary interval between the expectation and the accomplishment of an erotic act is that the faun himself is a creative reader who wants to theorize the mechanisms responsible for the production of his obsessive fantasy scenarios.

In an often-cited and much-discussed passage, the faun steps back to analyze his fantasy accomplishments, providing us with a kind of "art poétique" on the nature of creative inspiration:

> Le jonc vaste et jumeau dont sous l'azur on joue:
> Qui, détournant à soi le trouble de la joue,
> Rêve, dans un solo long, que nous amusions
> La beauté d'alentour par des confusions
> Fausses entre elle-même et notre chant crédule;
> Et de faire aussi haut que l'amour se module
> Evanouir du songe ordinaire de dos
> Ou de flanc pur suivis avec mes regards clos,
> Une sonore, vaine et monotone ligne.
>
> (OC, 52)[38]

This conscious discussion of the relationship of art and desire is nothing but a theoretical analysis of the activity in which the faun has just been engaging, an explanation of or gloss on his previous fantasy performance. The reed which, plucked from nature, has been tamed into a flute, becomes an intermediary between nature and the faun-poet-musician. It redirects to itself the cheek's rhythms (the poet's breath of inspiration) but takes off in a solo, on its own, to transform that vibrating breath into music which the poet can now hear as if outside of himself. In this objectified dreaming somehow separate and yet emanating from its "inspirateur," the flute's music becomes a performance designed to amuse or entertain the surrounding beauty of nature. This entertainment appears to be the result of the faun-poet's ability to both divide himself from the scene of the flute's solo concert—becoming a kind of spectator or listener though he is also its source—and at the same time, allow a fantasy identification or "exquisite confusion" between himself and nature. It is as if he appropriates the beauty of nature only to recreate it fictively, literally expressing it for the benefit of nature's enjoyment. Though it is indeed a "false confusion" in that it is imaginary, the faun, standing back to witness it, can also believe in it. He is "crédule," credulous. Clearly, in that first imaginary balletic prelude, the faun had done just this. By confusing nature's rhythms with his own desiring energies, he was able to project before himself, for the benefit of the marsh's shores, an imaginary and orchestrated fantasy scenario which both contained and did not contain him. The ambivalent grammatical mood of "ondoie" as well as the faun's inability to name that animal whiteness suggested this false belief in or confusion with the scene.

More important, the faun shows us in this passage that it is the sexualized energy of desire that fuels those imaginary performances which art is. For in creating a concert both separate from and yet constituted by himself, any ordinary bodily desire for flesh re-directs or re-translates itself into music. Leo Bersani has referred to this modulation of love as a mechanism of sublimation by which desire multiplies its representations (*The Death*, 83). The description is indeed apt. For it is not a question of representing either nature or the poet's own inner theater but of modulating desirous impulses into art or music by moving away from both nature and a self in order to prolong both of their rhythms in an objectified performance. Moreover, this modulation of desire is the work of a backward glance, a glance with closed eyes ("regards clos"), which peers inside the faun's mind at the fictive representation of nature's beauty already inscribed there. And if this modulation of desire into music creates only one single vain and monotonous line, it is undoubtedly because this music, like a verse of Mallarmé's poetry, is rich enough to evoke an entire, sonorous concert.

As I suggested earlier, this remarkable passage is nothing but a reflection upon the imaginary performance the faun has just finished conducting. The faun is a kind of critic who is re-reading his own spectacle. Therefore, the faun is very much like those readers and critics who continually re-organize Mallarmé's writings. Although this act of critical reproduction is associated with most of Mallarmé's writing, the *Faune* is of particular significance because of the many re-readings of it in music and in dance. There are several versions of the *Faune*, from the musical re-readings of C. Lombardi and Debussy to the choreographic ones of Nijinsky, Serge Lifar, and Jerome Robbins.[39] Like Mallarmé's, the "Fauns" of Debussy and Nijinsky are considered to be the origins of modernity in each of their respective art forms. More recently, Mallarmé's work has also provided a tangential inspiration for much of the work of Pierre Boulez. The composer's "Troisième Sonate" for piano envisioned as a musical transposition of Mallarmé's *Livre* and his "Pli selon Pli/Portrait de Mallarmé" (itself re-written by Maurice Béjart's modern ballet "Pli selon Pli") both owe a debt to the "music" of Mallarmé.[40] This proliferation of musical and choreographic readings leads us to wonder what it is about Mallarmé's writing that causes repercussions in the performing arts.

The answer of course lies in the activities of the faun himself who loses his model in the very gesture of its re-creation, in those musical and choreographic scenes of desire that emanate from a theatricalized subjectivity. Many academic readers merely "narrativize" Mallarmé's texts in order to make sense out of them, yet these musical and choreographic readers are true to Mallarmé's own theories of reading and writing. In re-reading, they actually modulate the musicality of Mallarmé's writing through "exquisite confusions" of their own inner rhythms. They thereby create a plus value of signification, a multiplicity of meanings in art forms which are by nature antirepresentational and which do not, therefore, close circuits of interpretation. On the contrary, they prolong such circuits indefinitely. Indeed, these artists do not seek to represent or describe Mallarmé's poems, but to engage in the activities of the faun. Each appropriates the poem through a gaze adequate to reduce it to an absence. Then, out of an exquisite but false confusion of themselves and Mallarmé's text, each re-writes it, in a new means of textual expression.

On this subject, Pierre Boulez writes: "Le poème est centre de la musique, mais il est devenu absent de la musique, telle la forme d'un objet restitué par la lave, alors que l'objet lui-même a disparu—telle encore la pétrification d'un objet à la fois RECONNaissable et MÉCONNaissable."[41] Like the faun's "original scene," Boulez's composition silences the poem, or more precisely, petrifies its shape in the mobile matter of sound. Therefore, just as the faun modulates his desire for the nymphs into fantasy fictions that both suggest their immediate presence and mark their inevitable absence, in Boulez's music the poem is both recognizable and unrecognizable.

This paradoxical notion of petrifying a poem in music is particularly striking in light of Boulez's fascination with Mallarmé's *Livre*. For in his project for this "Ideal Book," Mallarmé conceived of writing as an architecturally stable framework whose interior would produce an infinite variety of mobile readings (OC, 662–63).[42] Likewise, Boulez designs his "Troisième Sonate" as a fixed compositive structure full of internal reflections and movable, interchangeable parts whereas Béjart creates a ballet in which the internal reflections of dancers moving in space result, by the end, in the construction of a fixed architectural form. Whereas Mallarmé, writing his *Livre*, wanted to "borrow back" the essential principles of music and dance, these re-readers may be said to reverse the process. Therefore, although I am not interested in studying either Boulez's sonata or Béjart's ballet here, I am interested in underscoring the fact that Mallarmé's writing has produced a number of performative readings which in turn demand more performative readings in an endless chain of slightly altered repetitions that actualize Mallarmé's notion of virtual theater.[43]

As the fate of his *L'Après-midi d'un faune* illustrates, Mallarmé has captured in writing a virtual or potential performance that these re-readers strive to repeat. This is only true, however, because the impossible contours of his supposedly unrealizable "Ideal Book" are already inscribed within the poet's own virtual plays. With their multidirectional lines of thought, their lack of communicative logic, and their mobile fragments contained within a structured compositive design, Mallarmé's virtual plays already resemble a musical or choreographic composition, a continually renewable performance of endlessly shifting perspectives. They can never be read or presented in the same way twice. Like Boulez's sonata or Béjart's ballet, the virtual plays are inevitably and eternally "in progress."[44] Just as one reading of the faun's fantasy invites another, ad infinitum, so Debussy's composition invites Nijinsky's, Nijinsky's, Lifar's and Lifar's, Robbins's or Boulez's, Béjart's. We might say, thus, that this series of artistic re-readings of Mallarmé in music and in dance repeatedly modulates an original text into a new, highly mobile performance. And the internal virtuality of each of these performances in turn invites yet more performances. Therefore, in the guise of a conclusion that cannot ever be, I propose that this is the logical result of the many manifestations of the poet's virtual theater. For Mallarmé's virtual theater is not only a particular set of writing strategies—found in all virtual plays—designed to re-present and re-evoke the functioning of the fantasm, nor is it uniquely a way of problematizing the relationship of a "philosophical" subject to the psychoanalytic scenes of his own theatricalized subjectivity, but, indeed, a way of amusing Mallarmé and his readers through false confusions of his virtuality and the actualizing force of our own credulous songs . . .

Notes

INTRODUCTION. WHAT IS VIRTUAL THEATER?

1. Freud, *The Interpretation of Dreams*, 649.

2. Mallarmé, "Crise de vers," *Oeuvres complètes*, 366. My translation. I shall have more to say about Mallarmé's dispersions in my last chapter.

3. Notable exclusions from my study can be found in the work of Musset, Mérimée, and Gautier, as well as more modern examples to be found in Valéry, Queneau, Duras, and Blanchot. I am thinking in particular of Alfred de Musset's *Le Spectacle dans un fauteuil;* Prosper Mérimée's *Théâtre de Clara Gazul;* Théophile Gautier's "Une Larme du diable"; Paul Valéry's "L'Ame et la danse"; Marguerite Duras's *India Song*, which she refers to as "texte théâtre film," and her *L'Homme atlantique;* Raymond Queneau's *Le Vol d'Icare;* and Maurice Blanchot's *L'Attente/L'Oubli.* Another obvious example and model for many of these plays is of course Goethe's *Faust.*

4. Mallarmé speaks of his era as an interregnum in his "Autobiographie," *Oeuvres complètes*, 664. Flaubert speaks of his as unstable and transitional in his *Correspondance*, 2:34.

5. Jean-Louis Baudry compares Plato's cave to Freud's cinematic metaphors for a psychical apparatus in order to theorize this reversal

in his "Le Dispositif." The theme of this reversal is also taken up by Jacques Derrida in the opening of his essay on Mallarmé, "La Double Séance," in *La Dissémination*, 216.

6. In his "Theatrum philosophicum" (*Language, Counter-Memory, Practice*, 166), Michel Foucault presents the history of philosophy as a series of attempts to overturn Platonism. He then proposes a spatial and Freudian theatricality similar to the one I am suggesting in a discussion of the ways in which the philosophical discourse of Gilles Deleuze steps outside of this history.

7. In this context, the history of Virtual Theater is designed in part to counter the arguments put forth by Barish in *The Antitheatrical Prejudice*. In his examination of the Platonic tradition of antitheatrical prejudice in literature and philosophy, Barish studies, among other things, closet dramas and unrepresentable plays which, like Plato and for similar reasons, appear to reject the exigencies of theatrical representation. I, on the contrary, am interested in discussing those plays which, in rejecting the classical esthetics of representation, also theorize and perform the theatricality of thought by using the figure and structure of the theater to illustrate the nature of subjectivity. Rather than being "antitheatrical" because they assume that acting confuses identities, the authors of Virtual Theater exploit the theatricality of Plato's dialogues to emphasize what they see as the inescapable inevitability of that very confusion.

8. Starobinski, "Hamlet et Freud," 2117–18.

9. Laplanche and Pontalis, "Fantasme originaire, fantasmes des origines, origine du fantasme." This essay has been translated as "Fantasy and the Origins of Sexuality"; hereafter, this English translation is cited as "Fantasy" in the text.

10. Lacoue-Labarthe talks about Freud's desire for medical and philosophical mastery and the theatricality that "strangely" disrupts it in "La Scène est primitive," *Le Sujet de la philosophie (Typographie I)*, 209.

11. For an overview of modern theory's use of figures of theatricality to describe itself, see the opening of Brewer's "Performing Theory," 13–19.

12. Sigmund Freud to Wilhelm Fleiss, 15 October 1897, in Masson, ed., *The Complete Letters of Sigmund Freud to Wilhelm Fleiss 1887–1904*, 272–73.

13. Borch-Jacobsen has suggested this analogy in *Le Sujet freudien*, 29.

14. Though it is primarily concerned with cinema rather than theater, the collective *Esthétique du film*, edited by Aumont et al., 176–80, offers an intelligent synopsis of the ramifications of Lacan's redefinition of the Oedipal triangle.

15. Translations of many of the most important essays by these authors, including Baudry's "Le Dispositif," can be found in Cha, ed., *Apparatus. Cinematographic Apparatus: Selected Writings*. See also Christian Metz, "The Fiction Film and Its Spectator: A Metapsychological Study"; and Aumont et al., *Esthétique du film*.

16. On the role of the theater in the work of these philosophers, see Deleuze and Guattari, *L'Anti-Oedipe*; Lyotard, *Economie libidinale* and *Des dispositifs pulsionnels*; Lacoue-Labarthe, *Le Sujet de la philosophie* and "Typographie," 167–271. See also Kofman, "L'Espace de la césure," in *Mélancolie de l'art*, 71–86; Derrida, *Writing and Difference*; and Lacoue-Labarthe's brief overview of this antitheater movement in "La Scène est primitive," 188–89.

17. Of particular interest is Lyotard's "La Dent, la paume," in which Cage and Cunningham are used as examples of an ideal, energetic theater; see *Des dispositifs pulsionnels*, 102–4. (This essay has been translated by Knap and Benamou as "The Tooth, the Palm.") However, at the end of their *L'Anti-Oedipe*, Deleuze and Guattari also imagine an ideal version of their schizophrenia in "modern art."

18. This tendency is well argued by Foucault in "Theatrum philosophicum," 171. See also Brewer, "Performing Theory," 15–16.

CHAPTER 1. FROM PLATO TO DIDEROT

1. Lacoue-Labarthe and Nancy, *L'Absolu littéraire* (hereafter *L'Absolu*). All further references in the text will be to this original French edition, although the theoretical portions of this book have been translated as *The Literary Absolute: The Theory of Literature in German Romanticism*.

2. In this context, "literature" is a concept designed to evoke "*la théorie elle-même comme littérature* ou, cela revient au même, la littérature se produisant en produisant sa propre théorie. L'Absolu littéraire, c'est aussi, et peut-être avant tout, cette absolue *opération littéraire*" (*L'Absolu*, 22). Translation: "*theory itself as literature*, or in other words, literature producing itself as it produces its own

theory. The literary absolute is also, and perhaps above all, this absolute literary operation" (*Literary Absolute*, trans. Barnard and Lester, 12).

3. This emphasis on the mixing of genres is part of a massive reappraisal of Platonico-Aristotelian poetics, a desire to go beyond that which the poetics and rhetoric of antiquity had constituted as genres (*L'Absolu*, 272–77; *Literary Absolute*, 88–91). As Gérard Genette explains it, however, antiquity's "genres" had less to do with literary genres as such than with distinctions between direct and indirect modes of utterance, between *diegetic* or first-person discourse and *mimetic* or third-person discourse. See Genette, "'Genres,' 'types,' 'modes.'" See also Lacoue-Labarthe and Nancy's discussion of the relevance of this distinction to German Romanticism's theories of genre in *L'Absolu*, 142, n. 15.

4. The translators of Bakhtin's *The Dialogic Imagination* explain: "Dialogism is the characteristic epistemological mode of a world dominated by heteroglossia. Everything means, is understood, as a part of a greater whole—there is a constant interaction between meanings, all of which have the potential of conditioning others. A word, discourse, language or culture undergoes 'dialogization' when it becomes relativized, de-privileged, aware of competing definitions for the same things." *The Dialogic Imagination*, 426–27. Lacoue-Labarthe and Nancy do not make specific reference to Bakhtin's "dialogism" in *L'Absolu littéraire* but the reference does appear in a short article that can be seen as the prelude to it: "Le Dialogue des genres," 150, n. 8.

5. This Ideal Book remained unrealized and unrealizable but the desire to write it resulted in various experimental forms or "genres" including fragments, ideas, letters, dialogues, and unfinished novels (*L'Absolu*, 263–64).

6. See Jaeger's discussion of the eighteenth- and nineteenth-century polemics about Platonism as a dogmatic system versus a movement of dialectic in his *Paideia: The Ideals of Greek Culture*, 2:77–79, 87–88.

7. For a discussion of Nietzsche's lectures on Plato see Lacoue-Labarthe in "Nietzsche Apocryphe," *Le Sujet de la philosophie (Typographie 1)*, 100–105. On the question of monologic versus polyphonic traditions, see Jauss, "'Le Neveu de Rameau' Dialogique et dialectique," 146–47.

8. The idea that Diderot's work signals the beginning of a modern "literary" philosophy has been associated, by Derrida, with

a reversal of Platonic Idealism. See *La Dissémination*, 216, n. 2. Creech and Jauss argue, for different reasons, that Diderot's position is more subtly intricated with Plato's. In his *Thresholds of Representation*, Creech states that Diderot is not interested in a "preexisting Ideal" but in an effect of ideality produced within the representation itself (172–74). Jauss proposes that *Le Neveu* stands at the threshold of a historic turning point when esthetics shifts away from a principle of imitation toward a theory of creation, while philosophy shifts away from an ideal realm of Truth and Beauty toward a notion of the autonomy of an individual's ethics ("'Le Neveu de Rameau' Dialogique et dialectique," 160). For Jauss, the Nephew himself is a tragic figure since he can envision these mutations without being able to cross the threshold; I would propose that the *Neveu* performs precisely these shifts by picturing the Nephew himself as only one side of the creative mind, one side of a purely mental contradiction swallowed up, at least momentarily, in the representation of the creative act itself. Incorporating Derrida's, Creech's, and Jauss's positions, I believe that Diderot's work does represent a "modern" breaking point but one that repeats, rather than reverses, Platonic Idealism to arrive at new or modern perspectives. This repetition obviously emphasizes the theatrical or polyphonic Plato I shall be discussing. For further insight on the nature of the breaking point that Diderot's work envisions, see also Jochen Schulte-Sasse's afterword to Caplan's *Framed Narratives: Diderot's Genealogy of the Beholder*, 101–13.

9. See Freud, "Psychopathic Characters on the Stage," 7:305–6, and Barish, *The Anti-Theatrical Prejudice*, 28–31.

10. Laplanche and Pontalis discuss the history of "foreclosure" or "forclusion" in both Freudian and Lacanian thought in their *Vocabulaire de la psychanalyse*, 163–67.

11. For further discussion of the question of the writer in dialogues in a historical perspective, see Lacoue-Labarthe and Nancy, "Le Dialogue des genres." On the likeness of the actor and the philosopher, see Lacoue-Labarthe, "Diderot, le paradoxe et la mimésis."

12. Barish points out that in the *Laws*, Plato exhorts men to imitate the "ideal character" of others in order to reinforce desirable behavior patterns but Barish also concedes that this is a narrow definition of imitation (*The Anti-Theatrical Prejudice*, 21–22). Barish also points out that the dialogues are conducted in a "mimetic mode" (11). On this issue see Karl R. Popper—as quoted by Barish (14, n. 16)—who suggests that for Plato, politics itself is an "art of composition." See also Jaeger, *Paideia*, 2:90–91, and Genette,

"Frontières du récit," 49–70. I, like the French authors, am interested in underscoring the theatrical nature of dialogue as a writing practice.

13. I have borrowed "theatrum philosophicum" from Foucault's "Theatrum philosophicum" (in *Language, Counter-Memory, Practice*), in which he highlights the theatrical self-portrait of postmodern philosophy. Discussing the work of Gilles Deleuze, Foucault refers to this portrait as the repositioning of philosophy in our time because it returns to Platonism rather than attempting to overturn it ("Theatrum Philosophicum," trans., Bouchard, 166). According to Foucault, Deleuze leads Platonism out of a logic of truth and falsehood or simulacrum and perfect model and thereby makes of Platonism a philosophy of material "events," a joyous metaphysics in which philosophy is theatricalized, that is, "multiplied, polyscenic . . . broken into separate scenes" ("Theatrum Philosophicum," trans. Bouchard, 171). In light of my argument in favor of a "Virtual Theater," however, this repositioning is not really new; it merely repeats the work of Diderot and of the German philosophers.

14. Curtius, *European Literature and the Latin Middle Ages*, 138. See Benjamin Jowett, trans. *The Dialogues of Plato*, 4:145–480. See also Jaeger's discussion of the world/stage metaphor, *Paideia*, 3:203, 225–26.

15. I have borrowed these distinctions in the nature of truth from Jauss's discussion of the Socratic dialogue in "'Le Neveu de Rameau' Dialogique et dialectique," 146–47. See also Jaeger, *Paideia*, 2:162–73. On the mathematical metaphor of the circle for dialectic apprehension, see Jaeger, 3:208.

16. Vernant, "Oedipe sans complexes," *Mythe et tragédie en Grèce ancienne*, 80.

17. Jaeger is more thorough in distinguishing the roles of Aeschylus, Sophocles, and Euripides but offers essentially the same point of view in his *Paideia* (1:251–79).

18. Kerckhove, "A Theory of Greek Tragedy," 34.

19. On the unresolvable nature of the Platonic dialogue, see Koyre, *Introduction à la lecture de Platon*, 15–19; and Jaeger, *Paideia*, 2:90–91, 105–6.

20. See Jauss's discussion of Bakhtin's study of the "polyphonic" novels of Rabelais and Dostoievski ("'Le Neveu de Rameau' Dialogique et dialectique," 147) as well as Bakhtin's own discussion of the shift from the epic to the novel as a breakdown in the hierarchy governing an author's relationship to his or her world already antici-

pated by the Socratic dialogues in "Epic and Novel." See *The Dialogic Imagination*, 22–31.

21. In their "Le Dialogue des genres," Lacoue-Labarthe and Nancy suggest that the age of the Sophists, the Renaissance, and the age of the French Revolution were privileged moments for the literary exploitation of the dialogue (150). I am excluding the dialogues of the Renaissance as I am particularly interested in attending to modernism's re-reading of Plato's dialogues as a theatrical problem. In the context of "le drame poétique," Peter Szondi also points out that this antigenre appears at moments of heightened sensitivity when classical forms of theater are questioned. Quoting F. W. Wodtke, he notes: "En Allemagne ce fut l'effet du sentimentalisme du XVIIIe siècle, des périodes préromantique et romantique, de la fin du XIXe siècle, du symbolisme, de l'impressionnisme, puis de l'expressionisme" (In Germany, it was the effect of the sentimentality of the eighteenth century, of the pre-Romantic and Romantic periods, of the end of the nineteenth century, of Symbolism, of Impressionism, then of Expressionism). *Poésies et poétiques de la modernité*, 75. See also Bakhtin. *Dialogic Imagination*, 31.

22. Jauss argues that the Socratic dialogue is not really open since it assumes a latent truth, established from the outset, to which the polyphonic exchange is designed ultimately to lead, but one may wonder whether he is not succumbing here to Aristotle's prejudice. I would argue, after Koyre, that Plato's dialogues are open. On this question, see Jaeger's distinctions between Plato's openness and Aristotle's tendency toward closure, *Paideia*, 2:162–73, as well as Fischer's "Cartography of Inner Space," 220–21.

23. I am grateful to Jean-Marie Diot for initiating my inquiry into this association by proposing it in an unpublished paper entitled "Theatrical (Non-) Staging and the Crises of Western Thought."

24. Although the authors do not deal with the cosmological sphere, it is clear that one could also include, as does F. W. J. Schelling, the revolution or crisis proposed by the Newtonian system of gravitation and its first discoverer, Kepler, thus completing the circle of similarities to Greek culture. See the conclusion to Schelling's *System of Transcendental Idealism* in David Simpson, ed., *German Aesthetic and Literary Criticism*, 126.

25. According to Harris, "It was for a long time generally held that this essay was written by Schelling, or by Schelling and Hölderlin together, and sent to Hegel (presumably in a letter that is now lost), who copied it out, either wholly or in part, because he found it

interesting." See Harris, *Hegel's Development: Toward the Sunlight 1770–1801*, 249. Curiously, Fuhrmans asserts that this text was written by Hegel, although he includes it in his collection of Schelling's letters. See Fuhrmans, ed., *F. W. J. Schelling*, 69. For further information on this problem, see also Schüler, "Zur Chronologie von Hegels Jugendschriften"; Firchow, *Friedrich Schlegel's Lucinda and the Fragments*, 143–256; and Blanchot's discussion of the *Athenaeum* in *L'Entretien infini*, translated into English by Esch and Balfour in "*The Athenaeum* by Maurice Blanchot."

26. *L'Absolu*, 54. The original text as it is quoted by Fuhrmans (*F. W. J. Schelling*, 70) reads "Ich bin nun überzeugt, daß der höchste Akt der Vernunft, der, indem sie alle Ideen umfaßt, ein ästhetischer Akt ist, und daß *Warheit und Güte, nur in der Schönheit* verschwistert sind—der Philosoph muß eben so viel ästhetische Kraft besitzen als der Dichter. Die Menschen ohne ästhetischen Sinn sind unsere Buchstabenphilosophen. Die Philosophie des Geistes ist eine ästhetische Philos." The following English translation is found in Harris, *Hegel's Development*, 511: "I am now convinced that the highest act of Reason, the one through which it encompasses all Ideas, is an aesthetic act, and that *truth and goodness only become sisters in beauty*—the philosopher must possess just as much aesthetic power as the poet. Men without aesthetic sense is what the philosophers-of-the-letter of our times [*unsere Buchstabenphilosophen*] are. The philosophy of the spirit is an aesthetic philosophy."

27. This self-conscious subject is free because the notions of God or immortality are now contained within the self. In the same manifesto, we read "La première Idée est naturellement la représentation de *moi-même* comme un être absolument libre. Avec l'être libre, conscient de soi, surgit en même temps tout un *monde*—à partir du néant—la seule véritable et pensable *création à partir du néant*" (*L'Absolu*, 53). The original text as quoted by Fuhrmans (*F. W. J. Schelling*, 69) but reconstructed to conform to its English translation, reads "Die erste Idee ist natürl<ich> d<ie> Vorst<ellung> *von mir selbst,* als einem absolut freien Wesen. Mit dem freyen, selbstbewußten Wesen tritt zugleich eine ganze Welt—aus dem Nichts hervor—die einzig wahre und gedenkbare *Schöpfung aus nichts*." English translation by Harris (*Hegel's Development*, 510): "The first Idea is, of course, the presentation [Vorst<ellung>] of *my self* as an absolutely free entity [*Wesen*]. Along with the free, self-conscious essence there stands forth—out of nothing—an entire *world*—the one true and thinkable creation out of nothing." In the same text, we

also read "Absolute Freiheit aller Geister, die d<ie> intellektuelle Welt in sich tragen, u<nd> weder Gott noch Unsterblichkeit außer sich suchen dürfen" (Fuhrmans, 70). In English: "Absolute freedom of all spirits who bear the intellectual world in themselves, and cannot seek either God or immortality outside themselves" (Harris, 511). It is interesting to note here the origins of Mallarmean Idealism as well, both in the notion of creating an individual world out of nothingness and in the idea that this world is produced in a self-conscious act.

28. Lacoue-Labarthe and Nancy repeatedly insist on the importance of Diderot's role in the theoretical work of the German Romantics. See Lacoue-Labarthe, "Diderot, le paradoxe et la mimésis," 277; Lacoue-Labarthe and Nancy, L'Absolu littéraire, 285; and "Dialogue des genres," 154. In a more general context, consider also Gita May's comment that as an art critic Diderot anticipates Romantic revolution in "Neoclassical, Rococo, or Preromantic? Diderot's Esthetic Quest," in Undank and Josephs, eds., Diderot Digression and Dispersion, 191.

29. Jauss disagrees with this association of Diderot and the German Romantics; he dissects Hegel's reading of Le Neveu to show that the dialogue does not answer questions opened only later by German Idealism ("'Le Neveu de Rameau' Dialogique et dialectique," 160). According to Jauss, Diderot's dialogue creates a rupture between idealism and materialism (161) or between the individual and society but it does not reconcile or "dialecticize" these contradictions (163). Though I would agree with Jauss's assessment of Hegel's "faulty" reading of Diderot, I would also argue that Le Neveu does, nonetheless, materialize the idealism of the German philosophers. For it does objectify a philosophy of the mind by inserting it within the confines of literature and by supposing that this mind can only be conceived as a theater.

30. Julia Kristeva also makes this point but insists that Diderot's Le Neveu de Rameau stages a dissolution of theocratic hierarchy. See her "La Musique parlée," 156.

31. Jauss, "'Le Neveu de Rameau' Dialogique et dialectique," 147. See also Bakhtin's discussion of the Menippean satire as a product of the disintegration of the Socratic dialogue and as the sign of a shift in the temporal center of artistic orientation because it "placed on the same temporally valorized plane the author and his readers . . . the world and [its] heroes" (Dialogic Imagination, 26−27).

32. Lacoue-Labarthe and Nancy agree with Jauss's reading of the

origins of Diderot's "satire" but add that this satire is first and foremost a mixed genre and thus the sign par excellence of the instability of the speaking subject (*L'Absolu*, 276). They further explain that the Latin "satura" indicated a mix of genres and gave a name to what Aristotle could only refer to as an "anonymous" genre in the *Poetics*. It designated the Socratic dialogue, the mimes of Sophron and Xenarque, as well as other poetic forms that created a "dangerous indistinction" between poetic and theoretical discourse (271). See also their "Le Dialogue des genres," 149–51.

33. Diderot, *Le Neveu de Rameau*, 3. All further references to this text indicate this edition. All translations of passages taken from *Le Neveu* are modified versions of those offered by Leonard Tancock, trans., *Rameau's Nephew* and *D'Alembert's Dream* (hereafter Tancock). Note, however, that these translations do not account for an interesting proliferation of personal pronouns in this and other passages, which my further analyses will clarify: "Come rain or shine, my custom is to go for a stroll in the Palais-Royal every afternoon at about five. I am always to be seen there alone, sitting on a seat in the Allée d'Argenson, meditating. I hold discussions with myself on politics, love, taste or philosophy, and let my thoughts wander in complete abandon, leaving them free to follow the first wise or foolish idea that comes along, like those young rakes we see in the Allée de Foy who run after a giddy-looking little piece with a laughing face, sparkling eye and tip-tilted nose, only to leave her for another, accosting them all, but sticking to none. In my case my thoughts are my wenches" (Tancock, 33).

34. Kristeva, "La Musique parlée," 167. On the question of the other in the self or the self as other, see Creech's "Diderot's 'Ideal Model,'" in *Thresholds of Representation*, 93; and Lionel Gossman's and Elizabeth MacArthur's "Diderot's Displaced *Paradoxe*," in Undank and Josephs, eds., *Diderot Digression and Dispersion*, 117.

35. Translation by Tancock (35–36), modified: "You were anxious to know this man's name, and now you do. He is the nephew of that famous musician who has delivered us from the plainsong of Lully. . . . / He accosts me. . . . Aha, there you are, Mr. Philosopher, and what are you doing here among all this lot of idlers? Are you wasting your time, too, pushing the wood about? This is a disparaging way of referring to the games of chess and women. / I: No, but when I've nothing better to do I enjoy for a moment watching those who push well."

36. Diderot, "Paradoxe sur le comédien," 1008. See also Lacoue-Labarthe's discussion of the paradox of genius in "Diderot, le paradoxe et la mimésis," where the question of the indeterminate nature of the speaking subject is also at issue. See Kofman's "La ressemblance des portraits: L'imitation selon Diderot," in *Mélancolie de l'art*, 37–70, where Diderot's theory of imitation is presented in light of Aristotle's double mimesis.

37. Jauss notes Moi's tendency to change the subject when he has been outwitted by Rameau's questionable morality and can only respond affectively (" 'Le Neveu de Rameau' Dialogique et dialectique," 164). In fact, this is one reason why, according to Jauss, we should see the Nephew and not the philosopher in the role of Socrates (158–59). However convincing Jauss's argument may be, this identification of one role for the Nephew seems as useless or indifferent to the question of subjectivity posed by *Le Neveu* as that long list of critics attributing Diderot's position to one or the other of the protagonists. See Jauss's fine survey of scholarship on this issue (152).

38. See Freud, *The Interpretation of Dreams*, 133–35; and Moore, *Training an Actor: The Stanislavski System in Class*.

39. All translations of passages from the "Paradoxe" are my own: "Casually reclining on a chaise longue, arms crossed, eyes closed, immobile, she is able, by following her dream from memory, to hear herself, see herself, judge herself, and judge the impressions she will elicit. At this moment, she is double: the little Clairon and the great Agrippina."

40. In his discussion of Diderot's program for becoming an author as it is outlined in *De la poésie dramatique*, Creech also notes the splitting of the self into subject and object or spectator and actor. See "Diderot's 'Ideal Model,' " 92.

41. Following are modified translations by Tancock for each of the passages taken from this scene and cited in this paragraph. First: "He: . . . how many times have I said to myself: Well, Rameau, there are ten thousand good tables in Paris, each laid for fifteen or twenty, and of all of those places, there is not one for you! . . . couldn't you manage to lie, swear, perjure, promise, fulfill or back out like anybody else? . . . couldn't you encourage that young man to speak to Mademoiselle and persuade Mademoiselle to listen to him, like anybody else?" (49). Then: "—But what about Daddy? —Yes, of course your Daddy will be a bit upset at first. —And then Mummy, who is always telling me to be a good girl? —Old wives' tales that don't

mean a thing" (50). Finally: "Already her heart is bounding with joy. You fiddle with a bit of paper between your fingers . . . What's that? —Nothing" (50).

42. In his "Diderot, le paradoxe et la mimésis," Lacoue-Labarthe makes a distinction between passive and active mimesis. The first is a passive "dispossession" of self of which Diderot, like Plato, disapproves; the second is a deliberate and voluntary dispossession of self necessary to creativity (280). The first might describe Rameau's usual histrionics whereas the second describes the philosopher/writer. On this subject, he also cites Diderot, himself, in correspondence with an actress: "Je sais aussi m'aliéner, talent sans lequel on ne fait rien qui vaille" (281; "I also know how to alienate myself, a talent without which one is worth nothing").

43. Translation by Tancock (98), modified: "Song is an imitation, by means of the sounds of a scale (invented by art or inspired by nature, as you please), either by the voice or by an instrument, of the physical sounds or accents of passion; and you see that by changing the necessary variables, the same definition would apply exactly to painting, eloquence, sculpture or poetry."

44. Translation by Tancock (104), modified: "What did I not see him do? He was weeping, laughing, sighing, his gaze was tender, tranquil or furious: he was a woman swooning with grief, he was a poor wretch abandoned in the depth of his despair, a temple rising into view, birds falling silent at eventide, waters murmuring in a cool, solitary place or tumbling in torrents down the mountain side, a thunderstorm, a hurricane, the shrieks of the dying mingled with the howling of the tempest and the crash of thunder; he was night with its shadows, he was darkness and silence, for even silence itself is depicted by sound."

45. Translation by Tancock (104), modified: "By now he was quite beside himself. Knocked out with fatigue, like a man coming out of a deep sleep or long trance, he stood there motionless, dazed, astonished. He kept looking about himself, like a man who has lost his way and who is trying to recognize the place in which he finds himself."

46. This performance might be seen as one of those moments to which Jay Caplan refers, during which the philosopher is overwhelmed by feelings. According to Caplan, such moments signal the inability of thought to grasp reality, and the breakdown of dialogue as a mode suitable to the representation of thought (*Framed Narratives*, 7). I agree with Caplan's analysis of these moments but would

suggest that whereas dialogue in *Le Neveu* renders the work of conscious thought, music and identification with it may be a technique for representing the work of unconscious thought.

47. This scene seems to suppose a distinction noted by Lionel Gossman and Elizabeth MacArthur between "an external, rational Other" which one incorporates into the self, that is, which one controls or manipulates, and "an internal Other, perhaps neither accepted nor rational," which disrupts the self's coherence and which Diderot finds disquieting ("Diderot's Displaced *Paradoxe*," 117–18). Whereas the former defines the work of the actor as a societal manipulator (Rameau as a mediator of love intrigues), the latter defines that loss of conscious identity necessary to creativity.

48. See the discussion by Laplanche and Pontalis of the fantasm as a theatrical structure in "Fantasy and the Origins of Sexuality."

49. The following definitions of fugal writing have been borrowed from Sadie, ed., *The New Grove Dictionary of Music and Musicians*, 7 : 9–20. However, caution dictates that any formal features of the fugue be understood generally since, as it is noted in the dictionary entry, music theory has erected formal models which do not necessarily bear resemblance to the fugues of actual composers.

CHAPTER 2. MIXED LITERATURE AND PHILOSOPHY

1. Poulet, *Entre Moi et Moi*, 9, 27–28.

2. In his *Théâtre et pré-cinéma*, 138, Hassan El Nouty points out that before *Hernani* in 1830, there was no real Romantic French tragedy, only mimodramas and melodramas with happy endings. In this context, see Curtius's discussion of the effect of August Wilhelm Schlegel's unfavorable comparison of Racine and Euripides which, under the influence of Madame de Staël, was to give support to French Romanticism and its dramatic forms. Curtius, "Friedrich Schlegel and France," in *Essays on European Literature*, 98. Albert Thibaudet also notes that Schlegel's attack on Racine combines with the publication of *De l'Allemagne* in 1813 to further fuel nationalistic debates about the theater; see *Histoire de la littérature française*, 50, 90.

3. Duchet, "Théâtre, histoire et politique," 285.

4. El Nouty, *Théâtre et pré-cinéma*, 273. See also El Nouty's comments on Hugo's use of voices in a crowd in the fifth act of *Cromwell*, 131.

5. Prior, *The Language of Tragedy*, 220.

6. Salomon, "Préface," 27–29.

7. Musset, "Avis au lecteur" in "La Coupe et les lèvres," from *Un Spectacle dans un fauteuil.*

8. El Nouty does make an exception for Flaubert's "psycho-drama" (*Théâtre et pré-cinéma*, 277–78), to which I shall return in chapter 4. It is precisely this kind of exception that has created the need for a term such as "Virtual Theater."

9. Abrams, *The Mirror and the Lamp*, 84–88, 145–46. Affron, *A Stage for Poets*, 11, 11–18.

10. I have borrowed the heading from Raymond Bellour's article "L'Ego Hugo" contained in the Massin edition of Hugo's complete works. Quotation is from Hugo, *Littérature et philosophie mêlées*, 1:7. My translation: "Why, indeed, should we not confront more often than we do individual revolutions with societal revolutions?" All translations from Hugo's *Littérature et philosophie mêlées* are my own.

11. Lacoue-Labarthe, "Présentation."

12. Thibaudet, *Histoire de la littérature française*, 122.

13. Hugo, *Littérature et philosophie mêlées*, 1:7 (hereafter cited as *Littérature* in the text).

14. My translation: "All of that goes, comes, advances, retreats, intermingles, connects, thrusts itself, contradicts itself, argues with itself, believes, doubts, gropes along, denies, affirms, without visible goal, without exterior order, without apparent law; and yet . . . in the midst of all these contradictory ideas that buzz at the same time in this chaos of generous illusions and loyal preconceptions . . . one senses the sprouting and the movement of an element which will one day assimilate all the others, the spirit of liberty [or liberty of thought], which the author's instincts will apply first to art, then by an irresistible development of logic, to society; so that for this author . . . literary ideas will correct political ideas."

15. My translation: "In times such as ours, when events so rapidly change the aspects of doctrines and of men, he [the author] thought that it would perhaps not be a spectacle without lesson [to present] the development of a serious and righteous mind that had not yet been directly involved in any political thing and that had silently accomplished all its revolutions upon itself, with no other goal than the satisfaction of its conscience."

16. My translation: "The author believes that all those among

our contemporaries who in good faith will make the same folding back onto themselves, will not find less profound modifications in their thought, if they have had the wisdom and disinterest to allow that thought its free development in the presence of facts and results."

17. My translation: "If we were permitted to risk a conjecture as to what must be the outcome of art, we would say that in our opinion, a few years from now, art, without renouncing all its other forms, will sum itself up more specially in the essential and culminating form of drama. ... Also, the few remarks we shall make about drama are applicable in our way of thinking ... to poetry in its entirety, and that which applies to poetry applies to art in its entirety."

18. El Nouty discusses the importance of this polemic historically as a conflict between "le montrer" and "le dire" in the introduction to his *Théâtre et pré-cinéma*, 9-64.

19. My translation: "Drama, without leaving the impartial limits of art, has a national mission, a social mission, a human mission. When he [the author] sees each night the people so intelligent and so advanced, who have made of Paris the central city of progress, cluster together in a crowd before a curtain ... he questions himself with severity and introspection about the philosophical usefulness of his work.... The poet also bears the burden of souls.... The theater, we repeat, is a thing that teaches and civilizes."

20. Lacoue-Labarthe discusses the Aristotelian notion of mimesis with new emphasis on its corrective or pharmaceutical nature in "Diderot, le Paradoxe et la mimésis," 273.

21. My translation: "It is through true paintings of the eternal nature that each one carries within; it is by taking ourselves, you, me, us, them, everyone, by our irresistible emotions of father, of son, of mother, of brother and of sister, of friend and of enemy, of lover and of mistress, of man and of wife; ... it is by probing with the *speculum* of genius our conscience, our opinions, our illusions, our prejudices; it is by stirring up all that is in the shadow in the depths of our entrails; in a word, it is by casting ... great quantities of daylight onto the human heart, this chaos whence the *fiat lux* of the poet pulls a world! —It is thus and not otherwise. —And, we repeat, the more profound, disinterested, general, and universal the dramatic creator will be in his work, the better will he accomplish his mission with regard to both his contemporaries and posterity."

22. Barthes, "Texte (Théorie du)," 1014. My translation: "It is the 'function' of the text only to 'theatricalize' . . . this work through which the encounter of the subject and language is produced."

23. Vigny, *Le Journal d'un poète*, 1:352–53. My translation: "I must therefore say that I thought I had isolated within myself two beings quite distinct one from the other, the *dramatic me*, that lives with activity and violence, that feels with pain or drunkenness, that acts with energy or perseverance, and the *philosophical me* that separates itself daily from the other me, that disdains it, judges it, criticizes it, analyzes it, watches it pass by, and laughs or cries at its mistakes as would a guardian angel. The two persons will speak in turn in this book, and I am convinced that the sound of their voice will be easily recognized." All further translations from Vigny's writings are my own.

24. Vigny, *Oeuvres complètes*, 2:904. All further references to Vigny's writings including *Stello*, *Daphné*, and *Le Journal d'un poète* are from this two-volume edition. My translation: "I present these considerations, not to set forth principles, but to explain my own and to help understand what ideas made me decide to impress upon my works the form I have given them."

25. My translation: "(*To be placed in the preface of my next drama*). There are in works of art two points of view. One philosophical, the other poetic. —The philosophical point of view must support the work, drama, or book, from one pole to the other precisely as does the axis of a globe, but the globe in its rounded form complete with these varied and brilliant colors is an image of the axis of art which must always be in sight, while turning around the philosophical thought and carrying it off in its atmosphere. . . . To warm up rather than to teach."

26. My translation: "I have long searched for which secret aversion kept me away from writing for the theater, strange aversion in me whose main instinct or talent is dramatic composition. In analyzing theatrical art, I found it. It is that there is in this art one part that remains forever floating, that of the *playacting* which belongs to the actor, and that which is called *playacting* is nothing more than the expression of sentiments, the designing of paintings and of scenes, that is to say, three of the sources of emotion."

27. My translation: "Stopped the project of *Daphné* which was not simple enough. This is too tragic for a poem. It is a Drama that I cannot save for the stage because no government would allow its representation."

28. The same is true of other of Vigny's projected dramas such as *Astrolabe* or *Grégoire VII*. For further commentary on these dramas, one can refer to the Conard edition of Vigny's *Journal*, 1:238, 240, 386, 433.

29. My translation: "I cannot overcome the attraction I have always had for Julian the Apostate. If metempsychosis exists, I was that man. He is the man whose role, life, character would have been most appropriate for me in history."

30. My translation: "*Julian the Apostate*. Since he always spoke Greek, I will write the drama of the Stoics in prose. . . . The drama will be entitled "The Stoics." This work which I've dreamed about for so many years does not yet have its definitive form in my mind. It's coming closer. When I see it well enough, I shall write it." Then: "*Julian the Apostate.* / I am pursued ceaselessly by this thought. To paint the interior battle of the soul in this great man, preserver of the *Roman Empire* and foreseeing the invasion of Barbarism. Fearing Christianity because it weakens the *defense* of the Empire by discouraging *warriors* from *war*. [He] discusses this question with Saint Martin. Entitle the play: *The Stoics.*"

31. My translation: "Wrote the chapter: "Christ and Antichrist." —Let there be at the end of the volume an Imaginary Dialogue Between Julian and Jesus. —Stello hears it distinctly. / —*Love*, the Poet, Stello, is searching for beauty and goodness; *Intelligence*, the Philosopher, Docteur Noir, is searching for the true. . . . / You see, says Docteur Noir, that Lamuel would have done better to throw his ideas [on paper] as you will yours, in an entirely philosophical or poetic form, rather than throwing himself headlong into the stream in order to reverse its flow. But he could do only what he did because he was neither wholly a poet nor wholly a philosopher."

32. My translation: "He thought he saw before him the melancholy faces of Gilbert, of Chatterton, and of André Chénier, and the firm and inflexible voice of Docteur Noir resounded still smooth in his ears. . . . he caught himself dreaming about the people in the Universe who had best understood the sadness of life: the Jews."

33. My translation: "Phèdre counsels Julian to leave life because he's destroying the human race. / Dr. N. —What then is your plan? What is at the back of your thoughts? Stello leans forward, receives a few words in his ear. / —It is, says Lamuel, this new passion to assist humanity. . . . / That's not it, says Docteur Noir. —he is fooling himself and is mistaken about himself. / —Let us read . . . *Daphné* follows."

34. See Benveniste, "L'Appareil formel de l'énonciation." We shall see a similar if more subtle exploitation of this same phenomenon in Flaubert's *La Tentation de Saint Antoine* in chapter 4.

35. My translation: "—An extreme sensitivity, repressed at the beginning of childhood . . . remained locked away in the most secret corner of the heart. —The world never again saw more than ideas, the result of the prompt and exact work of intelligence. —Docteur Noir alone appeared in me, Stello was hidden."

36. Milner, ed., *Littérature française: Le Romantisme, I: 1820–1843*.

37. My translation: "THE THEATER (SYMBOL). —For Rachel. The journalist to the act[ress?]. —The passion of the world is to see. . . . —It is for that [reason] that they created the Theater, but the Theater speaks only of the past or accounts for present events only in very roundabout allusions. What was needed was an everyday theater where great personages would come in the morning to play their role of the previous evening, or in the evening, the role they'd played in the morning . . . without the spectators needing to leave their homes; this Theater has been made. This Theater is a journal. . . . / He who each day makes these living personages move according to his own pleasure, he who presents them in his theater with whatever meaning and in whatever light he pleases, he who builds them up or shrinks them down according to his own pleasure, he is the journalist! this will be you tomorrow if you wish! see if you find this occupation extensive enough!"

38. Translation by Guy Daniels in Stendahl, *Racine and Shakespeare*, 24: "I have arrived at the last confines of what logic can grasp in poetry." All modified versions of Daniel's translations of *Racine et Shakespeare* (hereafter Daniels) will be so indicated. Those appearing without reference to Daniels are my own.

39. As Henri Martineau notes, between 1804 and 1830, Stendhal would work and rework his most complete dramatic project, *Letellier*. See *Le Calendrier de Stendhal*, 133–41. Modeled after Molière's *Tartuffe*, *Letellier* proposed to represent a modern-day conflict of censorship between a talented young author, Chapelle, and Letellier, a thinly masked portrayal of Julien-Louis Geoffroy and other such extremely oppressive censors. However, the project was from its inception undermined because of its subject matter and its blatantly designated living models. Though it may indeed have been thus a mirror of its times, *Letellier* was destined, for this reason, to

self-destruct. See Stendhal's introduction to the characters in "Letellier," *Théâtre*, 3:37.

40. Like *Letellier*, Stendhal's two plays written in defense of his theories, *Le Retour de l'île d'Elbe* and *Lanfranc ou le poète*, were simply more theatricalized versions of Stendhal's own personal concerns, experiments in the creation of theatrical self-representations. See, however, El Nouty's discussion of *Le Retour*, in *Théâtre et pré-cinéma*, 119–21.

41. Stendhal, *Racine et Shakespeare* (Paris: Calmann-Levy, n.d.) 7. All further page references to these pamphlets in the text indicate this edition.

42. Blin, *Stendhal et les problèmes du roman*, 53–59.

43. It is not my intention to enter into the polemics surrounding the question of Realism in recent critical studies from Georg Lukács to Fredric Jameson. Rather, I am concerned with the theatrical nature of Stendhal's mirror esthetic and the ways in which it displaces its own gesture at "objective" or "realist" representation. For a provocative overview of the Realist debate and its ramifications, see Jameson, "Reflections on the Brecht-Lukács Debate," in *The Ideologies of Theory*, 2:133–47, and his "The Ideology of the Text," 1:17–71. For a consideration of the ways in which Stendhal's "real" may overlap onto Lacan's, see also Jameson's notion that Lacan's "real" is "simply History itself" in "Imaginary and Symbolic in Lacan," in ibid., 1:75–115. Finally, for further discussion of the mirror esthetic in Stendhal's novel *Le Rouge et le Noir*, see my "Stendhal's Theaters."

44. My translation: "Illusion therefore signifies the act of a man who believes a thing that is not, as in dreams, for example. . . . But [at the theater] these moments are infinitely brief, lasting, for example, a half-second or a quarter-second."

45. Freud, *The Interpretation of Dreams*, 83. See also Freud, "Psychopathic Characters on the Stage."

46. Mannoni, *Clefs pour l'Imaginaire ou l'Autre Scène*. See also Green, *Un Oeil en trop*.

47. Brombert, "Stendhal et les 'douceurs de la prison,'" in *La Prison romantique*, 83.

48. Starobinski, "Stendhal pseudonyme," in *L'Oeil Vivant*, 219–21, 224.

49. Stendhal, *Souvenirs d'égotisme*, 70.

50. Roger Fayolle notes that as of 1834 Stendhal gives up his

dreams of writing for the theater: "Je regarde le roman comme la comédie du XIXe siècle." In Fayolle, ed., *Racine et Shakespeare*, 43.

51. Translation by Daniels (26), modified: "This marks the end of the dialogue between the two adversaries, a dialogue that I actually witnessed in the pit of the theatre on Chantereine Street, and whose participants I could name if I wished."

52. Translation by Daniels (19), modified: "Why, I will say to the partisans of *Classicism*, do you demand that the action depicted in a tragedy take place in not more than twenty-four or thirty-six hours, and that the setting represented on the stage not change, or at any rate, as Voltaire puts it, that the changes of setting not extend beyond the different rooms of a palace? / THE ACADEMICIAN: Because it is not credible that an action represented in two hours should encompass a week or a month; or that in the space of a few moments the actors should go from Venice to Cyprus, as in Shakespeare's *Othello*, or from Scotland to the English court, as in *Macbeth*. / THE ROMANTIC: Not only is that incredible and impossible; but it is likewise impossible that the action encompass twenty-four or thirty-six hours." Stendhal appends a footnote that reads "Dialogue of Hermès Visconti in the *Conciliatore*, Milan, 1818."

53. Though it might be possible to draw a relationship between this triangular structure and the Oedipal triangle, I am not interested in making that association here. On the contrary, I am underscoring the importance of the triangle's relationship to the theater and thereby displacing the Oedipal question. For a discussion of the Oedipal complex in Stendhal, see Leo Bersani, "The Paranoid Hero in Stendhal," in *A Future for Astyanax*, 106–27; and "Stendhalian Prisons and Salons," in *Balzac to Beckett*, 91–139.

54. It is true for example, that the Stendhalian hero always finds himself caught between being both a spectator and an actor and for this reason always "writes" his own fate, so to speak. As Starobinski has shown, he plays roles to seduce women and then feels ridiculous watching himself play (Starobinski, "Stendhal pseudonyme," 226–28). In fact, this theatrical gap, unconsciously present in Hugo's journal, constitutes, in Stendhal's novels, the hero's tragic flaw. For further discussion of this phenomenon in *Le Rouge et le noir* specifically, see my "Stendhal's Theaters."

55. The following brief historical overview is intended to be only that. For greater detail, see Bakhtin's discussion of the relationship between the breakdown of the Socratic dialogue and the origin of the

novel in "Epic and Novel" in *Dialogic Imagination*, 3–40, as well as Lacoue-Labarthe and Nancy's "Le Dialogue des genres," in which they trace the dialogue's encounter with literature from an historical perspective.

56. Translation by Daniels (89), modified: "Such is Plato: an impassioned soul, a sublime poet, a captivating poet, a writer of the first rank, and a puerile reasoner. See . . . the quaint arguments advanced by Socrates." Note also that in his essay "Victor Cousin" of 1827, Stendhal comments further on Plato's dissimulation: "Qu'est-ce encore que Platon? C'est un esprit d'une trempe si haute qu'en le lisant on le sent supérieur à l'opinion exclusive qu'il plaide par la bouche de Socrate." In *Mélanges de littérature*, 3:235. My translation: "What then is Plato? He is a mind of such high caliber that while reading him, one feels him to be superior to the exclusive opinion he pleads through the mouth of Socrates."

57. In this context one might also note Stendhal's conception of the artifice of presentation characteristic of the work of the genius, what Stendhal sees as the "great man," whether painter, musician, or writer. In his "Réponse à quelques objections" provoked by the first *Racine et Shakespeare*, for example, Stendhal points out that the great artist, like Racine, as opposed to the simple "peintre-miroir," like Carlo Goldoni (*Racine et Shakespeare*, 100–101), does not simply represent a real before which the ideal spectator may enjoy a moment of dramatic pleasure, but absorbs that real through sensitive perception becoming the very substance on which nature or reality leaves its impressions (122). It is from this model that the artist then borrows his representation, a bit like Diderot's actor. On this subject, see my "Stendhal's Theaters."

58. This heading is my translation of Mallarmé's phrase "le seul théâtre de notre esprit, prototype du reste," in "Hamlet," *Oeuvres complètes*, 300.

59. The following discussion of Freud and his critics is put forth in a different context in my "Why Go to the Theater?" 73–78.

60. Starobinski, "Hamlet et Freud," 2117.

61. The distinction between these two forms of desire is one I am borrowing from Lyotard's *Des dispositifs pulsionnels*, 281.

62. A similar criticism of Deleuze and Guattari is made by Leo Bersani in *A Future for Astyanax*, 8–9. For further insight into Lyotard's specific attitudes toward Freud's theatrical metaphor, see his "The Unconscious as mise-en-scène" and his "Par-delà la repré-

sentation" which appears as a preface to the French translation of Anton Ehrenzweig's *The Hidden Order of Art, L'Ordre caché de l'art.*

63. Green, *Un Oeil en trop*, 12. Though a translation of this passage can be found in Green, *The Tragic Effect: The Oedipus Complex in Tragedy*, 2, I believe my own translation to be more exact: "Fantasy would be [best approximated] by an association with a certain form of theatre made up of a narrator who would speak about an action occurring in a place that he designates as outside of himself, all while, at the same time, not being a stranger to it."

CHAPTER 3. LIBERATED THEATER

1. Epigraph from Hugo, *Oeuvres poétiques*, 660.
2. Gaudon, "Hugo." Ascoli, *Le Théâtre romantique.*
3. Barrère, *Hugo, l'homme et l'oeuvre*, republished as *Hugo.*
4. Barrère, *La Fantaisie de Victor Hugo.*
5. As quoted by Barrère, *La Fantaisie de Victor Hugo*, 2:398. My translation: "Playable alone in that ideal theater that each man has in his mind." All translations of all of Hugo's writings are my own. They are literal and explanatory rather than poetic.
6. Hugo, *Théâtre complet*, 2:1903. References to this edition are abbreviated in the text as *TC.*
7. Charles Affron points out that the "sub-genre" of armchair theater is less related to the fiasco of *Les Burgraves* than to Hugo's ironic perspective into his own art (*A Stage for Poets*, 84). Henri Peyre notes that between 1850 and 1860, Hugo was working arduously at investing his philosophical ideas with a poetic form but points out that during this period, a general pessimism swept over all of Europe. See *Victor Hugo: Philosophy and Poetry*, 50. Claude Gély, in his *Victor Hugo poète de l'intimité*, associates exile with Hugo's new and profound return to autoexamination and contemplation: ". . . enfin dépouillé de tout ce qui le dérobait à la lucidité de son propre regard, enfin libéré à l'égard de tout ce qui le détournait de l'essentielle 'contemplation'" (383; ". . . finally stripped of all that was hiding his own look from lucidity, finally freed with regard to all that was turning him away from the essential 'contemplation'"). Gély also sees *Les Contemplations* as the work in which, by the grace of mystic revelations, literature and philosophy are mixed (408).

8. Hugo, *William Shakespeare*, 160. References to this piece are abbreviated in the text as *WS*. My translation: "The poet philosophizes because he imagines."

9. Albouy, *Mythographies*, 100–101, 176–77.

10. Levaillant, *La Crise mystique de Victor Hugo*, 74–76. According to Levaillant, this mystical endeavor was first introduced by Madame de Girardin who originally enticed the participants by promising that they could speak with the spirit of Léopoldine, Hugo's drowned daughter. Her apparition fueled a continued interest in this type of "spiritual" dialogue.

11. As quoted by Delalande, *Victor Hugo à Hauteville House*, 21, n. 2. My translation: "I had found by meditation alone several of the results which today make up the revelation[s] of the table . . . I had perceived others which remained in my mind in the form of confused outlines. . . . Today the things which I had seen in their entirety are confirmed by the table, and the 'semi-things' are completed by it."

12. Hugo refers to his crisis and the philosophical doubts it engenders in the *Journal de l'exil* and the *Livre des tables*. See the *Oeuvres complètes*, 9:1165-1487, 1495. See also Levaillant, *La Crise mystique de Victor Hugo*.

13. Hugo, *Oeuvres complètes*, 9:1366. References to this edition of Hugo's complete works are indicated in the text as Massin. It is perhaps important to note that Maurice Levaillant was the first to discover and publish *Le Prologue mystique* in his *La Crise mystique de Victor Hugo*. He also notes that it was Hugo himself who later gave the piece a title (282).

14. My translation: "Starry sky. Serene night. The stars sparkle. Their sparkling murmurs mysterious words. Suddenly, two of these stars undergo a strange development and become enormous; and as if the spectators' opera glasses had been transformed into magic telescopes, they all hear these words coming from two monstrous globes."

15. See Barrère's references to the theme of Hugo "entendant" and "voyant" (a "listener" or "knower" and a "seer") as well as his discussion of Hugo's theories of animism during the crisis years in *La Fantaisie de Victor Hugo*, 2:81.

16. My translation: "A FRANK SPARROW, coming out from under the leaves and flapping its wings. / Everyone out! / At the signal given by the sparrow, an extraordinary movement agitates the forest. It seems that everything is awakening and coming to life. Things be-

come beings. Flowers take on the appearance of women. One could say that the minds of plants poke out their heads from under the leaves and begin to chatter. Everything speaks, everything murmurs, everything whispers. Quarrels here and there. All the stems bend pell-mell toward each other. The wind comes and goes. Birds, butterflies, flies come and go. Earthworms stand up outside their holes as if prey to a mysterious rut. Odors and rays of light embrace. In the clusters of trees, the sun produces all possible shades of green. During the entire scene, mosses, plants, birds, flies mix together in groups that decompose and recompose incessantly. In corners, flowers groom themselves, the happy ones adjusting their necklaces of dew, the melancholy making their teardrop of rain shine in the sun. The pond water imitates the shimmering of silver gauze. Nests give little cries. For the seer [clairvoyant], it is an immense tumult; for man, it is an immense peace."

17. My translation: "I blame / God for having made man in two pieces / of which one is a woman." Then: "To love! ludicrous adventure. / Man is made to dream in the depths of nature."

18. My translation: "THE WAGTAIL / Let's make a horrible uproar. / DENARIUS, in contemplation. / Fresh silence!"

19. My translation: "DENARIUS / All is enigma and all is word / Oh! I feel the forest full of the chimera! / Creation is a somber grammar / The invisible, mixed with the real, changes a ray / Into a look, and the flower and the tree into vision."

20. My translation: "Everything sings a mysterious opera here. . . . / An invisible ear hears scales sounding out. . . . / (pushing himself deeper into his dream) / Why not? I would be a primitive man. . . . / And I would savor, alone in my green stall, / Many scores executed for me / By the wind/musician in the forest/orchestra."

21. My translation: "I am crazy. My mind flounders in the middle of Chompré. / "No, let us remain in the true, in the grass, in the field. / Being a wolf is enough, let us not be a faun. / . . . / The true suffices. Let us be a simple philosopher. . . . / While humanity was sucking its thumb, fine, / The fable had its value. But man is a has-been, / Hell! Right now, the human mind wears a wig, / And our reason shakes a mind now out of style. / To believe in nymphs is stupid [bestial]. One has to be real."

22. My translation: "I want to bathe my feverish forehead / In your breasts! to roll myself up in your beds!"

23. My translation: "DENARIUS / This woman has a heavenly

sparkle in her eye. / She's Diana, or Psyche! / THE SPARROW /
Her, she's mademoiselle Balminette, seamstress in residence, / Number three, Bear Street." Then: "Yes, that's the ideal, the figure [I]
dreamed! / Oh! that white dress lifted up for an instant! / The lightning bolt of paradise!" Finally: "THE PEBBLE, to the stream, /
Without us, if we had not turned up the Wench's skirt, / This Clown
ran the risk of becoming Plato."

24. Kristeva, "The System and the Speaking Subject."

25. My translation: "THE SPARROW, looking around himself
/ Oh, my word! This is the court, / this forest! It's Versailles and the
oval window . . . / (to a tuft of heather) / Hello, La Bruyère. [Mr.
Heather] / (to a tree branch) / Hello, Rameau. [Mr. Branch] / (to a
crow on the crag) / Hello, Corneille. [Mr. Crow] / (to the water lily)
/ Hello, Boileau. [Mr. Drink-Water]."

26. Genette, "Silences de Flaubert," 222–43.

27. On the importance of *aparté* and other dramatic techniques
such as the use of gestures and objects to develop dramatic logic, see
Butor, "Le Théâtre de Victor Hugo."

28. Charles Affron sees the plastic configuration of the stage setting as an image of antithesis. As he puts it, "We see on the stage two
distinct realms, the liberty of the enclosed cloister opposed to the
slavery of the open world beyond." As this universe is absurd, according to Affron, not only do "the play's spatial relationships have
the potential for dramatic and poetic movement built into them" but
this intolerable system is ripe for transformation by the "imposition
of values consistent with Hugo's universe" (*A Stage for Poets*, 99).

29. See Riffaterre's study of Aïrolo's role in the stylistic structure
of the play in "Un exemple symboliste chez Victor Hugo."

30. Jamati's comparative study of *L'Epée* and *Les Châtiments*
emphasizes the play's revolutionary appeal to insurrection. See "Dans
l'atmosphère des *Châtiments*."

31. My translation: "THE MARGRAVE, hidden behind the
hedge. / There is fury in my soul. / She watches the children, and bit
by bit, listens to them. —While they speak without seeing her, she
approaches them step by step."

32. My translation: "LEO / . . . Lower your veil, Lea. I respect
you. / Don't be afraid of me. / A SATYR, in the woods / An entirely
suspicious sentence."

33. My translation: "CONVERSATION OF THE WAVES /
under water / The scene takes place at the Porte-Saint-Martin, in the

middle of the sea, during the drama: *The Storm.* / KIDS: [and] WAVES} / Romarin, Filasse / Boilu, Popard / Grimebodin, Bigaru / Talotte, Quine-au-lièvre / Bigarreau / FIRST WAVE / Hey, Titi, you stepped on my hand. / SECOND WAVE / Sir, you're bothering me." Then: "(This comes after a serious and terrible dialogue of the winds in a polar storm. The two scenes are in the same play)."

34. Albouy, *La Création mythologique chez Victor Hugo*, 179, n. 1.

35. My translation: "Is it wrong for an author to be an author to the point of bringing to life in the depths of his thinking stereotypes—more or less real—in which he incarnates his ideas? Does the author have the right to push creation to the point of causing the characters of his drama to exist above and beyond that drama? When the enthusiastic young man *who used to sing*, when the miserable and joyous child, when these two beings who suffered and sang have fallen, is it permitted to open their tombs a bit, in order to allow their voices to escape like breaths from the shadow? If the reader answers yes, he will not reject this book."

36. The circularity of desire and of Hugo's total composition may explain why the manuscript of 1886 places *La Forêt mouillée*, the earliest composition, at the end of the *Théâtre en liberté*. See Hugo, *Théâtre complet*, 2:1907.

37. My translation: "These waves, this ebb and flow, this terrible coming and going . . . this calm after the storm, these infernos and these paradises of the eternally moved immensity, this infinite, this unfathomable, all this can be in one mind and if it is, this mind is called genius . . . and it is the same thing to look at these souls or to look at the ocean."

38. My translation: "What does the probe bring you back, promontory into this mystery? What do you see? Conjectures tremble, doctrines quiver, hypotheses float; all of human philosophy vacillates with a somber breath[ing] before this opening. . . . One presses the abyss with questions. Nothing more."

39. As quoted by Barrère, *La Fantaisie de Victor Hugo*, 2:346. My translation: "Every dreamer has within himself this imaginary world. This summit of dreams is beneath the skull of every poet as the mountain [is] beneath the sky. It's a vague kingdom full of the inexpressible movement of the chimera."

CHAPTER 4. THE DYNAMIC UNIVERSE OF
FLAUBERT'S *TENTATION*

1. Epigraph from Flaubert, *Correspondance*, 6:385. Citations
from Flaubert's correspondence (hereafter abbreviated *C* in the text)
refer to this edition unless otherwise indicated. All translations of the
correspondence are my own: "In the midst of my grief, I'm finishing
my *Saint Anthony*. It is the work of a lifetime because the first idea
came to me in 1845 in Gênes before a painting by Breughel, and
since that time, I've not stopped dreaming about it and doing related
readings."

2. Exceptions to this rule include the psychoanalytic readings of
La Tentation offered by Theodor Reik, "[Flaubert and His *Tempta-
tion of Saint Anthony*]," and Laurence Porter, "Projection as Ego
Defense in Flaubert's *Tentation de saint Antoine*," both reprinted in
Porter, ed., *Critical Essays on Gustave Flaubert*, 145–64. Though
Reik does show clear and provocative relationships between "saint
Flaubert" and Saint Antoine, and Porter discovers the psychoanalytic
dimensions of Flaubert's "drama of personality" (162), their reliance
on ego psychology has, in my opinion, diminished the strength of
their arguments. I will be referring, on occasion, to some of Porter's
insights but will shift the emphasis of his reading away from ego
psychology and toward the problems posed by a structural reading
of Flaubert's use of the theatrical metaphor for the conscious/uncon-
scious mind.

3. Those who have noted the theatrical form of *La Tentation* include Michel Foucault, "La Bibliothèque fantastique"; El Nouty,
"Au delà du Spectacle: Le Genre de *La Tentation de Saint Antoine*,"
in *Théâtre et pré-cinéma*; Brombert, "*La Tentation de saint Antoine*:
The Debaucheries of the Mind," in *The Novels of Flaubert*; Ginsberg, *Flaubert Writing: A Study in Narrative Strategies*; and Bem,
*Désir et savoir dans l'oeuvre de Flaubert—Etude de "La Tentation
de saint Antoine."* See also Buck, *Gustave Flaubert*.

4. This categorizing of Flaubert's work is a tendency that persists
despite the recent understanding of Romanticism, in terms of what
Lacoue-Labarthe and Nancy call the "literary absolute," the study
of the genre that *is* literature (*L'Absolu littéraire*, 21). It also persists
despite Roland Barthes's concept of the "texte" as a field of work
that can be truly interdisciplinary. In "Texte (Théorie du)" and "De
l'oeuvre au texte," such distinctions become irrelevant. Though most

critics discussing Flaubert rely upon this Structuralist notion of text
and of modernism, many seem to have forgotten them in their endless efforts to make Flaubert more and more modern. Recent studies
of Flaubertian Realism are specifically interested in counterbalancing
Structuralism's overestimation of formal concerns and its dismissal
of referential or representational aspects of Flaubert's writing. These
studies often call themselves "post-Structuralist" or "postmodern."
As a response to the 1974 Cerisy colloquium *La Production du sens
chez Flaubert* Claudine Gothot-Mersch, ed.—but see also the collected essays of the Centre d'Histoire et d'analyse des manuscrits
modernes, Raymonde Debray-Genette, ed., *Flaubert à l'oeuvre*—
Diana Knight, for example, articulates an entire generation's reac-
tions to Structuralism's seemingly limited concerns: "Calling attention to writing as writing and to the methods of literature need not
demand the complete loss of illusion, nor the devaluation of 'subject
matter.' " Knight, *Flaubert's Characters: The Language of Illusion*,
2. In so arguing she echoes the general tone of Majewski and Schor,
eds., *Flaubert and Postmodernism*, and underscores the renewed interest in the place or role of historicity in literary theory. The neglect
of Flaubert's *La Tentation* in this realm seems particularly ironic in
light of *La Tentation*'s formal writing strategies since, as Baudelaire's
commentaries on *Madame Bovary* suggest, they may lay bare the
skeletons of his other novels, thus commenting on the esthetic production of realism as an artifice, a game of points of view and pluralized poetic voices. That is, the application to *La Tentation* of the
kinds of narrative techniques illustrated by Rousset in his work on
Madame Bovary might, in light of its much more open exploitation
of historical documentation, yield surprisingly fruitful insights. For
it is clear that relations of writer to narrator and narrator to character are openly explored in *La Tentation* and in formal, even physical
ways that could make Baudelaire's argument all the more topical.
See Rousset, "Madame Bovary ou le livre sur rien."

5. Kovács, *Le Rêve et la vie*; 65–66, 79–98.

6. Brombert, *The Novels of Flaubert*. Baudelaire, "Madame Bovary, par Gustave Flaubert."

7. Culler, *Flaubert: The Uses of Uncertainty*, 68.

8. The designation of "family idiot" refers to Sartre's three-
volume study of Flaubert: *L'Idiot de la famille: Gustave Flaubert de
1821 à 1857*. The psychology of the psychopath is outlined by Reik,
"[Flaubert and his *Temptation of Saint Anthony*]" and by Charles
Bernheimer, "The Psychogenesis of Flaubert's Style: Matter, Meta-

phor and Metamorphosis," in *Flaubert and Kafka: Studies in Psychopathic Structure*. Comments on Flaubert's epileptic fits can be found in Porter, *Critical Essays on Gustave Flaubert*, 152; in Pommier, "Les Maladies de Gustave Flaubert"; and in Pontalis "La Maladie de Flaubert."

9. Leyla Perrone-Moisés, "*Quidquid volueris*: The Scriptural Education," in Majewski and Schor, eds. *Flaubert and Postmodernism*, 139–40.

10. Each time Flaubert completed one of his "more mature" books, he repeatedly returned to his *Tentation*: after the first *Education sentimentale* in 1848–49, after *Madame Bovary* in 1856–57, and after *Salammbô* in 1874. In this light, Ginsberg's study of the problems confronted in and solved by the three versions offers an interesting and useful way of seeing the significance of *La Tentation* in Flaubert's oeuvre without entering into questionable distinctions such as "Romanticism" and "Realism." On relations between techniques used in *La Tentation* and in other works, see *Flaubert Writing: A Study in Narrative Strategies*, esp. 47, 77–78, 80–83, 137–40.

11. My translation: "We came along, we others, either too early or too late. We shall have accomplished that most difficult and least glorious of things: the transition. In order to establish something lasting, a fixed base is necessary; the future torments us and the past holds us back. That is why the present escapes us."

12. Jean Bruneau refers to *Smarh* as an earlier avatar of *La Tentation* and as an example of Flaubert's early "philosophical years" in *Les Débuts littéraire de Gustave Flaubert*, 506–12. Brombert refers to the influence of Spinoza (*The Novels of Flaubert* 196, 200), as does Georges Poulet who also notes the contamination by readings of Kant and Hegel in "Flaubert," in *Etudes sur le temps humain*, 311. Porter also points out that the Devil "preaches a compound of Spinozistic doctrine and Kantian exposition of the limits of empirical knowledge" (*Critical Essays on Gustave Flaubert*, 159). Kovács discusses Flaubert's interest in scientific studies of psychology, *La Rêve et la vie*, 19–20.

13. No one has noticed that changes from version to version suppose a movement toward the theatrical. Nonetheless, comparative studies of the three versions can be seen in Porter's *Critical Essays*, in Bem's *Désir et savoir*, in Ginsberg's *Flaubert Writing*, and in two early articles: Madeleine, "Les Différents 'Etats' de la *Tentation de Saint Antoine*," and Mazel, "Les Trois Tentations de Saint Antoine."

Ginsberg notes that the final version is at least a third of the length of its original, that the percentage of narrative in it is greater (64), and that the opening scene changes from a setting represented as real to a theatrical stage (67). However, she also persists in showing that typographical distinctions do not really change Flaubert's narrative technique (65), thus minimizing the importance of the theatrical. Bem points out that the first version is a free, spontaneous expression later repressed by Flaubert's own censorship (43, 71). In light of this argument, it does seem obvious that what began as a lyric *gueulade* and a literal expression of the author's insides—indeed on many occasions Flaubert describes his original joy in effortlessly composing the first version (C, 2:81, 85, 86; 4:104, 111)—came to be tempered by methodical corrections in an effort to depersonalize its content. This is of course a reduction that suggests the same kind of painstaking attention to style recorded in Flaubert's correspondence during his composition of *Madame Bovary*.

14. Flaubert, *La Tentation de Saint Antoine*, 1–2. All further references to *La Tentation* are to this edition. All translations of the text are modified versions of those offered by Mrosovsky, trans., *The Temptation of Saint Anthony* (hereafter Mrosovsky), and will be so indicated. Here: "One more day! One more day gone!" (31–32).

15. Genette, "Flaubert par Proust," 12.

16. Translation by Mrosovsky (61–62), modified: "Surely I used to be less miserable! . . . I used to begin my orisons; then I always went down to the river . . . coming back up the rough track . . . I always enjoyed . . . always took . . . always felt as if a fountain of mercy were pouring into my heart from the height of heaven. It has now dried up. Why?"

17. Porter also discusses the replaying of initial images (*Critical Essays on Gustave Flaubert*, 154–162), noting the "emerging contents of the unconscious," but he does not emphasize the way in which *La Tentation* works its way back into earlier and earlier memories.

18. Translation by Mrosovsky (65), modified: "But I would have served my brothers better by simply becoming a priest. . . . Laymen are anyway not all damned, and it was up to me to become . . . say . . . a grammarian, or a philosopher. . . . But there's too much pride to these triumphs. Better to have been a soldier. I was quite hardy and tough. . . ."

19. Translation by Mrosovsky (94), modified: "Hypocrite, sinking into solitude the better to license your outbreaks of desire! You

abstain from meat, wine, baths, slaves and honors; but how you let your imagination provide you with banquets, perfumes, naked women and applauding crowds! Your chastity is only a more subtle corruption."

20. Translation by Mrosovsky (64), modified: "Ah! how I wish I could follow them! How often also I've gazed with envy at the long boats whose sails look like wings especially when they carried away people whom I'd made welcome! . . . Where do I get my obstinate commitment to the continuation of a life such as this?"

21. See Freud's discussion of displacement in the dream work in *The Interpretation of Dreams*, 340–44.

22. See Laplanche and Pontalis, "Fantasy and the Origins of Sexuality," 5, n. 12.

23. My translation: "Differentiate as much as possible the Entrances in the beginning so that St. Anthony [bends] [thinks] the sins rather than seeing them, or better, before seeing them."

24. Giving a general definition for the pattern of regression in dreams, Freud writes in *The Interpretation of Dreams*: "Dreams differ from day-dreams in their second characteristic: namely, in the fact of their ideational content being transformed from thoughts into sensory images to which belief is attached and which appear to be experienced. . . . It should also be remembered here that it is not only in dreams that such transformations of ideas into sensory images occur: they are also found in hallucinations and visions, which may appear as independent entities, so to say, in health or as symptoms in the psychoneuroses" (573–74). He explains: "The only way we can describe what happens in hallucinatory dreams is by saying that the excitation moves in a *backward* direction. Instead of being transmitted towards the *motor* end of the apparatus it moves towards the *sensory* end and finally reaches the perceptual system. If we describe as 'progressive' the direction taken by psychical processes arising from the unconscious during waking life, then we may speak of dreams as having a 'regressive' character" (581). See also the structural models Freud offers to illustrate the movement of unconscious desire in regression, 571–88.

25. In *The Interpretation of Dreams*, Freud explains that regression in dreams relies upon "the state of sleep and the changes in cathexis which it brings about at the sensory end of the apparatus." However, he also goes on to qualify this remark in terms that come closer to describing Antoine's particular situation: "In explaining regression in dreams, however, we must bear in mind the regressions

which also occur in pathological waking states. . . . For in those cases regression occurs in spite of a sensory current flowing without interruption in a forward direction. My explanation of hallucinations in hysteria and paranoia and of visions in mentally normal subjects is that they are in fact regressions—that is, thoughts transformed into images—but that the only thoughts that undergo this transformation are those which are intimately linked with memories that have been suppressed or have remained unconscious" (583).

26. Translation by Mrosovsky (72), modified: "Despite the uproar in his head, he is aware of a huge silence which cuts him off from the world. He tries to speak: impossible! It is as if the overall bond of his being were dissolving; and no longer resisting, Anthony falls on the mat."

27. As quoted by Bollème, *Préface à la vie d'écrivain*, 74. My translation: "This is why I love Art. There, at least, everything is liberty in this world of fictions. There, one satiates everything, one does everything, one is at the same time king and populace, active and passive, victim and priest. No limits; for you, humanity is a puppet with bells that one rings at the end of his sentence as [does] the juggler at the end of his foot (I have often, thus, avenged myself of existence; I have brought upon myself [or ironed into myself] many sweet things with my pen; I have given myself women, money, travels), how the soul curved in upon itself stretches out in this azure which stops [ends] only at the borders of the True."

28. On Baudelaire's concern with the moral ambiguity of the imagination see the poem "Au lecteur" (in *Oeuvres complètes*) and Bersani's discussion of it in *Baudelaire and Freud*, 26–29. For a general discussion relating Baudelaire to Flaubert's *Tentation*, see Brombert, *The Novels of Flaubert*.

29. Laplanche and Pontalis, *Vocabulaire de la psychanalyse*, 155.

30. See ibid., "Fantasme originaire" or the English "Fantasy and the Origins of Sexuality," as well as the references to its inception in the *Vocabulaire de la psychanalyse*.

31. Metz, "The Fiction Film and Its Spectator: A Metapsychological Study," 96.

32. Although the situation of the film spectator is materially different from that of a spectator at the theater because the latter faces real bodies on stage and therefore attends more to the represent*er* than to the represent*ation* (ibid., 101), Metz notes that this difference is only a question of the force and degrees of belief engendered in "The Cinematic Apparatus as Social Institution."

33. Borch-Jacobsen, *Le Sujet freudien*, 32.

34. Translation by Mrosovsky (73), modified: "Anthony, still with closed eyes, enjoys [as a sexual pleasure] his inaction; and he spreads his limbs [members] across the mat. It feels soft, more and more so, until it puffs out, lifts itself up, becomes a bed, the bed, a skiff; water laps against its sides. To the right and left two tongues of black earth are rising, [they are] topped by farmed fields, with a sycamore here and there. A ringing of bells, a drumming and a singing, echo in the distance: people are setting off for Canopus, to sleep by the temple of Serapis in order to have dreams. Anthony knows this; and he glides, driven by the wind, between the banks of the canal. . . . He is stretched out at the bottom of the boat, one oar trailing behind in the water. . . . The murmur of the little waves diminishes. A drowsiness overcomes him. He dreams that he is an Egyptian solitary. / Then, suddenly, he starts up. / Was I dreaming? . . . I can't have been, it was so vivid. My tongue's burning! I'm thirsty!"

35. Translation by Mrosovsky (78), modified: "One after another, Anthony comes upon all his old enemies. He recognizes some whom he had forgotten; he commits atrocities on these before he kills them. He disembowels, slits throats, beats out brains, drags old men by the beard, crushes children, strikes the wounded."

36. Translation by Mrosovsky (126, 134), modified: "He longs for the chance to pour out his life for the Saviour, not knowing whether he may not himself be one of these martyrs." Then, "I'm going mad. Steady now! Where was I? What happened?"

37. Translation by Mrosovsky (61), modified: "This is the Thebaid, high on a mountain, on a platform that curves to a half-moon, and is enclosed by large boulders. The hermit's cabin occupies the rear. It consists of mud and reeds, with a flat roof and no door. Inside it one distinguishes a pitcher and a loaf of black bread; in the middle, on a wooden slab, a fat book; . . . Ten steps away from the cabin stands a long cross planted in the soil; and at the platform's other end, . . . the Nile seems to spread like a lake at the foot of the cliff. The enclosure of rocks cuts off the view to right and left. But out in the desert, like beaches that would unfold, immense parallel ash-blond undulations stretch out one after the other, gradually rising. . . . Opposite, the sun sinks. In the north the sky is a shade of pearl-gray, while at its highest point crimson clouds, positioned like the tufts of a giant mane, comb out across the blue vault. These bars of flame become embrowned, the azure areas grow pale and nacre-

ous; . . . all now seems hard as bronze; and in the air floats a golden dust, so fine as to be indistinguishable from the vibration of the light. / SAINT ANTHONY / who has a long beard, long hair, and wears a goatskin tunic, is sitting cross-legged, making mats. As soon as the sun disappears he heaves a great sigh, and gazing at the horizon: / One more day! one more day gone!"

38. Lacan, "Le Stade du miroir comme formateur de la fonction du Je . . . ," in *Ecrits*, 96.

39. See Foucault's discussion of the way in which the images in each successive chapter of *La Tentation* become less and less possible but just as real as their predecessors as each new narrator creates spectators who narrate ad infinitum; "La Bibliothèque fantastique," 16–20.

40. Ginsberg, *Flaubert Writing*, 65, 138.

41. Porter, *Critical Essays on Gustave Flaubert*, (152–53, 158, and Ginsberg, *Flaubert Writing*, 67–68, trace the permutations of elements originating in the monologue and both note that this is a change skillfully adapted in the final *Tentation*.

42. Translation by Mrosovsky (126), modified: "This shock makes him open his eyes and he sees the Nile, clear and undulating in the white moonshine, like a great serpent in the middle of the sands. . . . And then a prison vault shuts in around him. Bars facing him create black lines on a blue background. . . . And opposite him, caged behind more bars, he perceives a lion walking about. . . . Beyond come gradually widening rings of people in symmetrical tiers, from the lowest enclosing the arena to the highest."

43. Flaubert himself mused about the problem of transitions between scenes or "links between pearls" in a letter to Louise Colet concerning the first version of *La Tentation*: "C'est une oeuvre manquée. Tu parles de perles. Mais les perles ne font pas le collier; c'est le fil. . . . *Saint Antoine* en manque; la déduction des idées sévèrement suivie n'a point son parallélisme dans l'enchaînement des faits" (C, 1:91; "It is a failure. You speak of pearls. But pearls don't make a necklace; the string does. . . . That is what is missing from *Saint Anthony*; the deduction of strictly followed ideas has not yet found its parallel in the unfolding of events"). Later, still working on transitions in the play, he describes the need to create a "lien logique . . . entre les différentes hallucinations du saint" (C, 4:31; "logical link . . . between the different hallucinations of the saint").

44. My translation: "Why do we have this mania of denying, of

putting down our past, of blushing about yesterday and of wanting the new religion to wipe away the old ones? . . . The heart in its affections, like humanity in its ideas, stretches out in ever-widening circles."

45. It is worth noting in the context of this mirror that just as Chapter IV of *La Tentation* began with a delving of point of view from general to specific, a similar effect is created in Chapter V where from a cinematic sweep through centuries of Eastern gods, the camera's eye zooms in to focus on one particular god out of whose navel surges a lotus carrying yet another, tinier god, and so on (120–24).

46. Lacan, "Kant avec Sade," in *Ecrits*, 774. See also Lacan's *Four Fundamental Concepts of Psycho-Analysis*, 209.

47. Lyon, "The Cinema of Lol V. Stein," 30.

48. My translation: "I am going back to *Graziella*. There is one paragraph in it, a whole page in length, all in infinitives: 'to get up in the morning, etc.' The man who adopts such modes of expression is tone deaf [has a bad ear]; he's not a writer. . . . I myself envision a style: a style that would be beautiful, that someone will invent some day, ten years or ten centuries from now, one that would be rhythmic like verse, precise like the language of the sciences, and with undulations, the humming of a cello, crests of fire; a style that would pierce your idea[s] like the thrust of a stiletto, and on which your thought[s] would sail easily across smooth surfaces, as when one floats along in a canoe with a good tail wind behind."

49. See Descamps, "Béjart parle de Flaubert."

CHAPTER 5. VIRTUALITY, ACTUALITY, AND
STÉPHANE MALLARMÉ

1. Epigraph is from Mallarmé, *Oeuvres complètes*, 328. References to Mallarmé's complete works are abbreviated in the text as OC. All translations of passages from Mallarmé's writings are my own unless otherwise indicated. I would like to note that Mallarmé's play with syntax and multiple meanings renders any translation of his writing subjective and approximative. My translation of the epigraph: "A theater, inherent in the mind, whoever has looked at nature with a certain eye carries it [this theater] with him, résumé of types and harmonies; in the same way the volume opening parallel

pages confronts them." Mallarmé's statement about *L'Après-midi d'un faune* is from Mallarmé, *Correspondance 1862–1871*, 166. All further references to Mallarmé's correspondence indicate this edition (*Correspondance*), unless otherwise noted.

2. On the relevance of Mallarmé's notions of theater to the future development of symbolist drama, see Block, *Mallarmé and the Symbolist Drama*; Kermode, "Poet and Dancer before Diaghilev" and his *Romantic Image*; Lehmann, *The Symbolist Aesthetic in France 1885–1895*; Bablet, *Esthétique générale du décor de théâtre de 1870 à 1914*; Bernard, *Mallarmé et la musique*; Pridden, *The Art of the Dance in French Literature*; and Szondi, "Sept leçons sur Hérodïade," in *Poésies et poétiques de la modernité*, 73–141. Although there has been a great deal of work on Mallarmé's figurative theaters, the most notable includes Derrida, "La Double Séance," in *La Dissémination*, 199–317; Scherer, *Le "Livre" de Mallarmé*; Richard, *L'Univers imaginaire de Mallarmé*; Kristeva, "Quelques Problèmes de sémiotique littéraire à propos d'un texte de Mallarmé: *Un Coup de dés*" and her *La Révolution du langage poétique*; Johnson's "Poetry and Performative Language," Sonnenfeld's "Mallarmé: The Poet as Actor as Reader," and Barko's "The Dancer and the Becoming of Language."

3. Though none of the aforementioned critics exploit the ambivalence toward the theater that I am interested in circumscribing, one notable exception to the two dichotomous positions pro and contra theater outlined in note 2 is Peter Szondi. Szondi does not discuss Mallarmé's elaboration of a theatrical apparatus but he does note that Mallarmé's ambivalent description of the *Faune*'s theater is not to be ignored ("Sept leçons sur *Hérodïade*," 120). Although these two "plays" are not the only examples of virtual theater in Mallarmé's poetry, they are alike and yet different from any of the other theaters in that they rely upon the dramatic formats of monologue and dialogue in order to create the space of an imaginary theater. In this way, they also resemble the other virtual plays discussed in the preceding chapters.

4. As Peter Szondi has remarked in his study of *Hérodiade*, the play is at the same time a model for poetic dramas written at the end of the nineteenth century and a signpost leading to an evolution in future conceptions of dramatic form (ibid., 111).

5. On Mallarmé's particular interest in dance and music, see his "Autobiographie" written for Verlaine in which he notes: "Voilà

toute ma vie dénudée d'anecdotes. . . . Quelques apparitions partout où l'on monte un ballet, où l'on joue de l'orgue, mes deux passions d'art presque contradictoires, mais dont le sens éclatera, et c'est tout" (*OC*, 664). My translation: "Here is my life stripped of anecdotes. . . . A few appearances anywhere there is a ballet or someone playing the organ, my two almost contradictory passions for art but whose meaning will shatter, and that's all." Scherer, *Le "Livre" de Mallarmé*, 38–43.

6. Mallarmé's reconception of the *Faune* is repeated for *Hérodïade* when, having already completed its "Scène," he begins work on its "Ouverture musicale." At that time he writes: "Je commence *Hérodïade*, non plus tragédie, mais poème" (*Correspondance*, 174; "I'm beginning *Hérodïade*, no longer tragedy, but poem"). Whether or not this shift actually marks a movement away from the stageworthy is still open to debate. I would argue that the "Scène" is as virtual as the "Ouverture." However, this reconception of *Hérodïade* does mark a movement away from the dialogic exchange of the "Scène" and toward the monologic symphony in writing of the "Ouverture." Wolf discusses useless or fruitless attempts to determine whether the "Scène" is stageworthy or not by reducing the question of the stageworthy to a question of narrative logic which critics tend to find in the piece but which, according to Wolf's analysis, is not really there (*Eros Under Glass*, 16–18). Similarly, Peter Szondi (in "Sept leçons") compares Thibaudet's and Block's positions in order to point out that neither really asks the right question: "Il ne s'agit pas de savoir si l'oeuvre ferait son effet sur la scène ou non; il s'agit de dégager les rapports entre ce poème et les lois de la scène" (86; "It is not a question of knowing if the work would be effective on stage or not; it is a question of figuring out relationships between this poem and the laws of the stage"). For Szondi, *Hérodïade* breaks certain of these scenic laws through its fragmentation of characters, its substitution of narrative for dramatic action, and its general tendency toward dematerialization (84–89).

7. Translation from Bersani, *The Death of Stéphane Mallarmé*, 84 n. 1, modified: "Yes, *I know it*, we are only vain forms of matter, empty and yet sublime for we have invented God and our own soul. So sublime, my friend, that I want to offer myself this spectacle of matter, having consciousness of being and, nonetheless, throwing itself wildly into the Dream it [consciousness] knows does not exist, singing [of] the Soul and all such divine impressions amassed within

us since the earliest times and that proclaim, in the face of the Nothing that is truth, these glorious lies! Such is the plan of my lyric volume."

8. See also Davies, *Mallarmé et le rêve d'Hérodïade*, and Wolf, *Eros Under Glass.*

9. These and all further translations of Mallarmé's *Hérodïade* and *L'Après-midi d'un faune* are modified versions of those offered by Cohn, *Toward the Poems of Mallarmé* (hereafter Cohn). Translations lacking any reference to Cohn are my own. First: "O mirror! / . . . distressed / By dreams and seeking my memories which are / Like leaves under your ice with its deep hole, / . . . in your severe fountain, / I have recognized the nakedness of my scattered dream!" (72). Then: "And your solitary sister, O my eternal sister, / My dream will mount toward you: such already / Rare limpidity of a heart that dreamed it . . ." (78).

10. See Wolf's likening of *Hérodïade* to Freud's psychical apparatus (*Eros Under Glass*, 13), as well as Lacan's notion, in "Le Stade du miroir," that the mirror apparatus is a drama that offers the lure of a spatial identification (93).

11. My translation: "His solitary drama! and which, sometimes, so much does this walker in a labyrinth of trouble and grief prolong its circuits with the suspense of an unaccomplished act, seems the spectacle itself [of] why the footlights as well as the quasi-moral golden space they border [protect and interdict] exist, for there is no other subject, mark my words: the antagonism drawn by misfortune between man's dreams and the fatalities of his existence."

12. This shift is easily associated with Mallarmé's so-called Impressionist esthetic: "Peindre non la chose mais l'effet qu'elle produit" (*Correspondance*, 137; "Paint not the thing but the effect it produces").

13. Translation by Cohn (60), modified: "One of them . . . / Seems, garbed in departed [bird] flights and phantom / Like an aroma which carries, O roses! an aroma. . . ."

14. Robert Greer Cohn (60) points out that "os" (bones) might well have been a misprint of "ors" (golds).

15. In this way Mallarmé does predict the future evolution of conceptions of stage space in the work of, say, Diaghilev or of Gordon Craig. See Bablet, *Esthétique générale du décor de théâtre de 1870 à 1914.*

16. My translation: "When a sign of scattered, general beauty isolates itself before one's gaze, flower, wave, cloud, and jewel, etc.,

if, in us, the exclusive way of knowing it consists in juxtaposing it [this aspect of it] to our own spiritual nudity so that this nudity feels it to be analogous to itself and appropriates it in some exquisite confusion of that same nudity and this form in flight—through nothing but the rite alone, there, enunciation of the Idea, does the dancer not appear [to be] half the element responsible, half humanity apt to confuse itself there, in the floating of daydreams? The operation, or poetry, par excellence and the theater."

17. In her "The Dancer and the Becoming of Language," Carol Barko comments upon Mallarmé's theater in the following very apt way: "The theater is not merely a metaphor for the activity of language, but also a spatial framework embodying the distance between subject and object necessary for self-reading" (173–74).

18. On the image of the rotating bar that I have likened to a proscenium arch, see Lyotard's *Economie libidinale*, 35–36.

19. Translation by Cohn (62–63) modified: "Magic shadow with symbolic charms! / A voice, long evocation of the past, / Is it mine ready to break into incantation? / Still in the yellow folds of thought / Dragging, old, like a perfumed star / Over a confused mass of cold monstrances / Through the old holes and the stiffened folds / Pierced just like the rhythm and the pure lacework / Of the shroud letting through its beautiful stitches / The old veiled bursting desperately mount / Rises: (oh, what a distance is hidden in those calls!)"

20. Translation by Cohn (63–64), modified: "The old veiled bursting of the insolent redness, / Of the voice languishing, nul, without acolyte, / Will it cast its gold in last splendors, / [Will] It [rise] still, the hymn with pleading verses, / In the hour of agony and funereal struggles! / And, through silence and the black shadows / All alike goes back into the ancient past, / Fatal, vanquished, monotonous, tired, / Just as the water of ancient basins grows resigned."

21. For a further discussion of Mallarmé's Romantic esthetics, see Ellmann, "Spacing Out: A Double Entendre on Mallarmé."

22. This same mirror esthetic is repeated in the "Sonnet en -yx" in which both the décor of the empty room (the author is gone) and the constellations beyond are reflected (*OC*, 68–69).

23. My translation: "[What is] its particular enchantment if not to free, from a handful of dust or reality without enclosing it, in the book—even as text—the volatile dispersion, that is the mind which has nothing to do with anything other than the musicality of all things."

24. My translation: "Yes, as an opera with neither accompani-

ment nor song, but spoken; now the book will attempt to suffice to half-open the interior stage and to whisper its echoes. A versified ensemble makes for an ideal representation ... one portion inclines in a rhythm or movement of thought, to which is opposed an other contradictory design."

25. My translations: First, "The book hesitates such as it is, an outlet, indifferent, into which the other empties itself." Then, "The Book, where the satisfied mind lives ... does not call for a reader's approach ... it takes place all alone: fact, being. ... The buried meanings mobilize themselves and transform, into a choir, the pages." Note here, however, that the word "fact" can also be interpreted as a verb, meaning "done" or "accomplished."

26. Thibaudet, *La Poésie de Stéphane Mallarmé*, 388.

27. Leo Bersani discusses the stabilizing and mobilizing features of the "Ouverture," specifically the way in which it becomes an "immobile verbal block, a mass in which the only movement is one of shimmering internal reflections." *The Death of Stéphane Mallarmé*, 13.

28. Mannoni, *Clefs*, 164. See also chapter 1.

29. My translation: "Dance alone, by virtue of its evolutions, along with mime seems to me to necessitate a real space or the stage. / In a pinch, paper suffices to evoke any play: assisted by his multiple personality, each being able to play it for himself within [on the inside], which is not the case when it comes to pirouettes."

30. My translation: "The author, from his evils, dragons he has pampered, or from a [his] mirth, must establish himself, in the text, [as] the spiritual histrion. / Floor boards, chandelier, obscured fabrics, and liquefaction of mirrors, in the real order [or in the order of the real], but including the excessive leaps of our aerated form around a stopping [or plumb-line], on foot, of virile stature, a Place presents itself, scene, the raising before everyone of the spectacle of Self; there, due to the intermediaries of light, of flesh, and of laughs the sacrifice that is made there, relative to his personality, [by] the one who inspires, a complete end, or it is, in a strange resurrection, finished with that one: whose reverberated and henceforth vain verb exhales itself through the orchestral chimera. / An audience [or a place for an audience], he celebrates himself, anonymously, in the hero."

31. The burying of the poet's literal, biological self and his subsequent resurrection in the work he leaves behind is the recurring theme of the *Tombeaux* poems. For an insightful discussion of this

kind of death, see Leo Bersani, *The Death of Stéphane Mallarmé*, 25-35.

32. On the evolution of Mallarmé's *Faune*, see Mondor's *Histoire d'un faune.*

33. Translation by Cohn (13-14), modified: "THE FAUN: These nymphs, I want them perpetuated. / So clear, / Their light incarnadine, that it lilts in the air / Drowsy with tufted slumbers."

34. Translation by Cohn (15-16), modified: "Did *I* love a dream? / My doubt, confused mass of ancient night, ends / In many a subtle bough, which, [having] remained the true / Woods themselves, proves, alas! that alone *I* offered *myself* / For triumph the ideal absence of roses. / Let us reflect . . . / or what if the women *you* are glossing / Represent a wish of *your* fabulous senses!"

35. Translation by Cohn (18), modified: "No water murmurs except for that which my flute pours / . . . and the only wind . . . / Is, on the horizon un-stirred by so much as a wrinkle, / The visible and serene artificial breath / Of inspiration, which regains heaven."

36. Translation by Cohn (19), modified: "O Sicilian banks of a calm marsh / That my vanity plunders before the envy of suns, / Tacit beneath the flowers of sparks, TELL / *'That I was cutting here the hollow reeds tamed* / *'By talent; when, on the glaucous gold of distant* / *'Greeneries dedicating their vine to wellsprings,* / *'Undulates an animal whiteness in repose:* / *'And [Tell] that at the slow prelude when the pipes begin* / *'This flight of swans, no! of naiads flees* / *'Or plunges . . .'"*

37. Translations by Cohn, modified: "'*My eye, piercing the reeds, darted at each nape . . .* / *'And the splendid bath of hair disappears . . .* / *'I run . . .* (24-25). Then: *'I ravish them without disentangling them, and flee* / *'To this clump . . .* / *'Where our struggle with the fading daylight is the same"* (26).

38. Two inspired readings of this passage can be found in Mauron, *Mallarmé l'obscur*, 68; and in Bersani, *The Death of Stéphane Mallarmé*, 81-83. Translation by Bersani, *The Death of Stéphane Mallarmé* (98, n. 41), modified: "The vast and twin reed on which one plays under the blue sky: / Which, diverting to itself the cheek's agitation, / Dreams, in a long solo, that we were beguiling / The surrounding beauty by fictive / Confusions between itself and our credulous song, / And [dreams] of making—as high as love modulates— / Vanish from the every day dream of a back / Or of a pure side followed by closed eyes, / A sonorous, illusory and monotonous line."

39. Suzanne Bernard has collected a partial list of musical compositions derived from Mallarmé's poems in her *Mallarmé et la musique*, 162–63.

40. Stoïanova discusses Boulez's compositions inspired by Mallarmé in *Geste-texte-musique*, 96.

41. As quoted by Stoïanova, *Geste-texte-musique*, 157. My translation: "The poem is [the] center of the music, but it has become absent from the music, like an object's form restored by lava, even though the object itself has disappeared—or like the petrification of an object at once Recognizable and Unrecognizable."

42. In *Le Livre* Mallarmé notes, for example: "Le volume, malgré l'impression fixe, devient, par ce jeu, mobile. De mort, il devient vie." (Scherer, *Le "Livre" de Mallarmé*, 409). My translation: "The volume, fixed impression notwithstanding, becomes, by this play, mobile. From death, it becomes life."

43. Stoïanova presents a wonderful study of the play of stability and mobility in both *Le Livre* and Boulez's sonata; see *Geste-texte-musique*, 95–156.

44. As Mallarmé notes in *Le Livre* (Scherer, 82B):

2 lect. par an
   chacun invitant
      l'autre.
2 read.[ings] [ers] a year
   each inviting
      the other.

Works Consulted

Abraham, Pierre, and Roland Desne. *Manuel d'histoire littéraire de la France*, vol. 5. Paris: Editions Sociales, 1977.

Abrams, Meyer Howard. *The Mirror and the Lamp: Romantic Theory and the Critical Tradition*. New York: Norton, 1958.

Affron, Charles. *A Stage for Poets: Studies in the Theater of Hugo and Musset*. Princeton, N.J.: Princeton Univ. Press, 1971.

Albouy, Pierre. *La Création mythologique chez Victor Hugo*. Paris: José Corti, 1963.

———. *Mythographies*. Paris: José Corti, 1976.

Allévy, Marie Antoinette. *La Mise en scène en France dans la première moitié du dix-neuvième siècle*. Paris: Droz, 1938.

Alter, Robert. *A Lion for Love: A Critical Biography of Stendhal*. Cambridge: Harvard Univ. Press, 1986.

Ascoli, Georges. *Le Théâtre romantique*. Paris: Centre de documentation universitaire, n.d.

Aumont, Jacques, et al., eds. *Esthétique du film*. Paris: Nathan, 1983.

Bablet, Denis. *Esthétique générale du décor de théâtre de 1870 à 1914*. Paris: Editions du Centre National de la Recherche Scientifique, 1965.

———. *La Mise en scène contemporaine*. Brussels: La Renaissance du livre, 1968.

Bakhtin, Mikhail Mikhailovich. *The Dialogic Imagination*. Trans. Caryl Emerson and Michael Holquist. Austin: Univ. of Texas Press, 1981.

Barish, Jonas. *The Anti-Theatrical Prejudice*. Berkeley and Los Angeles: Univ. of California Press, 1981.

Barko, Carol. "The Dancer and the Becoming of Language." *Yale French Studies* 54 (1976): 173–87.

Barrère, Jean-Bertrand. *Hugo, l'homme et l'oeuvre*. Paris: Boivin, 1952.

———. *La Fantaisie de Victor Hugo*. 3 vols. Paris: José Corti, 1960.

———. *Hugo*. Paris: Hatier, 1967.

Barthes, Roland. "De l'oeuvre au texte." *Revue d'Esthétique* 24.3 (1967): 225–32.

———. *L'Empire des signes*. Geneva: Editions d'Art Albert Skira, 1970.

———. *S/Z*. Paris: Seuil, 1970.

———. *Le Degré zéro de l'écriture*. 2d ed., 1953; rpt. Paris: Seuil, 1972.

———. *Le Plaisir du texte*. Paris: Seuil, 1973.

———. "La Peinture et l'écriture des signes." *Coloquio artes* 20 (Dec. 1974): n.p.

———. "Texte (Théorie du)." *Encyclopedia Universalis* 15 (1975): 1013–17.

———. *Image Music Text*. trans. Stephen Heath. New York: Hill and Wang, 1977.

Baudelaire, Charles. "Madame Bovary, par Gustave Flaubert." In *Oeuvres complètes*. 2 vols. Paris: Club du meilleur livre, 1955, 2:51–62.

———. *Les Fleurs du mal*. In *Oeuvres complètes*, ed. Claude Pichois. Paris: Gallimard, 1961.

Baudry, Jean-Louis. "Le Dispositif." *Communications* 23 (1975): 56–72.

Bem, Jeanne. *Désir et savoir dans l'oeuvre de Flaubert—Etude de "La Tentation de saint Antoine."* Paris: Editions de la Baconnière, 1979.

Benoist, Jean-Marie. "The End of Structuralism." *Twentieth Century Studies* 3 (May 1970): 31–54.

Benveniste, Emile. *Problèmes de linguistique générale*. Paris: Gallimard, 1966.

———. "L'Appareil formel de l'énonciation." *Langages* 17 (1970): 12–18.

Bernard, Suzanne. *Mallarmé et la musique*. Paris: Nizet, 1959.

Bernheimer, Charles. *Flaubert and Kafka: Studies in Psychopathic Structure*. New Haven, Conn.: Yale Univ. Press, 1982.

Bersani, Leo. *Balzac to Beckett: Center and Circumference in French Fiction*. New York: Oxford Univ. Press, 1970.

―――. *Baudelaire and Freud*. Berkeley and Los Angeles: Univ. of California Press, 1977.

―――. *The Death of Stéphane Mallarmé*. Cambridge: Cambridge Univ. Press, 1982.

―――. *A Future for Astyanax: Character and Desire in Literature*. New York: Columbia Univ. Press, 1984.

Blanchot, Maurice. *Faux Pas*. Paris: Gallimard, 1943.

―――. *La Part du feu*. Paris: Gallimard, 1949.

―――. *L'Espace littéraire*. Paris: Gallimard, 1955.

―――. *Le Livre à venir*. Paris: Gallimard, 1959.

―――. *L'Attente/L'Oubli*. Paris: Gallimard, 1962.

―――. *L'Entretien infini*. Paris: Gallimard, 1969.

Blin, Georges. *Stendhal et les problèmes du roman*. Paris: José Corti, 1954.

Block, Haskell. *Mallarmé and the Symbolist Drama*. Detroit: Wayne State Univ. Press, 1963.

Bollème, Geneviève. *Préface à la vie d'écrivain*. Paris: Seuil, 1963.

Bonnefoy, Georges. *La Pensée religieuse et morale d'Alfred de Vigny*. Paris: Hachette, 1964.

Borch-Jacobsen, Mikkel. *Le Sujet freudien*. Paris: Aubier-Flammarion, 1982.

Borch-Jacobsen, Mikkel, Eric Michaud, and Jean-Luc Nancy. *Hypnoses*. Paris: Galilée, 1984.

Boyle, Nicholas. *Landmarks of World Literature: Goethe Faust. Part One*. Cambridge: Cambridge Univ. Press, 1987.

Brewer, Maria Minich. "Performing Theory." *Theater Journal* 37.1 (March 1985): 13–30.

Brombert, Victor. *The Novels of Flaubert: A Study of Themes and Techniques*. Princeton, N.J.: Princeton Univ. Press, 1966.

―――. *Flaubert*. Paris: Seuil, 1971.

―――. *La Prison romantique*. Paris: José Corti, 1975.

―――. *Victor Hugo and the Visionary Novel*. Cambridge: Harvard Univ. Press, 1984.

Bruneau, Jean. *Les Débuts littéraires de Gustave Flaubert*. Paris: Armand Colin, 1962.

Buck, Stratton. *Gustave Flaubert*. New York: Twayne, 1966.

Butor, Michel. "Le Théâtre de Victor Hugo." *La Nouvelle Revue Francaise* 12 (Nov.–Dec. 1964): 862–78, 1073–81; 13 (Jan. 1965): 105–13.

Caplan, Jay. *Framed Narratives: Diderot's Genealogy of the Beholder.* Minneapolis: Univ. of Minnesota Press, 1985.

Cha, Theresa Hak Kyung, ed. *Apparatus. Cinematographic Apparatus: Selected Writings.* New York: Tanam Press, 1980.

Chartier, Alain. *La Belle Dame sans mercy.* Ed. Arthur Piaget. Geneva: Droz, 1949.

Cohn, Robert Greer. *Toward the Poems of Mallarmé.* Berkeley and Los Angeles: Univ. of California Press, 1965.

Coomaraswamy, Ananda K. and Duggérata Gopalakrishnayya. *The Mirror of Gesture: Being the ABINAYADARPANA OF NANDIKES-VARA.* New York: E. Weyhe, 1963.

Creech, James. *Thresholds of Representation.* Columbus: Ohio State Univ. Press, 1968.

Culler, Jonathan. *Structuralist Poetics: Structuralism, Linguistics, and the Study of Literature.* London: Routledge and Kegan Paul, 1975.

———. *Flaubert: The Uses of Uncertainty.* 2d ed. 1974; rpt. Ithaca, N.Y.: Cornell Univ. Press, 1985.

Curtius, Ernst Robert. *European Literature and the Latin Middle Ages.* Trans. Willard R. Trask. New York: Pantheon, 1953.

———. "Friedrich Schlegel and France." In *Essays on European Literature.* trans. Michael Kowal. Princeton, N.J.: Princeton Univ. Press, 1973.

Damisch, Hubert. "Dynamique Libidinale." *L'Arc* 64 (1976): 53–59.

Davies, Gardner. *Les Noces d'Hérodiade.* Paris: Gallimard, 1959.

———. *Mallarmé et le rêve d'Hérodiade.* Paris: José Corti, 1978.

Debray-Genette, Raymonde, ed. *Flaubert à l'oeuvre.* Paris: Flammarion, 1980.

Delalande, Jean. *Victor Hugo à Hauteville House.* Paris: Albin Michel, 1947.

Deleuze, Gilles, and Félix Guattari. *L'Anti-Oedipe.* Paris: Minuit, 1972.

Delfel, Guy. *L'Esthétique de Stéphane Mallarmé.* Paris: Flammarion, 1951.

de Man, Paul. *Blindness and Insight: Essays in the Rhetoric of Contemporary Criticism.* 2d ed. Minneapolis: Univ. of Minnesota Press, 1983.

————. *The Rhetoric of Romanticism.* New York: Columbia Univ. Press, 1984.

Derrida, Jacques. *L'Ecriture et la différence.* Paris: Seuil, 1967.

————. *La Dissémination.* Paris: Seuil, 1972.

————. *Writing and Difference.* Trans. Alan Bass. Chicago: Univ. of Chicago Press, 1978.

Descamps, Christian. "Béjart parle de Flaubert." *L'Arc* 79 (May 1980): 44–48.

Diderot, Denis. *Le Neveu de Rameau.* Ed. Jean Fabre. Genève: Droz, 1950.

————. "Paradoxe sur le comédien." *Oeuvres.* Paris: Gallimard, 1951.

————. *Rameau's Nephew* and *D'Alembert's Dream.* Trans. Leonard Tancock. 5th ed. New York: Penguin, 1981.

Diot, Jean-Marie. "Theatrical (Non-) Staging and the Crises of Western Thought." Unpublished paper, University of Oregon, 1987.

Doyle, Ruth Lestha. *Victor Hugo's Drama: An Annotated Bibliography 1900–1980.* Westport, Conn.: Greenwood Press, 1981.

Duchet, Claude. "Théâtre, histoire et politique." In *Romantisme et politique.* Paris: A. Michel, 1969.

Dufrenne, Mikel. "Doutes sur la 'libidiné.'" *L'Arc* 64 (1976): 13–27.

Duras, Marguerite. *India Song.* Paris: Gallimard, 1973.

————. *L'Homme atlantique.* Paris: Minuit, 1982.

Ehrenzweig, Anton. *The Hidden Order of Art: A Study in the Psychology of Artistic Imagination.* Berkeley and Los Angeles: Univ. of California Press, 1969.

Ellmann, Maud. "Spacing Out: A Double Entendre on Mallarmé." *Oxford Literary Review* (1976): 22–31.

El Nouty, Hassan. *Théâtre et pré-cinéma.* Paris: Nizet, 1978.

Esch, Deborah, and Ian Balfour, trans. "*The Athenaeum* by Maurice Blanchot." *Studies in Romanticism* 22.2 (Summer 1983): 163–72.

Fayolle, Roger, ed. "Introduction." Stendhal, *Racine et Shakespeare.* Paris: Garnier-Flammarion, 1970, 21–43.

Felman, Shoshana, ed. *Literature and Psychoanalysis.* Baltimore: Johns Hopkins Univ. Press, 1982.

Firchow, Peter. *Friedrich Schlegel's Lucinda and the Fragments.* Minneapolis: Univ. of Minnesota Press, 1971.

Fischer, Roland. "Cartography of Inner Space." In *Hallucinations, Behavior, Experience and Theory*, ed. R. K. Siegel and L. J. West. New York: Wiley, 1975, 197–239.

Flaubert, Gustave. *La Tentation de Saint Antoine*. Paris: Louis Conard, 1924.

———. *Correspondance*. 9 vols. Paris: Louis Conard, 1926–33.

———. *Oeuvres Complètes*. 22 vols. Paris: Louis Conard, 1924–33.

Foster, Hal, ed. *The Anti-Aesthetic: Essays on Postmodern Culture*. Port Townsend, Wash.: Bay Press, 1983.

Foster, Susan Leigh. *Reading Dancing: Bodies and Subjects in Contemporary American Dance*. Berkeley and Los Angeles: Univ. of California Press, 1986.

Foucault, Michel. "Preface." Flaubert, *La Tentation de Saint Antoine*. Paris: Gallimard, 1967, 7–33.

———. *Language, Counter-Memory, Practice*. Ed. Donald F. Bouchard. Trans. Donald F. Bouchard and Sherry Simon. Ithaca, N.Y.: Cornell Univ. Press, 1977.

Francastel, Pierre. "Le Théâtre est-il un art visuel?" In *Le Lieu théâtral dans la société moderne*. Ed. Denis Bablet and Jean Jacquot. Paris: Editions du Centre National de la Recherche Scientifique, 1963, 77–83.

———. *Etudes de sociologie de l'art*. Paris: Denoël, 1970.

Freud, Sigmund. "Psychopathic Characters on the Stage." *The Standard Edition of the Complete Psychological Works of Sigmund Freud*. Trans. James Strachey. 24 vols. London: Hogarth Press, 1953, 7:305–10.

———. *Jokes and Their Relation to the Unconscious*. Trans. James Strachey. New York: Norton, 1960.

———. *Beyond the Pleasure Principle*. Trans. James Strachey. New York: Norton, 1961.

———. *The Interpretation of Dreams*. Trans. James Strachey. 5th ed., 1913; rpt. New York: Avon, 1965.

Fried, Michael. *Absorption and Theatricality: Painting and Beholder in the Age of Diderot*. Berkeley and Los Angeles: Univ. of California Press, 1980.

Fuhrmans, Horst, ed. *F. W. J. Schelling: Briefe und Dokumente, Band I 1775–1809*. Bonn: H. Bouvier, 1962.

Gaudon, Jean. "Hugo." In *Enciclopedia dello Spettacolo*, ed. Silvio d'Amico. 10 vols. Rome: Le Maschere, 1954–63, 6:426–34.

Gautier, Théophile. *Histoire de l'art dramatique*. Leipzig: Hetzel, 1858.

———. *Souvenirs de théâtre, d'art et de critique*. Paris: Charpentier, 1883.

———. *Histoire du romantisme*. Paris: Charpentier, 1890.

———. "Une Larme du diable." *Théâtre: Mystère, comédies et ballets.* Ed. Eugène Fasquelle. Paris: Charpentier, 1912, 1–52.

Gély, Claude. *Victor Hugo poète de l'intimité.* Paris: Nizet, 1969.

Genette, Gérard. "Silences de Flaubert." *Figures I.* Paris: Seuil, 1966, 223–43.

———. "Frontières du récit." *Figures II.* Paris: Seuil, 1969, 49–70.

———. *Mimologiques.* Paris: Seuil, 1976.

———. " 'Genres,'types,' 'modes.' " *Poétique* 32 (1977): 389–421.

———. "Flaubert par Proust." *L'Arc* 79 (May 1980): 3–17.

———. "Frontiers of Narrative." In *Figures of Literary Discourse,* trans. Marie-Rose Logan. New York: Columbia Univ. Press, 1982, 127–44.

Ginsberg, Michal Peled. *Flaubert Writing: A Study in Narrative Strategies.* Stanford, Calif.: Stanford Univ. Press, 1986.

Goethe, Johann Wolfgang von. *Faust: Part One.* Trans. Philip Wayne. New York: Penguin, 1949.

———. *Faust: Part Two.* Trans. Philip Wayne. New York: Penguin, 1959.

Gothot-Mersch, Claudine, ed. *La Production du sens chez Flaubert.* Paris: Union general d'editions, 1975.

Gould, Evlyn. "Stendhal's Theaters." *French Forum* 12.3 (1987): 289–301.

———. "Why Go to the Theater?" *Journal of Dramatic Theory and Criticism,* 2.1 (1987): 69–86.

Green, André. *Un Oeil en trop.* Paris: Minuit, 1969.

———. *The Tragic Effect: The Oedipus Complex in Tragedy.* Trans. Alan Sheridan. Cambridge: Cambridge Univ. Press, 1979.

Harari, Josué V., ed. *Textual Strategies: Perspectives in Post-Structuralist Criticism.* Ithaca, N.Y.: Cornell Univ. Press, 1979.

Harris, H. S. *Hegel's Development: Toward the Sunlight 1770–1801.* Oxford: Clarendon, 1972.

Hugo, Victor. *William Shakespeare.* Paris: J. Hetzel, 1894.

———. *Oeuvres poétiques complètes.* Ed. Francis Bouvet. Paris: Jean-Jacques Pauvert, 1961.

———. *Théâtre complet.* 2 vols. Paris: Gallimard, 1964.

———. *Actes et paroles.* vol. 3 Paris: Editions Rencontre, 1968.

———. *Oeuvres complètes.* Ed. Jean Massin. 18 vols. Paris: Club français du livre, 1968.

———. *Littérature et philosophie mêlées.* Ed. Anthony R. W. James. 2 vols. Paris: Klincksieck, 1976.

Humphrey, Doris. *The Art of Making Dances.* New York: Grove, 1959.

Jaeger, Werner. *Paideia: The Ideals of Greek Culture.* Trans. Gilbert Highet. 3 vols. New York: Oxford Univ. Press, 1939–45.

Jamati, Paul. "Dans l'atmosphère des *Châtiments.*" *Europe* 31 (Sept. 1953): 84–87.

Jameson, Fredric. *The Political Unconscious: Narrative as a Socially Symbolic Act.* Ithaca, N.Y.: Cornell Univ. Press, 1981.

———. *The Ideologies of Theory: Essays 1971–1986.* 2 vols. Minneapolis: Univ. of Minnesota Press, 1988.

Jauss, Hans Robert. *Aesthetic Experience and Literary Hermeneutics.* Trans. Michael Shaw. Minneapolis: Univ. of Minnesota Press, 1982.

———. "'Le Neveu de Rameau' Dialogique et dialectique (ou: Diderot lecteur de Socrate et Hegel lecteur de Diderot)." *Revue de Métaphysique et de Morale* 2 (1984): 145–81.

Johnson, Barbara. "Poetry and Performative Language." *Yale French Studies* 54 (1976): 140–58.

Josephs, Herbert. *Diderot's Dialogue of Language and Gesture.* Columbus: Ohio State Univ. Press, 1969.

Jowett, Benjamin, trans. *The Dialogues of Plato.* 4 vols. Oxford: Clarendon Press, 1871.

Kerckhove, Derrick de. "A Theory of Greek Tragedy." *Sub-Stance,* 29 (1981): 23–36.

Kermode, Frank. "Poet and Dancer before Diaghilev." In *Puzzles and Epiphanies.* London: Routledge and Kegan Paul, n.d., 1–28.

———. *Romantic Image.* London: Routledge, 1957.

Kirstein, Lincoln. *A Short History of Classical Theatrical Dancing.* 2d ed., 1935; rpt. New York: Dance Horizons, 1974.

Knight, Diana. *Flaubert's Characters: The Language of Illusion.* Cambridge: Cambridge Univ. Press, 1985.

Kofman, Sarah. *L'Enfance de l'art.* Paris: Payot, 1970.

———. *Nietzsche et la scène philosophique.* Paris: Union générale d'editions, 1979.

———. *Mélancolie de l'art.* Paris: Galilée, 1985.

Kovács, Katherine Singer. *Le Rêve et la vie: A Theatrical Experiment by Gustave Flaubert.* Lexington, Ky.: Harvard Studies in Romance Languages, no. 38, 1981.

Koyre, Alexandre. *Introduction à la lecture de Platon.* Paris: Gallimard, 1962.

Kravis, Judy. *The Prose of Mallarmé: The Evolution of a Literary*

Language. Cambridge: Cambridge Univ. Press, 1976.

Kristeva, Julia. "Quelques Problèmes de sémiotique littéraire à propos d'un texte de Mallarmé: *Un Coup de dés*." In *Essais de sémiotique poétique*, ed. Algirdas Julien Greimas. Paris: Larousse, 1972, 208–34.

———. "The Semiotic Activity." *Screen* 14.1–2 (Summer 1973): 25–39.

———. "The System and the Speaking Subject." *Times Literary Supplement* 736.3 (Oct. 1973): 1249–50.

———. *La Révolution du langage poétique*. Paris: Seuil, 1974.

———. *Recherches pour une sémanalyse*. Paris: Seuil, 1976.

———. "La Musique parlée ou remarques sur la subjectivité dans la fiction à propos du '*Neveu de Rameau*.' " In *Langue et Langages de Leibniz à l'Encyclopédie*, ed. Michèle Duchet and Michèle Jalley. Paris: 10/18, 1977, 153–224.

Lacan, Jacques. *Ecrits*. Paris: Seuil, 1966.

———. *The Four Fundamental Concepts of Psycho-Analysis*. Trans. Alan Sheridan. London: Hogarth, 1977.

Lacoue-Labarthe, Philippe. "Présentation." *Poétique* 21 (1975): 1–2.

———. *Le Sujet de la philosophie (Typographie 1)*. Paris: Aubier-Flammarion, 1979.

———. "Typographie." *Mimésis des articulations*. Paris: Aubier-Flammarion, 1975.

———. "Diderot, le paradoxe et la mimésis." *Poétique* 43 (1980): 267–81.

Lacoue-Labarthe, Philippe, and Jean-Luc Nancy. "Le Dialogue des genres." *Poétique* 21 (1975): 148–75.

———. *L'Absolu littéraire*. Paris: Seuil, 1978.

———. *The Literary Absolute: The Theory of Literature in German Romanticism*. Trans. Philip Barnard and Cheryl Lester. Albany: State Univ. of New York Press, 1988.

Laplanche, Jean. *Vie et mort en psychanalyse*. Paris: Flammarion, 1979.

Laplanche, Jean, and J.-B. Pontalis. "L'Inconscient: Une étude psychanalytique." *Les Temps Modernes* 183 (July 1961): 81–129.

———. "Fantasme originaire, fantasmes des origines, origine du fantasme." *Les Temps modernes* 19.215 (April 1964): 1833–68.

———. "Fantasy and the Origins of Sexuality." *International Journal of Psycho-Analysis* 49 (1968): 1–17.

———. *Vocabulaire de la psychanalyse*. Paris: Presses universitaires de France, 1973.

Leclaire, Serge. *Psychanalyser: Un essai sur l'ordre de l'inconscient et la pratique de la lettre.* Paris: Seuil, 1968.

Lehmann, A. G. *The Symbolist Aesthetic in France 1885–1895.* 2d ed., 1950; rpt. Oxford: Basil Blackwell, 1968.

Lesschaeve, Jacqueline, ed. and trans. *Merce Cunningham: Le Danseur et la danse.* Paris: Pierre Belfond, 1980.

Levaillant, Maurice. *La Crise mystique de Victor Hugo.* Paris: José Corti, 1954.

Levinson, André. "Stéphane Mallarmé métaphysicien du ballet." *La Revue Musicale* 1 (Nov. 1923): 21–33.

Lyon, Elisabeth. "The Cinema of Lol V. Stein." *Camera Obscura 6* (Fall 1980): 7–41.

Lyotard, Jean-François. *Des dispositifs pulsionnels.* Paris: Union générale d'editions, 1973.

———. *Economie libidinale.* Paris: Minuit, 1974.

———. "Par-delà la représentation." In *L'Ordre caché de l'art,* ed. Anton Ehrenzweig. Paris: Gallimard, 1974.

———. "The Tooth, the Palm." Trans. Anne Knap and Michel Benamou. *Sub-Stance* 15 (1976): 105–10.

———. "The Unconscious as mise-en-scène." In *Performance in Postmodern Culture,* ed. Michel Benamou. Milwaukee: Center for Twentieth-Century Studies, Univ. of Wisconsin, 1977, 87–98.

Madeleine, Jacques. "Les Différents 'Etats' de la *Tentation de Saint Antoine.*" *Revue d'Histoire Littéraire de la France* 15 (1908): 620–41.

Majewski, Henry F., and Naomi Schor, eds. *Flaubert and Postmodernism.* Lincoln: Univ. of Nebraska Press, 1984.

Mallarmé, Stéphane. *Oeuvres complètes.* Ed. Henri Mondor and G. Jean-Aubry. Paris: Gallimard, 1945.

———. *Correspondance 1862–1871.* Ed. Henri Mondor. Paris: Gallimard, 1959.

Mannoni, Octave. *Freud.* Paris: Seuil, 1968.

———. *Clefs pour l'Imaginaire ou l'Autre Scène.* Paris: Seuil, 1969.

Martineau, Henri. *Le Calendrier de Stendhal.* Paris: Le Divan, 1933.

Masson, Jeffrey Moussaieff, ed. and trans. *The Complete Letters of Sigmund Freud to Wilhelm Fleiss 1887–1904.* Cambridge: Harvard Univ. Press, 1985.

Mauron, Charles. *Mallarmé l'obscur.* Paris: Denoël, 1941.

———. *Mallarmé.* Paris: Seuil, 1964.

———. *L'Inconscient dans l'oeuvre et la vie de Racine.* 2d ed., 1957; rpt. Paris: José Corti, 1969.

Mazel, Henri. "Les Trois Tentations de Saint Antoine." *Mercure de France* (Dec. 1921): 626–43.

Mehlman, Jeffrey. *Revolution and Repetition.* Berkeley and Los Angeles: Univ. of California Press, 1977.

Meltzer, Françoise, ed. *The Trial(s) of Psychoanalysis.* Chicago: Univ. of Chicago Press, 1988.

Mérimée, Prosper. *Théâtre de Clara Gazul.* Ed. Pierre Salomon. Paris: Garnier-Flammarion, 1968.

Metz, Christian. *Essais sur la signification au cinéma.* I. Paris: Klincksieck, 1968.

———. *Langage et cinéma.* Paris: Larousse, 1971.

———. "Le Signifiant Imaginaire." *Communications* 23 (1975): 3–55.

———. "The Fiction Film and Its Spectator: A Metapsychological Study." *New Literary History* 8 (1976): 75–105.

———. "The Cinematic Apparatus as Social Institution—An Interview with Christian Metz." *Discourse* 1 (1979): 16–18.

Milner, Max, ed. *Littérature française: Le Romantisme, I: 1820–1843.* Paris: Arthaud, 1973.

Mitterand, Henri, ed. *L'Esthétique du film.* Paris: Editions Fernand Nathan, 1983.

Molinari, Cesare. *Theater through the Ages.* Trans. Colin Hammer. New York: McGraw-Hill, 1975.

Mondor, Henri. *Vie de Mallarmé.* 2 vols. Paris: Gallimard, 1940–41.

———. *Propos sur la poésie.* Monaco: Editions du Rocher, 1946.

———. *Histoire d'un faune.* Paris: Gallimard, 1948.

Moore, Sonia. *Training an Actor: The Stanislavski System in Class.* New York: Penguin, 1968.

Mrosovsky, Kitty, trans. *The Temptation of Saint Antony.* Ithaca, N.Y.: Cornell Univ. Press, 1980.

Musset, Alfred de. *Un Spectacle dans un fauteuil. Théâtre I.* Paris: Garnier-Flammarion, 1964.

Nagler, Alois Maria. *A Source Book in Theatrical History.* 2nd ed., 1952; rpt. New York: Dover, 1959.

Nietzsche, Friedrich. *The Birth of Tragedy.* Trans. Francis Golffing. New York: Doubleday, 1956.

Nisard, D. *Histoire de la littérature française,* vol. 4. Paris: Firmin Didot Frères, 1867.

Noulet, Emilie. *Vingt poèmes de Stéphane Mallarmé.* Geneva: Droz, 1967.

Peyre, Henri M. *Qu'est-ce que le romantisme?* Paris: Presses universitaires de France, 1971.

———. *Hugo, sa vie, son oeuvre.* Paris: Presses Universitaires de France, 1972.

———. *Victor Hugo: Philosophy and Poetry.* Trans. Roda P. Roberts. University: Univ. of Alabama Press, 1980.

Plato. *The Republic.* Trans. and Ed. Desmond Lee. 2d ed., 1955; rpt. New York: Penguin, 1974.

Pommier, Jean. "Les Maladies de Gustave Flaubert." In *Dialogues avec le passé.* Paris: Nizet, 1967. 281–328.

Pontalis, J.-B. "La Maladie de Flaubert." *Les Temps Modernes* 98.103 (Jan.–June 1954): 1646–59, 1889–1902.

Porter, Laurence M., ed. *Critical Essays on Gustave Flaubert.* Boston: G. K. Hall, 1986.

Poulet, Georges. *Etudes sur le temps humain.* Paris: Plon, 1950.

———. *Entre Moi et Moi.* Paris: José Corti, 1977.

Praz, Mario. *The Romantic Agony.* Trans. Angus Davidson. New York: World, 1933.

Pridden, Dierdre. *The Art of the Dance in French Literature.* London: Routledge and Kegan Paul, 1952.

Prior, Moody Erasmus. *The Language of Tragedy.* 2d ed. Bloomington: Indiana Univ. Press, 1966.

Quéant, Gilles, and Frédéric Towarnicki. *Encyclopédie du théâtre contemporain.* 2 vols. Paris: Les Publications de France, 1957.

Queneau, Raymond. *Le Vol d'Icare.* Paris: Gallimard, 1968.

Quinet, Edgar. *Ahasvérus. Oeuvres complètes,* vols. 10–11. Paris: Librairie Germer-Baillière, 1843.

Richard, Jean-Pierre. *L'Univers imaginaire de Mallarmé.* Paris: Seuil, 1961.

———. *Etudes sur le Romantisme.* Paris: Seuil, 1970.

———. *Littérature et sensation.* Paris: Seuil, 1970.

Riffaterre, Michael. "Un exemple symboliste chez Victor Hugo." *L'Esprit Créateur* 5 (Fall 1965): 162–73.

Rousset, Jean. "Madame Bovary ou le livre sur rien." *Forme et Signification.* Paris: José Corti, 1962, 109–33.

Sadie, Stanley, ed. *The New Grove Dictionary of Music and Musicians.* 20 vols. London: Macmillan, 1980.

Salomon, Pierre. "Préface." Prosper Mérimée, *Théâtre de Clara Gazul.* Paris: Garnier-Flammarion, 1968, 17–33.

Sartre, Jean-Paul. *L'Idiot de la famille: Gustave Flaubert de 1821 à 1857.* 3 vols. Paris: Gallimard, 1971–72.

Scherer, Jacques. Le *"Livre" de Mallarmé*. 2nd ed., 1957; rpt. Paris: Gallimard, 1977.

Schüler, Gisela. "Zur Chronologie von Hegels Jugendschriften." *HegelStudien* 2 (1963): 111–59.

Seznec, Jean. *Nouvelles Etudes sur la Tentation de Saint Antoine*. London: Warburg Institute, 1949.

Simpson, David, ed. *German Aesthetic and Literary Criticism*. Cambridge: Cambridge Univ. Press, 1984.

Sonnenfeld, Albert. "Mallarmé: The Poet as Actor as Reader." *Yale French Studies* 54 (1976): 159–72.

Starobinski, Jean. *L'Oeil vivant*. Paris: Gallimard, 1961.

———. "Hamlet et Freud." *Les Temps Modernes* 253 (1967): 2113–35.

Steegmuller, Francis, ed. and trans. *The Letters of Gustave Flaubert 1830–1857*. Cambridge: Belknap Press of Harvard Univ. Press, 1980.

Stendhal. *Racine et Shakespeare*. Paris: Calmann-Levy, n.d.

———. *Théâtre*. 3 vols. Paris: Le Divan, 1931.

———. *Mélanges de littérature*. Vol. 3. Paris: Le Divan, 1933.

———. *Racine and Shakespeare*. Trans. Guy Daniels. New York: Corwell-Collier Press, 1962.

———. *Le Rouge et le noir*. Paris: Garnier-Flammarion, 1964.

———. *Vie de Henry Brulard*. Paris: Gallimard, 1973.

———. *Souvenirs d'égotisme*. Paris: Gallimard, 1983.

Stoïanova, Ivanka. "L'Enoncé musical." *Musique en Jeu* 23 (June 1975): 23–57.

———. *Geste-texte-musique*. Paris: Union générale d'editions, 1978.

Szondi, Peter. *Poésies et poétiques de la modernité*. Ed. Mayotte Bollack. Lille: Presses universitaires de Lille, 1981.

Thibaudet, Albert. *La Poésie de Stéphane Mallarmé*. Paris: Gallimard, 1926.

———. *Gustave Flaubert*. Paris: Gallimard, 1935.

———. *Histoire de la littérature française de 1789 à nos jours*. Paris: Librairie Stock, 1936.

Todorov, Tzvetan, ed. *Langages* 17 (1970).

Ubersfeld, Anne. *Le Roi et le buffon: Etude sur le théâtre de Hugo de 1830 à 1839*. Paris: José Corti, 1974.

———. *Lire le théâtre*. Paris: Editions sociales, 1978.

———. *L'Ecole du spectateur: Lire le théâtre II*. Paris: Editions sociales, 1981.

Undank, Jack, and Herbert Josephs, eds. *Diderot Digression and*

Dispersion. Lexington, Ky.: French Forum, 1984.

Valéry, Paul. *Eupalinos, L'Ame et la danse, Dialogue de l'arbre.* Paris: Gallimard, 1945.

———. *Ecrits divers sur Stéphane Mallarmé. Oeuvres complètes.* Paris: Gallimard, 1952.

Veinstein, André. *La Mise en scène théâtrale et sa condition esthétique.* Paris: Flammarion, 1955.

Vernant, Jean-Pierre. *Mythe et tragédie en Grèce ancienne.* Paris: Maspero, 1972.

Vigny, Alfred de. *Le Journal d'un poète.* Ed. Louis Conard. 8 vols. Paris: Louis Conard, 1935.

———. *Oeuvres complètes.* Ed. F. Baldensperger. 2 vols. Paris: Gallimard, 1948.

Weber, Samuel. *The Legend of Freud.* Minneapolis: Univ. of Minnesota Press, 1982.

Wetherhill, P. M., ed. *Flaubert: La Dimension du texte.* Manchester: Manchester Univ. Press, 1982.

Wolf, Mary Ellen. *Eros Under Glass: Psychoanalysis and Mallarmé's "Hérodïade."* Columbus: Ohio State Univ. Press, 1987.

Index

Absolu littéraire, L', (Lacoue-Labarthe and Nancy): concept of literature in, 181–82 n. 2; Ideal Book in, 35; Plato's dialogues in, 13; Romanticism in, 9–10, 18–20, 205–6 n. 4; satire in, 187–88 n. 32

Affron, Charles: on lyric poetry, 38; on Hugo's theater, 78, 200 n. 7, 203 n. 28

Albouy, Pierre, 79, 97

Antitheatricalism: Jonas Barish on, 11–12, 38–39, 180 n. 7; in Hugo, 78–79; in Plato, 76; in Vigny, 50–51

Apparatus, psychical: in Freud, 1, 4–6, 172; in Mallarmé, 142, 149, 162, 172. See also Fantasm

Après-midi d'un faune, L' (Mallarmé), 140, 141, 142–43, 165–77, 214 n. 3; anticipation of, in Hugo, 86–87; musical and choreographic versions of, 175–77

Aristotle, 16, 18, 189 n. 36, 193 n. 20; and Hugo, 46; and Flaubert, 126; and Freud, 12; and Stendhal, 70; on tragedy, 17

Ascoli, Georges, 78

Bakhtin, Mikhail: on Socratic dialogue, 17, 184–85 n. 20, 187 n. 31, 198–99 n. 55; dialogism of, 9, 182 n. 4

Baldensperger, F., 52

Ballanche, Pierre-Simon: Orphée, 38, 58

Ballet. See Dance

Barish, Jonas: on antitheatricalism, 11–12, 180 n. 7; on mimesis, 183–84 n. 12; on Romanticism, 38–39

Barko, Carol, 217 n. 17

Barrère, Jean-Bertrand, 78, 80

Barthes, Roland: on narrative, 147; on the "realist effect," 69; on the texte, 48, 205–6 n. 4

Designed by Chris L. Hotvedt
Composed by G & S Typesetter, Inc., in Sabon text and display
Printed by Thomson-Shore, Inc. on 50-lb. Glatfelter paper and
bound in Joanna's Arrestox A